THE LESSON
OF
CARL SCHMITT

THE LESSON OF CARL SCHMITT

Four Chapters on the Distinction between Political Theology and Political Philosophy

HEINRICH MEIER

Translated by Marcus Brainard

THE UNIVERSITY OF CHICAGO PRESS
Chicago & London

Heinrich Meier is director of the Carl Friedrich von Siemens Foundation in Munich. Among his other books is *Carl Schmitt and Leo Strauss: The Hidden Dialogue*, translated by J. Harvey Lomax (University of Chicago Press, 1995).

The University of Chicago Press, Chicago 60637
The University of Chicago Press, Ltd., London

Printed in the United States of America

07 06 05 04 03 02 01 00 99 98   1 2 3 4 5

ISBN: 0-226-51890-6 (cloth)

Originally published as *Die Lehre Carl Schmitts: Vier Kapitel zur Unterscheidung Politischer Theologie und Politischer Philosophie*, © 1994 J. B. Metzlersche Verlagsbuchhandlung und Carl Ernst Poeschel Verlag GmbH in Stuttgart.

Library of Congress Cataloging-in-Publication Data

Meier, Heinrich, 1953–
[Lehre Carl Schmitts. English]
The lesson of Carl Schmitt : four chapters on the distinction between political theology and political philosophy / Henrich Meier ; translated by Marcus Brainard.
p. cm.
Includes bibliographical refrences and index.
ISBN 0-226-51890-6 (cloth : alk. paper)
1. Schmitt, Carl, 1888—Contributions in political science. 2. Political science—Germany—Philosophy. 3. State, The. 4. Christianity and politics. 5 Church and state. I. Title.
JC263.S34M44513 1998
320′.092—dc21 98-23580
CIP

♾The paper used in this publication meets the minimum requirements of the American National Standard for Information Sciences—Permanence of Paper for Printed Library Materials, ANSI Z39.48-1992.

To Joseph Cropsey
political philosopher and honored friend

CONTENTS

TRANSLATOR'S FOREWORD

THE CHALLENGES posed to the translator by the present work begin already with its main title, *Die Lehre Carl Schmitts*, precisely because of the ambiguity of *Lehre*. Among its possible translations are 'doctrine', 'teaching', 'theory', and 'lesson'. Generally speaking, the German reader will understand *Lehre* first of all as 'doctrine' or 'teaching', and only secondarily as what one is to learn, that is, as a lesson. Since the ambiguity of this term cannot be replicated in English and since the author's intention is to make visible the lesson of Carl Schmitt's teaching, he has chosen *The Lesson of Carl Schmitt* as the title of this volume. By contrast, Schmitt certainly did not intend that *Lehre* in the subtitle of his *Politische Theologie*, namely, *Vier Kapitel zur Lehre von der Souveränität*, denote 'lesson' but rather 'teaching'. Although in the present volume *Lehre* has been translated by all of the aforementioned terms, wherever Schmitt's thought is specifically at issue, it is translated by either 'teaching' or 'lesson'; in the few cases in which reference is made to his doctrine, the word translated is *Doktrin*. However, the reader should be aware of the fact that beyond the immediate context of Schmitt's thought, or rather when matters that are not exclusive to it are at issue, 'doctrine' is likewise used to render *Doktrin*, but also *Lehre*—chiefly in constructions such as *Erbsündenlehre* (doctrine of original sin). Aside from the translation of Schmitt's *Verfassungslehre* (*Constitutional Theory*), 'theory' always renders *Theorie*.

Similarly, the translation of *Sache* presents difficulties due to ambiguity. It has at least three related meanings—that for which one struggles, the focal point or object of inquiry, and what one makes one's own or what is one's affair—and may be rendered as 'concern', 'issue', 'cause', 'affair', 'what is contested' or 'controversial', 'subject matter', or 'case'. The sentence with which Chapter I opens, for example, reads "Moralische Entrüstung ist nicht die Sache der Politischen Philosophie" and is rendered "Moral indignation is no affair of political philosophy." Here *Sache* is used in the third sense listed above. However, while moral indignation is not its affair, it is, as becomes clear in the subsequent sentences, an object of inquiry for political philosophy. Except in this initial sentence, *Sache* is rendered here only as 'cause'; and it should be noted that 'cause' translates only this word and must not be confused with 'cause' (*Ursache*) in the sense of that which produces an effect. Such a confusion would obscure the centrality of the *Sache* to the author's presentation, which is indicated by this work's subtitle: *Four Chapters on the Distinction between Political Theology and Political Philosophy*. At issue is nothing less than the distinction between the cause of political theology and that of political philosophy.

Regarding the choice of translations for individual terms and phrases, I have profited much from J. Harvey Lomax's translation of the author's *Carl Schmitt and Leo Strauss: The Hidden Dialogue* (Chicago 1995). As far as was possible, I have adopted his translations of key terms—such as 'figure' for *Gestalt* and 'carnality' for *'Leib'haftigkeit* (cf. his notes in ibid., 133 f.). The purpose of doing so was to aid the reader who wishes to read the present book in conjunction with the former, which is the author's express intention. Furthermore, throughout the present volume words have been translated consistently as far as was possible. Wherever it was thought to be helpful to the reader, the German word or phrase has been provided after the first English translation of it. In those cases in which additional explanation seemed called for, translator's notes (designated in the text by TN1, TN2, etc.) have been included.

My thanks go to Guido Heinrich (with whom I discussed many of my linguistic queries about this complex text), Raquel Ajona (who graciously located several English texts and translations for me), and J. Harvey Lomax (who was kind enough to read the first two chapters of the present translation and to provide me with a number of helpful comments and suggestions). All have helped to improve this translation greatly.

Finally I should like to express my gratitude to the Lynde and Harry Bradley Foundation, which provided me with a fellowship that has made the completion of this translation possible.

PREFACE TO THE AMERICAN EDITION

THREE YEARS AGO I mentioned, at the beginning of the Preface to the American edition of my book *Carl Schmitt and Leo Strauss: The Hidden Dialogue*, that a critic, who had perused the recent literature on Schmitt, came to the conclusion that over the past decade the slim volume had set the increasingly animated discussion surrounding Carl Schmitt on a new course and brought about "a theological turn of the debate." In the meantime, the interpretation of Schmitt as a representative of political theology—which was begun in 1988 in *Carl Schmitt and Leo Strauss* and further developed in 1994 in *The Lesson of Carl Schmitt: Four Chapters on the Distinction between Political Theology and Political Philosophy*[1]—has met with such a broad response, and the thesis that the center of Schmitt's thought is his faith in revelation has become for many already such a matter of course, that not long ago another critic thought he could tell the public that no one had ever claimed anything else about that center. In view of this development, I should like to take the opportunity afforded by the American edition of my final book on Schmitt to separate the present interpretation from various readings which have concealed or blurred it over the past years. Since the philosophical turn of the debate apparently has yet to occur or at least is not altogether evident, it seems fitting to note that the confrontation with precisely those aspects of *The Lesson of Carl Schmitt* which could contribute to a philosophical turn has hardly begun in Europe. Among the aspects I have in mind are, for example, the investigation that revolves around the significance of politics to self-knowledge and that, in particular, concerns the attempt to define one's own identity by defining the enemy; or the analysis of Schmitt's complex relationship to Thomas Hobbes; not to mention the critique of morality or even more obvious topics. However, readers inter-

1. *Carl Schmitt, Leo Strauss und "Der Begriff des Politischen". Zu einem Dialog unter Abwesenden* (Stuttgart 1988) and *Die Lehre Carl Schmitts. Vier Kapitel zur Unterscheidung Politischer Theologie und Politischer Philosophie* (Stuttgart/Weimar 1994).

ested in the philosophical debate might, as a first step, compare the exegesis of Schmitt's "Weisheit der Zelle" ["Wisdom from the Cell"] in the second chapter of the present book with the interpretation of the same text in Jacques Derrida's *Politiques de l'amitié*.[2] He has his commentary on Schmitt, which occupies the middle four of the *Politiques de l'amitié*'s ten chapters, culminate in that interpretation. Since I cannot address Derrida's remarkable book here, I should like at least to draw the reader's attention to it, for it is of some interest with regard to the distinction between political theology and political philosophy.[3]

When a thesis is on the verge of turning into or being worn down to a matter of course, it is time to give it back its resistance and to reinstate it in its original sharpness. We begin our *restitutio in integrum* by expressing in a manner that cannot be mistaken by anyone just what the present interpretation does not say and what it absolutely does not aim at: Its concern is not "to explain Schmitt by his Catholic background" or demonstrate his "assimilation to a dogmatically steeled knowledge" of Church authorities; nor does it attempt to reduce "Schmitt's entire work" to an "application of a theology" or to show that it is a "product of a Catholic weltanschauung," or even to "take up" the Ariadnean thread of the interpretation "from Catholic moral philosophy," or whatever else has been claimed along these lines in the reception of my work over the past years. The thesis that the center and the context of Schmitt's thought is to be determined as political theology has been understood by many to be a thesis about the all-decisive significance of Schmitt's Catholicism. Yet one will search both *Carl Schmitt and Leo Strauss* and *The Lesson of Carl Schmitt* in vain for any statements about Schmitt's Catholicism that might suggest such an equation. It is no accident that there is no mention of Schmitt's "basic Catholic character" or "basic Catholic attitude" or "basic Catholic stance." Instead, the attentive reader will find in the appropriate place the reference to the fact that in a public discussion that directly and expressly concerned the Catholic Church, Schmitt behaved, "as on so many occasions before and after, . . . more 'like a Protestant,'

2. Cf. Jacques Derrida, *Politiques de l'amitié* (Paris 1994), 184–193 and *The Lesson of Carl Schmitt*, 43–57 below. These are the first two in-depth interpretations of Schmitt's meditation on the enemy in his *Ex Captivitate Salus*. [TN: For conventions used in citation, see xxiv and for explanations of certain key terms, see ix f. and 175 f.]

3. In my Epilogue—"A Theological or a Philosophical Politics of Friendship?"—to the second, expanded edition of *Carl Schmitt, Leo Strauss und "Der Begriff des Politischen". Zu einem Dialog unter Abwesenden* (Stuttgart/Weimar 1998), 171–181 I have commented on Derrida's politics of friendship in greater detail.

neither respectful of the intermediate instances nor relying on representation, referring solely to his own faith or to the sovereign authority."[4]

The confessional "classification" neither moves on the level of Schmitt's problem nor does justice to his stature. Furthermore, inasmuch as the confessional classification suggests that one already knows sufficiently what is at stake, it is likely to distract us from what is most important, that is, what the confrontation with Schmitt requires of and has in store for us: to think Schmitt himself. But this is precisely what the thesis of political theology aims at. It is by means of this thesis that the foundational context of a thought is to be determined, the center of which is occupied by faith in revelation: it is a position that can be grasped in no other way than by thinking it to the point—both aiming at and starting from that point—at which this position, in accordance with its own claim or confession, commands thinking to stop. That the confessional identification of the locus of Schmitt's thought falls short of the mark has been shown quite clearly by recent, sometimes voluminous studies that seek out Schmitt in the context of the Catholic groupings and circles of friends to which he had maintained close contact at various points in his life and which shared not only many of his convictions but, not infrequently, his political hopes and fears as well. Studies of this kind can bring much to light about Schmitt's milieu that is of interest and provide us with other historical insights. From the bird's-eye view of "historicization," however, it is far too easy to lose sight of what distinguishes Schmitt from those of his contemporaries who, as we learn, held more or less the same "weltanschauung" and whose names have largely been forgotten today. That which thwarts the confessional classification and goes beyond mere historical interest is simply not seen, namely, those questions which precede Schmitt's doctrines, the intentions he pursues with his concepts and interventions, the way in which he accounts for his theorizing—in a word: once again, the foundational context of his thought or the real drama of his existence.

That the confrontation with political theology ultimately is not aimed at this or that doctrinal edifice, but rather concerns the foundation and assertion of an existential position, is the open secret of both *Carl Schmitt and Leo Strauss* and *The Lesson of Carl Schmitt*. If the political theologian wishes to remain in accord with himself, he must apply the fundamental demands of his theory to his own activity and grasp his theorizing as historical action that is subject to the commandment of obedience. For

4. Cf. *The Lesson of Carl Schmitt*, 146 f. below.

the commandment of obedience to the sovereign authority of God, and the primacy of historical action that arises from this commandment, are indispensable postulates of a political theory that claims to be grounded in faith in divine revelation. That the political theologian joins the postulates of his theory with his existence as a theoretician distinguishes him from a mere doctrinaire, who seeks, by referring to firm traditions or higher institutions, to relieve himself of problems that the commandment of obedience poses for "historical action" in general and for the "historical action" of the theoretician in particular. What sets the political theologian apart is, on the one hand, his awareness of the fact that the problems that emerge from the demands of political theology cannot be solved by means of reason and, on the other hand, the intransigence with which he nevertheless insists on the inevitability of those demands. This twofold orientation is expressed conspicuously in Schmitt's talk of the "blind anticipation of the commandment that is to be obeyed." One can say with good reason that, for the "Christian Epimetheus," historicism considerably sharpens the problematic with which the political theologian sees himself confronted. But the problematic is in itself by no means dependent on Schmitt's historicism. What haunts Schmitt his entire life in the form of the question of self-deception[5]—who offers protection from self-deception and how can he free himself from it—is something that some of the most important political theologians over the past two thousand years have sought to understand and master in the conflict of grace and justice. None of them—from Paul to Calvin, from Augustine to Luther—was satisfied by the proclamation of traditional doctrines.[6]

The rank of a political theologian becomes manifest not least with regard to the clarity with which he knows how to distinguish the existential position that corresponds to his teaching from the position that is fundamentally opposed to it. The question of his attitude towards political philosophy therefore cannot remain extrinsic to the proper understanding of his thought. It speaks for the coherence of Schmitt's position that, even if without a clear concept of it, he does have a good sense of the dividing line that separates him from the philosophers.[7] Only a critic who considers

5. See *Carl Schmitt and Leo Strauss*, 79–82 and *The Lesson of Carl Schmitt*, 18–20, 44–51, 85–89, 132–135, 167 below.

6. Concerning the most profound problematic with which the political theologian is faced, the problematic to which every other problem refers, cf. *The Lesson of Carl Schmitt*, 88–92 below.

7. Jacques Derrida characterizes Schmitt as, among other things, a "penseur catholique," "penseur traditionaliste et catholique du droit européen," "juriste hyper-traditionaliste de la droite catholique," "grand juriste conservateur catholique," "une sorte de néo-hegelien catholique qui a un besoin essentiel de se tenir à une pensée de la totalité"

what was most important to Schmitt to be of no significance or who is unable to see that the distinction between political theology and political philosophy concerns neither scholarly disciplines nor relatively independent domains of human thought and action, but rather an existential alternative, can dismiss the distinction between political theology and political philosophy as "scholastic." What could be less irrelevant than the opposition between a life that believes itself to be anchored in the certainty of divine revelation and one that places itself entirely on the ground of human wisdom? What could be less immaterial than the distinction between a thought that wants to move and conceive itself in the obedience of faith and one that is not bound by any authority and spares nothing from its questions? As for how that opposition determines a difference in the stance towards morality, politics, revelation, and history, and what consequence this distinction has for what the interpreter can learn in the confrontation with the oeuvre of each side, this becomes visible for whoever allows himself to think unreservedly the cause of the political theologian as well as that of the political philosopher and who makes every effort to understand both just as they have understood or understand themselves.[8]

One of the advantages of the distinction between political theology and political philosophy is that it preserves a conceptual symmetry. It allows a distinction in the cause—specifically in consideration of the question that is held to be central by both positions—without fostering any discrimination. The symmetry of the distinction presupposes not only that both sides recognize themselves in light of the determination of what separates them, but also that they can employ the concept that describes their respective positions to characterize themselves. In the sense we use it, therefore, the distinction only became possible as a result of the positive recasting of political theology that Schmitt achieved for it in this century. For until Schmitt appropriated the concept, 'political theology' was a term of criticism, attack, and defense. It served to characterize the position of *others*, with the intention of placing them in the wrong from the

(*Politiques de l'amitié*, 102, 108, 162; *Force de loi. Le "Fondement mystique de l'autorité"* [Paris 1994], 77; *Adieu à Emmanuel Lévinas* [Paris 1997], 161). This comparatively conventional classification fits with an underestimation of Schmitt's hardly conventional opposition to Heraclitus, Hegel, Nietzsche, and Heidegger, to name just those philosophers who are most important to Derrida in this context.

8. Regarding what the interpreter can learn in the confrontation with the oeuvre of a philosopher, see my writing, *Die Denkbewegung von Leo Strauss. Die Geschichte der Philosophie und die Intention des Philosophen* (Stuttgart/Weimar 1996), 41–43. By contrast, compare *Carl Schmitt and Leo Strauss*, 68–69 and *The Lesson of Carl Schmitt*, 86, 89, 92, 93 f. below.

very start. Only since the publication of Schmitt's treatise *Politische Theologie* in 1922 has the concept come to be used of one's *own* position or to denote an objective context without polemical intention. By liberating it from its old, negative valence, Schmitt has helped the concept 'political theology'—though he never speaks of its provenance or discusses its meaning[9]—to gain prominence over the past seventy-five years throughout the world, across all political and theological fronts as well as across disciplinary and national boundaries. Cause and concept could now be brought into accord.[10] However, the advantages of the distinction between political theology and political philosophy are not exhausted by its being based on the agreement of both positions regarding the fundamental difference between their causes and by its enabling both positions to adopt the respective concept for their self-characterization. In addition, the distinction can do justice to the self-understanding or the self-knowledge of both the representatives of political theology and those of political philosophy. A glance at the concepts 'political mythology' and 'political religions' suffices to draw out this advantage more clearly. It is not just that in the use of the labels 'political mythology' and 'political religions' the interest of "ideological criticism," or the intention to invalidate what is so labeled, is written, *sit venia verbo*, on their faces. Talk of "political religions" makes the truth claim of the criticized position disappear, as it were, into the observer's perception. It is no accident that "political religion" is referred to almost exclusively in the summarizing plural, in which differences of foundation or of the self-understanding of the protagonists are neglected. And as far as "political mythology" is concerned, its truth claim is negated already in the concept itself. The political mythologist may be quite clear about the aims he pursues in producing or spreading myths, yet he cannot possibly grasp himself in

9. That might explain in part why the question of political theology played almost no role in the Schmitt literature until 1988, even though Schmitt had visibly raised the flag *Politische Theologie* no less than three times in quite different historical moments (in 1922, 1934, and 1970). Under the headword 'political theology', nothing much more than the so-called secularization theorem was discussed. In the atrophied form of a thesis of the history of concepts or the philosophy of science, which supposedly had certain "correspondences," "analogies," and "structural identities" in theology and jurisprudence as its object, political theology led a shadow existence on the periphery of the debate—a diversion and detoxification that Schmitt himself fostered at times to the best of his ability (cf. *The Lesson of Carl Schmitt*, 30 n. 12 below). In view of such a concept of political theology, it should be of no surprise that Schmitt's "arcanum" remained inaccessible.

10. In *Carl Schmitt and Leo Strauss* (75–78) I have indicated the arsenal from which Schmitt took the concept and have explained the uses to which it was put. The caesura that the year 1922 represents in the history of the concept 'political theology' is noted in *The Lesson of Carl Schmitt*, 8 f. and 170–172 below.

the horizon of what he sees clearly to be untrue.[11] By contrast, the distinction between political theology and political philosophy helps to keep apart what does not belong together and yet, by disregarding what is most important, is frequently confounded,[12] because the distinction allows one to take radically seriously what deserves to be taken radically seriously.

If we wish to take Schmitt's truth claim seriously, we must confront his political theology. But, one might ask, what reason is there to take his claim seriously? Does historical tact require that we seek to understand a thinker of the past as he understood himself? Or do we have the moral duty to do justice to the thinking of the other as other, irrespective of the person? As long as we do not take Schmitt seriously as a political theologian, he remains for us beneath his possibilities and we remain beneath our own. We deprive ourselves of what the task of thinking Schmitt would reveal to us should we succeed: clarity about the cause of political theology. The damage is to us, not to Schmitt. To realize this, we do not even need to recall that we are dealing here with an author who made note of the maxim, "Don't give your enemies the chance to grasp you. As long as they do you wrong, they have not grasped you."[13] One does Schmitt wrong when one sees in him only a Catholic doctrinaire, a political

11. In precisely that book in which he discusses Georges Sorel's theory of myth for the first time and in which he sets off the "mythology of the national" from the "inferior mythology" of socialism, Schmitt—who is regarded by many critics as a representative of "political mythology"—states for the record his fundamental distance from "political mythology": "Of course, the ideal danger of such irrationalities is great. The last solidarities, of which at least some remnants still exist, are abolished in the pluralism of an incalculable number of myths. For political theology, that is polytheism, just as every myth is polytheistic. But one cannot ignore it as a strong tendency in the present." (*Die geistesgeschichtliche Lage des heutigen Parlamentarismus* [Munich/Leipzig 1923], 65; 2d ed. 1926, 89.) In the political theologian's attitude, freedom, obedience, and the requirement of constant self-reassurance enter into a peculiar union: The political theologian perceives something "as a strong tendency in the present" which he uses in his "historical action" and for which he can even make himself an advocate based on the obedience of his faith, while not identifying himself with that "tendency," i.e., while not for one moment losing sight of his own position and thus the abyss by which "political mythology" or any other current tendency is separated from the truth of faith. (In this connection see *The Lesson of Carl Schmitt*, 143–146 and consider 88 n. 56 below.)

12. Thus, to mention one example that long played a prominent role in the discussion of political theology, Rousseau's *religion civile* is a concept employed by political philosophy. The "articles of faith" which Rousseau postulates in *Du contrat social* IV, 8 "comme sentiments de sociabilité" are suggested by a political theoretician who was decidedly not a political theologian and who subjected the presuppositions of political theology to a far-reaching critique. Cf. *The Lesson of Carl Schmitt*, 86, 98 f. below.

13. Carl Schmitt, *Glossarium. Aufzeichnungen der Jahre 1947–1951* (Berlin 1991), 210; cf. 190, 216.

mythologist, or a spokesman for antiliberalism. Schmitt may have been all this and more to a certain degree. But none of these labels is sufficient to grasp him. And here lies one of the reasons for the response that the thesis of political theology has received over the past decade: Carl Schmitt cannot be adequately grasped if one does not grasp the center and the context of his thought as political theology.[14] The objection of several critics that the thesis aims at a unity that could be granted only for his early and later work, or that it results merely from a retrospective dissolving of the breaks and ruptures in his oeuvre, was so obvious that it determined the line of my argument from the very beginning. It was for that reason that I sought to verify the interpretation by focusing on Schmitt's two most important books, which can be assigned neither to the early nor to the later work and which to that point, to put it reservedly, were not yet referred to by everyone as obvious testimonies of Schmitt's "basic Catholic attitude": *Carl Schmitt and Leo Strauss* developed the thesis of political theology by means of an interpretation of the three editions of *Der Begriff des Politischen* from 1927, 1932, and 1933, and *The Lesson of Carl Schmitt* used *Der Leviathan in der Staatslehre des Thomas Hobbes* from 1938 as the test case for the entire exegesis.[15]

Another reason for the attention that the interpretation of Schmitt as a political theologian has received over the past years in the international debate is the growing interest in political theology. It gains its sustenance from quite different sources and can be observed in quarters that are separated by great distances. In conclusion, I would like to mention four aspects of this interest. The collapse of the Soviet empire and the worldwide erosion of Marxist hopes that preceded it have in many places inspired the search for a new certainty of faith. Revealed religions not only promise a security that none of the faded ideologies approach. What is more, they seem to offer an effective foothold for resisting the global triumph of the union of liberalism and capitalism, or rather to present an alternative to the secularism of modernity in its entirety. The weight that

14. To grasp the center and the context of a thought does not mean to go through every detail. Nor does it mean to equate the scholar with the thinker and to short-circuit the more technical sections of his work with the center. It especially does not mean to reduce the activity of the theoretician to the doctrinal contents he relays. Yet the only path that leads to the theoretician's thought is the one that begins its ascent with the results or sediments of his activity. We note this, with respect to the present volume's original German title, *Die Lehre Carl Schmitts*, for "those who judge books only by their titles" or who do not read to the end because they already know everything from the start.

15. The interpretation of the book on the Leviathan, with which the interpretation stands and falls, already formed the basis of *The Hidden Dialogue* (cf. 43 n. 40). Both writings were conceived at the same time.

both moments have in the antiwestern type of political-religious radicalism is obvious. Such radicalism is, however, just one, even if at present the most spectacular, variety of the revival of Islamic, Jewish, and Christian orthodoxies. Both the disenchantment of political-antireligious utopias and the expectations of salvation that are bound up with the establishment of a theocracy have restored an urgency to the question of the relationship between politics and religion that few granted it for a long time. Compared with the three viewpoints just sketched—the free-floating yearnings for a new absolutely binding commitment, the return of orthodoxies, and the reflection on the question of the theological-political foundations of the community—the fourth aspect seems to be of lesser significance. Still, it should not be underestimated given the intellectual climate in which a political theory that claims to be grounded in faith in divine revelation is gaining appeal and an audience. I am thinking of those diffuse expectations that in the broad stream of "postmodernity" revolve around the "*Ereignis*" (appropriating event), which, should it occur, will put an end to the "wandering in the deserts," and yet must not, if it is to show itself openly in its otherness, if it is to occur precisely as the "*Ereignis*," be made the object of a thinking that conceives, distinguishes, and therefore aims at dominance. Jean-François Lyotard has recalled the divine commandment given to Abraham to sacrifice Isaac and Abraham's faithful obedience as the paradigm of the "*Ereignis*"—of the unforeseeable call as well as the attitude in which one must answer it. The proximity of some "postmodern" authors not only to the famous religious writer from Copenhagen but also to the political theologian from Plettenberg in Westphalia is greater than it may at first seem. They are turned towards the decisive determinations of the latter's cause—authority, revelation, and obedience—in an intricate way, *dans un état de latence ou dans un état de langueur*.

Munich, February 1998 H. M.

PREFACE TO THE GERMAN EDITION

WITH THE *Four Chapters* presented here I bring to a close the discussion I began with *Carl Schmitt and Leo Strauss: The Hidden Dialogue*. The two publications are related to one another. They deal with one cause and are guided by one intention. The elenctic-protreptic character that links them will not escape the attentive reader any more than the differences in detail to which it gives rise. The whole is a report about some results of my occupation with Carl Schmitt's political theology. What seems to me to be of lasting importance in his political theology and what I intended to say about it is contained in this book and the previous one.

Munich, September 20, 1993 H. M.

ABBREVIATIONS OF FREQUENTLY CITED TEXTS BY CARL SCHMITT

BdP	*Der Begriff des Politischen* [*The Concept of the Political*] (the wording of the 1932 edition will be cited, whereas the pagination is from the 1963 edition)
BdP I	First edition of 1927
BdP II	Second edition of 1932
BdP III	Third edition of 1933
D	*Die Diktatur* [*The Dictatorship*]
DA	*Über die drei Arten des rechtswissenschaftlichen Denkens* [*On the Three Kinds of Jurisprudential Thought*]
DC	*Donoso Cortés in gesamteuropäischer Interpretation* [*Donoso Cortés in European Interpretation*]
ECS	*Ex Captivitate Salus*
G	*Glossarium*
GLP	*Die geistesgeschichtliche Lage des heutigen Parlamentarismus* [*The Spiritual-Historical Situation of Contemporary Parliamentarianism*]
L	*Der Leviathan in der Staatslehre des Thomas Hobbes* [*The Leviathan in the State Theory of Thomas Hobbes*]
LuL	*Legalität und Legitimität* [*Legality and Legitimacy*]
LuM	*Land und Meer* [*Land and Sea*]
NdE	*Der Nomos der Erde im Völkerrecht des Jus Publicum Europaeum* [*The Nomos of the Earth in the International Law of the* jus publicum Europaeum]
PR	*Politische Romantik* [*Political Romanticism*]
PT	*Politische Theologie* [*Political Theology*]
PT II	*Politische Theologie II* [*Political Theology II*]
PuB	*Positionen und Begriffe im Kampf mit Weimar–Genf–Versailles 1923–1939* [*Positions and Concepts in the Battle with Weimar–Genf–Versailles 1923–1939*]
RK	*Römischer Katholizismus und politische Form* [*Roman Catholicism and Political Form*]
SBV	*Staat, Bewegung, Volk* [*State, Movement, People*]
TdP	*Theorie des Partisanen* [*Theory of the Guerrilla*]

VA *Verfassungsrechtliche Aufsätze aus den Jahren 1924–1954* [*Essays on Constitutional Law from the Years 1924–1954*]

VL *Verfassungslehre* [*Constitutional Theory*]

VGO *Völkerrechtliche Großraumordnung mit Interventionsverbot für raumfremde Mächte* [*The Order of International Law based on* Großraum, *with a Prohibition of Intervention by Foreign Powers*]

In addition to those listed above, all titles of Schmitt's writings referred to in the present volume are translated. In the notes all titles that are not accompanied by an author's name are by Carl Schmitt. All references to 'Chapter' pertain to the present volume. The author's insertions have been placed in angle brackets '< >' and the translator's in square brackets '[ ]'. Page numbers are preceded by 'p.' or 'pp.' only where confusion might otherwise occur.

MORALITY, OR ONE'S OWN QUESTION AS A FIGURE

The enemy is our own question as a figure.
And he will hunt us, and we him, to the same end.
Theodor Däubler, "Sang an Palermo"

MORAL INDIGNATION is no affair of political philosophy. It constitutes no part of philosophy. It does, however, belong among philosophy's objects, and it matters to philosophy as something philosophy has to be on guard against. It numbers among the objects of philosophy insofar as morality is not an unquestioned presupposition or an unquestionable given for philosophy, but rather an object to be investigated or a problem. Moreover, employed as a diagnostic probe, the question concerning the principal objective and ultimate source of moral indignation is able to unleash a disclosive power which does not fall short of the potency of that other farther-reaching question concerning the "morality it (he) aims at."[1] Whoever deals with Carl Schmitt and his teaching does well to raise both questions and not to lose sight of either. How could one possibly turn a deaf ear to Nietzsche's maxim when faced with a theoretician who declares that "the demanding moral decision" is the "core of the political idea" and who views both, the political idea, as well as the moral, as either standing or falling with the theological?[2] And how could one not take hold of the Ariadnean thread made accessible by the question about the cardinal objects of this political theologian's indignation if one is to succeed in the attempt to find one's way through and penetrate to the center of the labyrinth of an oeuvre rich in historical turns and political convolutions, in deliberate deceptions and involuntary obscurities?

But does Schmitt not claim to be "a theoretician of pure politics," or if

1. Friedrich Nietzsche, *Jenseits von Gut und Böse*, aph. 6; cf. aphs. 19 and 211.

2. *Politische Theologie. Vier Kapitel zur Lehre von der Souveränität* [*Political Theology: Four Chapters on the Teaching of Sovereignty*] (Munich/Leipzig 1922), 56 (2d, rev. ed. 1934: 83); cf. 55 (82).

not this, then at least an "observer of political phenomena" who "persistently sticks to his political thinking"?[3] Has he not a reputation for having, as some hold, rigorously distinguished between the political and the moral or, as others say, completely torn them asunder? Is it not just this bifurcation that, in conjunction with Schmitt's critique of "humanitarian morality," with his rejection of "moralism," most persistently occupied and impressed the minds of both friend and enemy? Does not the aura of cold intrepidity and fascinating terror which in the eyes of many surround his name have its roots largely right here? And does not the same hold for the moral indignation which confronts him to a far greater extent? Whoever seeks to take his bearings by opinions about Schmitt moves in a maze that has rampantly overgrown Schmitt's own labyrinth and affords a view of little more than its outskirts. The admiration says something about the admirers; the indignation, a great deal about the indignant. However, the judgment expressed therein about the object of their admiration or indignation may well miss the point and thus bar rather than give access to what is most important. Might not the proclamation of a "pure politics" be the expression of a rhetoric, the severance of the political and the moral part of a strategy, both of which in the final analysis are based on a "demanding moral decision"? What if Schmitt's attacks on "humanitarian morality" and "moralism" were guided by moral motives? And finally: were the question concerning the morality Schmitt aims at ever able to be a meaningful question, one that elucidates the cause and furthers our knowledge, should it stop and fall silent before that to which Schmitt himself lays claim?

Let us take hold of the tail end of the thread and observe—on the authority of Schmitt, who bids us to be constantly on the lookout for the historical challenge of an oeuvre, a doctrine, a political-theological decision—first of all the moral tableau of the age, one sketched in Schmitt's earliest coherent critique. "Like everything that has a bad conscience," he writes during the First World War, "this age reveled in discussing its problematic character until the twinges of conscience ceased and it could

3. "Der Begriff des Politischen," first edition, 26 (in *Archiv für Sozialwissenschaft und Sozialpolitik* 58, no. 1 [September 1927]); second edition, 67 (*Der Begriff des Politischen. Mit einer Rede über das Zeitalter der Neutralisierungen und Entpolitisierungen* [*The Concept of the Political: With a Speech about the Age of Neutralizations and Depoliticizations*] [Munich/Leipzig 1932]; quotations of the second edition will be rendered in accordance with the original publication; however, the page numbers refer to the reprint, *Der Begriff des Politischen. Text von 1932 mit einem Vorwort und drei Corollarien* [Berlin 1963], in order to make it easier for the reader to locate the relevant passages). Concerning the bibliographical details of the different versions of the *BdP*, see my *Carl Schmitt and Leo Strauss: The Hidden Dialogue*, trans. J. Harvey Lomax (Chicago 1995), 6–7.

feel better since such reasoning was at least interesting. This age has characterized itself as the capitalistic, mechanistic, relativistic age, as the age of transport, of technology, of organization. Indeed, 'business' does seem to be its trademark, business as the superbly functioning means to some pathetic or senseless end, the universal priority of the means over the end, business which annihilates the individual such that he does not even feel his nullification and who thereby does not rely on an idea but at most on a few banalities and always only asserts that everything must go smoothly and without any needless friction. The achievement of vast, material wealth, which arose from the general preoccupation with means and calculation, was strange. Men have become poor devils; 'they know everything and believe nothing.' They are interested in everything and are enthusiastic about nothing. They understand everything; their scholars register in history, in nature, in men's own souls. They are judges of character, psychologists, and sociologists, and in the end they write a sociology of sociology. Wherever something does not go completely smoothly, an astute and deft analysis or a purposive organization is able to remedy the incommodity. Even the poor of this age, the wretched multitude, which is nothing but 'a shadow that hobbles off to work,' millions who yearn for freedom, prove themselves to be children of this spirit, which reduces everything to a formula of its consciousness and admits of no mysteries and no exuberance of the soul. They wanted heaven on earth, heaven as the result of trade and industry, a heaven that is really supposed to be here on earth, in Berlin, Paris, or New York, a heaven with swimming facilities, automobiles, and club chairs, a heaven in which the holy book would be the timetable. They did not want a God of love and grace; they had 'made' so much that was astonishing; why should they not 'make' the tower of an earthly heaven? After all, the most important and last things had already been secularized. Right had become might; loyalty, calculability; truth, generally acknowledged correctness; beauty, good taste; Christianity, a pacifist organization. A general substitution and forgery of values dominated their souls. A sublimely differentiated usefulness and harmfulness took the place of the distinction between good and evil. The confounding was horrific."[4]

This portrait, with which Schmitt in 1916 seeks to express the "moral meaning of the age,"[5] draws together nearly all the objects of importance which Schmitt encounters with indignation and abhorrence throughout

4. *Theodor Däublers "Nordlicht". Drei Studien über die Elemente, den Geist und die Aktualität des Werkes* [*Theodor Däubler's "Nordlicht": Three Studies on the Elements, the Spirit, and the Actuality of the Work*] (Munich 1916), 63–65.

5. *Theodor Däublers "Nordlicht,"* 68.

his life, or they can certainly be discerned in the portrait from a distance: The world as business, an idling machine that perpetuates itself with neither purpose nor end, a cleverly staged play of comprehensive mediation, balance and finesse—all no doubt interesting, yet without greatness, without fulfillment, without meaning, a state of deadness, of industrious boredom and endless idle chatter, devoid of any intense emotion, flat, without mystery and without magic. The progressive secularization, the fall from the truth of faith, the increasing godlessness, or, as he will say decades later: incapacity for God.[6] The hubris of men who replace Providence with the plans of their will and the calculation of their interests and who imagine themselves able to force the advent of an earthly paradise in which they would be relieved of having to decide between good and evil and from which the dire emergency would remain banned forever. From the beginning, it is the "age of security"[7] that provokes all of Schmitt's energies against it. It is the efforts, regardless of their provenance, to pave the way for such an age, it is every attempt to erect the unlimited dominion of security. Schmitt's indignation is aimed at those who abandon themselves to the belief "that everything in the world is an entirely human affair." He is outraged at those of his contemporaries who count solely on "fabulous success," which is "irrefutable": "big cities, luxury liners, and hygiene; the prison of the soul has become a cozy summer residence." They have the audacity to make provisions for everything, to want to organize everything, to rule over everything. *Ecce saeculum.* In this age everything seems to have been accounted for and thought of. "Except for the only case that matters."[8]

In the Epilogue to his last book, Schmitt in 1970—more than half a century after the early critique of the age—once again sketches a "counterimage" with stark contours in order "to discern [his] own position more clearly."[9] It culminates with the sentences: *Homo homini res mutanda / Nemo contra hominem nisi homo ipse.* In 1970 as in 1916, the belief "that everything in the world is an entirely human affair," that men place everything in the service of their power to plan and to utilize, that they subjugate everything to their wishes and desires, that they can *make* anything and everything, steadfastly remains at the center of Schmitt's

6. *Donoso Cortés in gesamteuropäischer Interpretation. Vier Aufsätze* [*Donoso Cortés in European Interpretation: Four Essays*] (Cologne 1950), 11.

7. *Theodor Däublers "Nordlicht,"* 66.

8. *Theodor Däublers "Nordlicht,"* 67, 69, 77.

9. *Politische Theologie II. Die Legende von der Erledigung jeder Politischen Theologie* [*Political Theology II: The Legend of the Disposal of Every Political Theology*] (Berlin 1970), 124.

countersketch. He fixes his standpoint by characterizing his adversary; he marks off his position *ex negativo* by opposing the presumptuousness of the Prometheans. *Eripuit fulmen caelo, nova fulmina mittit / Eripuit caelum deo, nova spatia struit.*[10] The hubris of the Titan, whom Schmitt ultimately considers his opponent, reaches its insuperable zenith in the Titan's refusal to grasp rebellion as rebellion, to perceive in any way the hubristic character of the anti-divine endeavor. The rebel disavows his rebellion. He denies fighting against an enemy. He believes himself able to evade the decision and the battle by concealing himself as a responsible subject in an "interminable process-progress" in order to emerge from the latter as a "New Man who produces himself." Moreover, the "process-progress," which is kept going by a mutually intensifying interplay of science, production, and consumption, is to produce "not only itself and the New Man, but also the conditions for the possibility of his own renewal of novelties"; "that means the opposite of a creation *out of* nothing, namely, the creation *of* nothing as the condition for the possibility of the self-creation of an ever New Worldliness."[11] The madness of the Promethean delusion is as plain as day. It can be heard in every single formulation that Schmitt chooses in order to depict the "thought-chains" in which the "autism" of an immanence has to move, an immanence "that is directed polemically against a theological transcendence" without wanting to admit it. The "New, purely worldly-human Science" may pass itself off as an "incessant process-progress of an expansion and renewal of nothing-more-than-worldly-human knowledge, both of which are driven onward by incessant human curiosity." But it cannot deceive Schmitt about its being "nothing but self-authorization." In it he discerns the "New Theology" it does not want to be and the "anti-divine self-deification" it has to be if there is a God who demands obedience. The world of the New Man would be the world of a New God. There would be no room for miracles in the realm "of purely worldly-human" security. One would encounter them with "disapproval." They could not be anything more than "acts of sabotage," of events that suggest the existence of an adversary.[12]

For Schmitt the rebellion of the Prometheans has many faces. It need

10. *PT II*, 126. The model which Schmitt follows with his hexameter is the verses of Cardinal Melchior de Polignac who in his *Anti-Lucretius sive de Deo et Natura* (Paris 1747) attacks the unfaith of the philosophers from Epicurus to Gassendi, Hobbes, and Spinoza (cf. *Glossarium. Aufzeichnungen der Jahre 1947–1951* [*Glossarium: Notes from the Years 1947–1951*] [Berlin 1991], 25 and 154). When Polignac uses the phrase "Eripuit fulmen Iovi," he is speaking of Epicurus.

11. *PT II*, 125.

12. *PT II*, 113–114, 125–126.

not go so far as the hallucination of that "process-progress" which "no longer admits of an *ovum* in an old or renewable sense," but "only a *novum*"; and with biting sarcasm Schmitt helps give it, in its hopeless attempt to escape its theological-political opponent, a "totally" autochthonous, independent expression: "all detheologizations, depoliticizations, dejuridifications, deideologizations, dehistoricizations, and further series of un-doings[TN1] directed towards a tabula rasa, fall to the side; the tabula rasa *de*-tabularizes itself and falls to the side along with the tabula."[13] The "tabula rasa of techno-industrial progress," which Schmitt sees as emerging from the drawing of anything and everything into the "functionalism of a calculable, causal sequence of events," is reprehensible enough; there is no additional need for it to renounce itself *in principiis*. Much the same holds for the aggressiveness "of the true movers and shakers" of progress, for the aggressiveness of technology and science as the "true aggressors."[14] The Promethean self-arrogation is expressed in the "evolutionist credo" that man, "biologically and by nature an exceedingly weak and needy being," creates a new world for himself on his own resources and on his own authority by dint of technology and science, a world "in which he is the strongest, indeed even the sole, being." Such self-arrogation manifests itself in every attempt at collective "self-salvation" and private "self-redemption." Schmitt sees self-arrogation in the self-authorization of those givers of meaning and big planners who have devoted themselves to work on the "Babylonian unity" of mankind, but also in the self-sufficiency of a life that gains its center on the path of autonomous thought. He sees it in the anarchic rejection of every authority, as well as in the bourgeois diligence to make the world "secure." The idylls of self-pleasure and the trouble-free character of the "Panians" draw near the paradises which the "religion of technicity" promises with "all the glories of an unleashed productive power and a power of consumption, which is increased to infinity." The naturalism of those who want to be true to the earth appears in the same pale light as the artificialism of those who reach for the stars. Whoever holds fast to "pure this-worldliness" or falls prey to it in his actions, turns against the transcendent God.[15]

13. *PT II*, 124.

14. "Der Gegensatz von Gemeinschaft und Gesellschaft als Beispiel einer zweigliedrigen Unterscheidung" [The Opposition of Community and Society as an Example of a Bipartite Distinction], in *Estudios Juridico-Sociales. Homenaje al Profesor Luis Legaz y Lacambra* (Santiago de Compostela 1960), 173; cf. *PT II*, 126.

15. *PT*, 45, 55–56 (64–65, 81–83); *Politische Romantik* [*Political Romanticism*], 2d ed. (a heavily revised and expanded version of the first edition of 1919) (Munich/Leipzig

Revolt and turning away, unfaith and disobedience, become open enmity wherever rebellion is raised to a principle, wherever it is asserted to be the most distinctive feature of man, declared to be the origin and determinative moment of his historical ascent. Nowhere does the enmity towards the omnipotent sovereign manifest itself more visibly for Schmitt, nowhere is the rebellion more openly proclaimed, than in Bakunin's anarchism. The Russian opposes what is most precious to Schmitt; he denies that of which Schmitt is most convinced. He attacks the truth of revelation and disavows the existence of God; he wants to do away with the State[TN2] and negates the universal claim of Roman Catholicism.[16] Under the slogan *Ni Dieu ni maître* he revolts "with Scythian fury" against all dominion, all order,[TN3] all hierarchy, against divine as well as human authority.[17] With his appearance Schmitt sees the "true enemy of all traditional concepts of Western European culture" enter the arena. It is from him—in whom, generations ahead of the "barbarians in the Rus-

1925), 137; *Die Lage der europäischen Rechtswissenschaft* [*The Situation of European Jurisprudence*] (Tübingen 1950), 32 (reprinted in *Verfassungsrechtliche Aufsätze aus den Jahren 1924–1954. Materialien zu einer Verfassungslehre* [*Essays in Constitutional Law from the Years 1924–1954: Materials for a Constitutional Theory*] [Berlin 1958], 426); *Ex Captivitate Salus. Erfahrungen der Zeit 1945–47* [*Ex Captivitate Salus: Experiences from the Years 1945–47*] (Cologne 1950), 49, 82–83, cf. 53, 88, 93; *DC*, 112; "Die Einheit der Welt" [The Unity of the World], in *Merkur* 6, no. 1 (January 1952): 1–2, 8–9; "Nehmen/Teilen/Weiden" [Taking/Dividing/Grazing] (1953), in *VA*, 495–496, 503–504; "Nomos-Nahme-Name" [Nomos-Appropriation-Name], in *Der beständige Aufbruch. Festschrift für Erich Przywara* (Nuremberg 1959), 102; *G*, 10, 47, 84, 148, 218, 264.

16. "Dieu étant tout, le monde réel et l'homme ne sont rien. Dieu étant la vérité, la justice, le bien, le beau, la puissance et la vie, l'homme est le mensonge, l'iniquité, le mal, la laideur, l'impuissance et la mort. Dieu étant le maître, l'homme est l'esclave. Incapable de trouver par lui-même la justice, la vérité et la vie éternelle, il ne peut y arriver qu'au moyen d'une révélation divine. Mais qui dit révélation, dit révélateurs, messies, prophètes, prêtres et législateurs inspirés par Dieu même; et ceux-là une fois reconnus comme les représentants de la Divinité sur la terre, comme les saints instituteurs de l'humanité, élus par Dieu même pour la diriger dans la voie du salut, ils doivent nécessairement exercer un pouvoir absolu. Tous les hommes leur doivent une obéissance illimitée et passive; car contre la Raison Divine il n'y a point de raison humaine, et contre la Justice de Dieu il n'y a point de justice terrestre qui tiennent. Esclaves de Dieu, les hommes doivent l'être aussi de l'Eglise et de l'Etat, en tant que ce dernier est consacré par l'Eglise. Voilà ce que, de toutes les religions qui existent ou qui ont existé, le christianisme a mieux compris que les autres, sans excepter même les antiques religions orientales, qui d'ailleurs n'ont embrassé que des peuples distincts et privilégiés, tandis que le christianisme a la prétention d'embrasser l'humanité tout entière; et voilà ce que, de toutes les sectes chrétiennes, le catholicisme romain a seul proclamé et réalisé avec une conséquence rigoureuse. C'est pourquoi le christianisme est la religion absolue, la dernière religion; et pourquoi l'Eglise apostolique et romaine est la seule conséquente, légitime et divine." Mikhail Bakunin, *Dieu et l'Etat* (1871), in *Œuvres complètes* (Leiden 1961 ff./Paris 1973 ff.), VIII, 98–99.

17. "Toute autorité temporelle ou humaine procède directement de l'autorité spirituelle ou divine." *OC* VIII, 173.

sian republic of soviets," Schmitt believes he discerns the most persistent adversary of politics and religion, of the Pope and God, of idea and spirit[18]—that he adopts the concept 'political theology', which has since been linked with Schmitt's name and which, like no other, deserves to be linked with his. Whereas Bakunin intends it to brand and mortally wound the opponent against whom he is waging his war, Schmitt makes the polemical concept his own so as to characterize his position by means of it and simultaneously to turn it against his opponent. He makes no mention of the original arsenal of the weapon, a weapon of which he henceforth avails himself; nor does he say a word about the battle in which he wrested it from his enemy. With it Bakunin fought against Mazzini.[19] He forged it for a war in which two irreconcilable armies face one another, the one under the banner of Satan, the other under the sign of God.[20] Schmitt uses the weapon in the same war. But he wants to help the latter camp to victory. What Bakunin negates in the name of Satan is

18. *PT*, 45, 49, 50, 55, 56 (64–65, 69, 71, 81, 83–84); *Römischer Katholizismus und politische Form* [*Roman Catholicism and Political Form*] (Hellerau 1923), 74–78 and 80 (2d, lightly rev. ed. [Munich 1925], 49–51 and 53); *Die geistesgeschichtliche Lage des heutigen Parlamentarismus* [*The Spiritual-Historical Situation of Contemporary Parliamentarianism*], 2d ed. (revised and expanded version of the first edition of 1923) (Munich/Leipzig 1926), 79, 83, 87; cf. *BdP*, 60, 64, and esp. the *third version* (Hamburg 1933), 45.

19. Bakunin, *La Théologie politique de Mazzini et l'Internationale* (St. Imier 1871; reprint, *OC* I). Schmitt makes no mention of this text. Yet he does say of Bakunin: "His battle against the Italian Mazzini is like the symbolic border skirmish of a vast world-historical upheaval which has greater proportions than the migration of the Germanic peoples [in the late Roman Empire]. For Bakunin, the Free Mason Mazzini's *faith in God* was, *just as all faith in God*, only proof of slavery and the *true root* of all evil, of all governmental and political authority; it was metaphysical centralism" (*RK*, 75 [49]; my emphasis). Furthermore, cf. the contrast drawn between Bakunin and Mazzini in the last sentence of that book, which, according to Schmitt's report in his *Politische Theologie*, was written "at the same time" as this "in March 1922." His *Politische Theologie* itself culminates in an attack on the enemy, on whom Schmitt trains his sights in choosing his title: the concluding sentence figures Bakunin as "the theologian of the anti-theological" and "the dictator of an anti-dictatorship." That Schmitt, precisely as far as the key terms and sentences of his work are concerned, quite consciously abstains from giving "references" can be shown by a number of examples. On this, see my *Carl Schmitt and Leo Strauss*, 46, 82, 95, 96; cf. 61–62. (Rudolph Sohm's writing, *Wesen und Ursprung des Katholizismus* [Berlin 1912], against which *Römischer Katholizismus und politische Form* is immediately directed, is likewise not mentioned by Schmitt.)

20. "Selon la doctrine mazzinienne aussi bien que chrétienne, la Mal c'est la révolte satanique de l'homme contre l'autorité divine, révolte dans la-quelle nous voyons au contraire le germe fécond de toutes les émancipations humaines. Comme les Fraticelli de la Bohême au XIVe siècle, les socialistes révolutionnaires se reconnaissent aujourd'hui par ces mots: *Au nom de celui à qui on a fait tort, salut.* Seulement Satan, le révolté vaincu mais non pacifié d'aujourd'hui s'appelle la *Commune de Paris*." *La Théologie politique de Mazzini*, *OC* I, 43–44 (cf. 45 and 72).

asserted by Schmitt in the name of God. And what is nothing but a man-made fiction for the atheistic anarchist, is God-given reality for the political theologian.

The most outspoken rebellion need not be the most threatening, nor the most conspicuous enmity the most decisive. It is rather unlikely that Satan will display his power most prominently where he is celebrated as the eternal rebel and world-liberator in the battle against God and State or where he, as in the Satanism of a Baudelaire, is formally enthroned with the fratricide Cain.[21] Truly satanic is—there is no doubt about it for Schmitt—the flight into invisibility. The Old Enemy prefers cunning, he is a virtuoso of disguise. He will attempt to avoid the open battle and will hardly enlist under his own flag. Instead of declaring war on someone or something, if not "on war itself," he is much more likely to promise peace and will make every effort to lull his adversary into a false sense of security. Measured by the consistency with which economic rationalism, having erected the "system of unswerving objectivity," cultivates and furthers such objectivity to the point where every government proves to be superfluous since "things govern themselves"; and compared with the disposal of theology and politics on the path of techno-industrial progress, Bakunin's battle looks like that of "a naive berserker."[22] For the assessment of the "moral meaning of the age," the anarchist is of less importance than the bourgeois, whose ubiquitous efficacy the anarchist does not even remotely approach. Thus it is not the anarchist, but rather the born embodiment of the system of accountability and calculation that is the focus of Schmitt's attention. The bourgeois is the promoter and the ultimate fulfillment of the "age of security" all in one. Schmitt sees in his figure an existence that is thoroughly determined by the need for security. Nothing is more important to the bourgeois than his security: security for life and limb, security from divine and human encroachment upon his private existence, security for undisturbed doings and dealings, security from any interference with the increase and enjoyment of his possessions. Nothing is more important to him than himself and his property. He seeks to evade every claim that places him in question in view of the whole. This explains both his attitude towards politics, which he wants to master through commerce and communication, and towards religion, which he declares to be a "private matter." He shuts his eyes to the inevitability of the "oppositions between good and evil, God and Devil, between whom there is an Either-Or which is a matter of life and death, an Either-Or that

21. Bakunin, *Dieu et l'Etat*, *OC* VIII, 88–89. *PT*, 55 (80–81).
22. *RK*, 74 (49).

knows no synthesis and no 'higher third,'" and he hopes that the definitive confrontation can be "eternally suspended by an eternal discussion."[23] No one is more receptive to the promise of *peace and security* than he. Revelation does not reach him. He succumbs easily to the temptation to abandon himself to the faith in the "limitless possibilities for change and happiness of the natural, this-worldly existence of man."[24] The sole miracles he tolerates are those "miracles" he himself works. For Schmitt the bourgeois epitomizes the man for whom the verse holds: "He locks himself in and locks God out."[25]

Schmitt's valuations have a common vanishing point. They refer to

23. *PT*, 50, 52, 54 (71, 75–76, 78–79); *RK*, 25, 42–43, 58–60 (17, 28, 38–39).

24. *BdP*, 93.

25. *BdP*, 62; "Recht und Raum" [Right and Space], in *Tymbos für Wilhelm Ahlmann* (Berlin 1951), 243. Schmitt does not stand alone among his contemporaries when he attacks the bourgeois and liberalism on behalf of Christianity. "According to their historical origin, the bourgeois soul and the bourgeois consciousness," we read in Nikolai Berdiajew's *Christentum und Klassenkampf* (Lucerne 1936), "are closely connected with the fall from Christianity and the decline of Christian spirituality. The forms of the bourgeois psychic attitude are anathema to a genuine Christian" (78–79). "The communist is . . . the definitive bourgeois, the bourgeois who has achieved his final victory, who has become the collective man, and who wants to expand his power over everything" (57). It is on account of this that "the coming realm of socialism becomes a realm of the definitive bourgeoisification of the world" (98; cf. 37–38, 55, 56). In the "spirit of the bourgeoisie," Berdiajew sees "in the final analysis the disavowal of the Cross, of the tragic principle of earthly existence" (58). In *Von der Würde des Christentums und der Unwürde der Christen* (Lucerne 1936), Berdiajew intensifies his reproach by making the charge that the "fundamental idea of the bourgeois" amounts to "striving for power and goods in the world without accepting the mystery of Golgatha. That is the chiliastic idea of the bourgeois; and the bourgeoisie is precisely nothing but the nonacceptance of Jesus Christ, nothing but his crucifixion. And even those who profess his word can crucify Jesus Christ" (51–52; cf. 39, 41, 42, 44, 48, 55). In the thirties Erik Peterson writes in his essay "Politik und Theologie": "The liberalism that asserts that theology and politics have nothing to do with one another, was the same liberalism that separated State and Church in politics and for which in theology the membership in the body of Christ was only a matter of personal opinion and Christian dogma was only a merely subjective expression of opinion. It is clear that a privatization of faith, such as that carried out by liberalism, had to have a detrimental effect on every aspect of dogmatics. There God was stripped as far as was possible of his transcendent character so that he could be absorbed into a private religious relation. There the God become Man became a liberal bourgeois who in fact worked no miracles but made up for it by preaching humanity, whose blood was in fact not a mystery but who died for his conviction, who in fact did not rise from the dead but lived on in the memory of those close to him, who in fact did not proclaim the end of the world and his Second Coming but taught us to see the beauty of the lilies in the countryside. There the Holy Spirit also was no longer honored as the third person of the Trinity but only related psychologically to the so-called religious experiences of one's own soul. The assertion that politics and religion have nothing to do with one another could therefore be implemented by liberalism only in such a way that the Christian faith was heretically distorted." (Unpublished manuscript, transcribed by Barbara Nichtweiß, 1–2. See Barbara Nichtweiß, *Erik Peterson. Neue Sicht auf Leben und Werk* [Freiburg i. Br. 1992], 820–821.)

what he is resolved to protect at all costs: the certainty of his faith. In defending the certainty of his faith, Schmitt defends the center of his existence, that which can alone support and preserve him. But in order for it to support and preserve him, he must defend in it the center of all things. Man's efforts "to give meaning" do not give any meaning, and his "positings of value" do not bring about anything that would be free of arbitrariness, that would deserve unqualified devotion and could lay claim to absolute validity. Only a certainty with respect to which all human security goes to ruin can satisfy Carl Schmitt's need for security; only the certainty of a power that radically surpasses every human capacity for control can guarantee the moral emphasis which puts an end to arbitrariness: the certainty of the God who demands obedience, rules absolutely, and judges in accordance with his own law. *One has not to be naturally pious, he has merely to have a passionate interest in genuine morality, i.e., in "categoric imperatives," in order to long with all his heart for revelation.* The *one* source that feeds Schmitt's indignation and polemic is his resolution to defend the seriousness of the moral decision. For Schmitt such resolution is the consequence and expression of his political theology. For in light of political theology, which subjects everything to the commandment of obedience, the defense of the moral decision itself appears to be a moral duty. Indignation is transformed from an affect of moral need into a morally imperative act, and the polemic is assigned the task of supplying the moral disjunction with validity, a disjunction that holds reality together in its innermost core.

Moral man's need for absolute validity longs for a world in which the moral Either-Or is everlastingly inscribed, for a reality in which the conflict of ultimate opposites is irrevocably anchored for man. His need aims at a reality that grasps him completely and that he is unable to comprehend, a reality that he, filled with emotion, can approach and that can fill him with holy reverence. Moral man longs for tragedy, and he conceives of the world in its image as fate and dispensation, as the indissoluble interconnection of guilt, judgment, and concealed meaning, of sin, punishment, and salvation. What appears to reason as incommensurable is here regarded by faith as the supreme confirmation of the irrefutability of the spirit of gravity. The necessity of making the moral decision, the imperative "Thou shalt!" reaches further than human insight. Seriousness is superior to all disputation, weighing, and understanding. For Providence has an effect through the "mysterious concatenation and entanglement of incontestably real events." Unraveling the mysteriousness is as a rule denied to the agents. For the moral need, however, all that matters is the sublime source from which the tragic reality descends; the mysteries it poses can only underscore its sublimity. "The core of the tragic event, the origin of tragic genuineness, is something so incontrovertible that no mortal can think it up and no genius can pull it out of his hat."[26] What for Schmitt constitutes the "non-relativizable" and "non-squanderable seriousness" of the tragedy portrayed by the poet, at the same time and first of all constitutes for him the non-relativizable and non-squanderable seriousness of the tragic event that on Schmitt's view forms the basis of the poetic portrayal of tragedy: "Time's irruption into the play" and history itself as ruled by divine Providence are "beyond all subjective invention." In both cases Schmitt lights upon an insuperable, unavailable power. He comes upon "an incontrovertible reality that no human mind thought up, but that is given, has happened, and is present from outside. The incontrovertible reality is the silent rock against which the play smashes and the breakers of genuine tragedy foam."[27] The rock of fate on which Schmitt builds is the stumbling block for the aspirations and plans of the Prometheans. Precisely that on which Schmitt's confidence is based—that seriousness will be steadfastly preserved for life—precisely that in which he places his hopes—to meet the non-relativizable, the absolute, the sublime—is suspended by "activistic metaphysics," which is devoted to the self-authorization and self-salvation of mankind.[28] All action and enterprising on the part of the Prometheans is aimed at the final conquest of tragedy. They strive for nothing less than its definitive end. Wherever man has become the "sole being" and men "can make anything," there is no longer any room for tragedy, nor, as a consequence, for the "demanding moral decision" that matters to Schmitt. This sums up Schmitt's intense enmity towards the descendants of the rebel god, and it makes sense that he seeks to ascertain his own position in contrast to their "counter-image." *First is the commandment, men come later.*

No absolute commandment without the omnipotent commander, no Christian morality without the Christian God, no security outside of the certainty of faith—Schmitt knows what is at stake in his decision about the enemy.[29] He determines his position in the awareness of the "most profound connections." His political theology accounts not only for the

26. *Hamlet oder Hekuba. Der Einbruch der Zeit in das Spiel* [*Hamlet or Hecuba: The Irruption of Time into the Play*] (Düsseldorf/Cologne 1956), 47; cf. *PR*, 104.

27. *Hamlet oder Hekuba*, 47, 54; cf. 48, 51, 55; *DC*, 114; *G*, 23, 24, 287.

28. *BdP*, 93; *ECS*, 49, 52–53; note the motto that Schmitt places at the outset of his book *Der Wert des Staates und die Bedeutung des Einzelnen* [*The Value of the State and the Significance of the Individual*] (Tübingen 1914).

29. Cf. Nietzsche, *Die fröhliche Wissenschaft*, aph. 343; in addition, see Schmitt, *Gespräch über die Macht und den Zugang zum Machthaber* [*Conversation about Power and Access to the Ruler*] (Pfullingen 1954), 20–23; *G*, 139.

insight "that if the theological disappears, so does the moral; if the moral disappears, so does the political," assuming that the theological or the moral could ever "disappear." Schmitt believes he knows beyond this and much more certainly "that the denial of original sin destroys all social order."[30] Consequently, one need not first wait for the general "incapacity for God," nor could anything be hoped for from a well-meaning "defense of the faith in God" for the maintenance of social order. However things may stand with the order for which faith in original sin is held to be indispensable, it certainly is so for Schmitt's political theology. The doctrine of original sin names the guarantor who insures the unavoidability of a radical Either-Or until the end of time: *I will put enmity between thy seed and her seed*. The belief in the truth of Genesis 3:15 is the foundation on which Schmitt's political theology is erected.[31] The doctrine of original sin is concerned with the opposition between good and evil, God and Satan, obedience and disobedience. At the same time, it confronts man himself with an ultimate Either-Or. The decision, the absolute *credo* or *non-credo* that it requires, thereby becomes the paradigm of the "demanding moral decision" as such. Schmitt conceives of the latter on the model of the former, as the fundamentally always identical, historically continually new repetition of the former. For this reason the "demanding moral decision" is his touchstone. For this reason the attitude towards "the moral" marks a dividing line of which Schmitt never loses sight.

The bourgeois has already been "sentenced" insofar as he wants to avoid the decision and seeks salvation in the "sphere of the unpolitical, risk-free private."[32] Sentence is passed on Bakunin, as the first to give "the battle against theology" the "complete consistency of an absolute naturalism," because "every moral and political decision" would be "paralyzed in a paradisiacal this-worldliness of immediate, natural life and unproblematic carnality," as he aspires to it by means of the final defeat of the enemy. The same holds for all those who wage war against the *patria potestas* and against monogamy in order "to preach" the return to the matriarchy as the "allegedly paradisiacal original state" of unspoiled love and friendship.[33] The *Nemo contra hominem nisi homo ipse* could not be in sharper conflict with the doctrine of original sin, and the way in which the Promethean self-authorization and self-salvation attacked

30. *PT*, 55 (82); *BdP* III, 45.

31. Cf. *BdP*, 67; *ECS*, 89–90.

32. *PT*, 52 (75); *BdP* III, 43.

33. *PT*, 55 (81–82); *GLP*, 83; "Gespräch über den Partisanen" [Conversation about the Guerrilla], in Joachim Schickel, ed., *Guerrilleros, Partisanen. Theorie und Praxis* (Munich 1970), 23.

by Schmitt behaves towards it is no less evident; for the will of man to lead his life based entirely on his own resources and his own efforts, following reason alone and his own judgment—*that* is the original sin: man's impudence does not begin when he believes that he can make *anything and everything*, but rather when he forgets that there is *nothing* that he may do on his own authority, i.e., outside of the realm of obedience. The romantic is defined by Schmitt as the virtual embodiment of the incapacity to make the demanding moral decision; the romantic, like the bourgeois in general, would like to adjourn and postpone the decision forever; the "higher third" to which he appeals when confronted with a choice is in truth "not a higher but another third, i.e., always the way out in the face of the Either-Or";[34] however, the matter does not rest there: religion, morality, and politics are for him nothing but "vehicles for his romantic interests" or just so many occasions to develop comprehensively his brilliant ego, which he raises to the "absolute center"; the romantic wants to defend the sovereignty of his limitless subjectivism against the seriousness of the political-theological reality inasmuch as he plays off one reality against the other, "never deciding in this intrigue of realities"; the romantic ego, which usurps God's place as the "final instance,"[TN4] lives in a "world without substance and without functional commitment, without firm guidance, without conclusion, and without definition, without decision, *without a last judgment*, continuing on without end, led only by the magic hand of chance"; the "secularization of God as a brilliant subject" conjures up a world in which all religious, moral, and political distinctions dissolve "into an interesting multitude of interpretations" and certainty evaporates into arbitrariness.[35] Matters are not much better with the aestheticist; wherever the aesthetic is made the absolute center, the "hierarchy of the spiritual[TN5] sphere," the true order is destroyed in its firm dispensation and determinate guidance; the aestheticist who finds satisfaction in the "completely amoral, natural enjoyment" of his aesthetic object or of his own achievement, in still more sublime consumption or in still more refined production, misses what is most important;[36] moral, religious, and political oppositions are transformed for him into noncommittal contrasts, delightful nuances of a work of art, a work which he may admire or at which he may try his own hand, but which by no means calls upon him to make the "great moral de-

34. *PR*, 162; cf. 21, 26, 83, 133, 169; *BdP*, 68.

35. *PR*, 22, 25 (my emphasis), 132, 222, 223; cf. 96–97, 104, 161, 168, 169, 172, 175, 177, 205, 207, 224.

36. *PR*, 21, 223; *BdP*, 83; cf. *RK*, 74 (49).

cision,"[37] to say nothing of its being able authoritatively, as a matter of life and death, to make him discharge his duty.[38] Finally Schmitt's touchstone proves itself—to cite a final example that is more than an example—with regard to Hegel; since in Hegel's construction of the philosophy of history "an exception never enters from the *outside*, outside of the immanence of the development," since as a result of the construction "opposing things penetrate one another and are incorporated into the overall development," the "*Either-Or* of the moral decision, the decided and decisive disjunction, has no place in this system";[39] like everything else, dictatorship, the opposition of good and evil, and even the enemy[40] are also "assimilated in the peristalsis of this world spirit";[41] the most profound reason for the fact that the "absoluteness of the moral disjunction" has no place in Hegel is that "at its core" Hegel's theory remains "ever in the contemplative realm" or that, put more precisely, Hegel as a philosopher persists in contemplation.[42]

37. Cf. *GLP*, 80, 83; notice 89.

38. "When the hierarchy of the spiritual sphere is dissolved, anything can become the center of spiritual life. But all that is spiritual, including art itself, is changed in its essence and even counterfeited when the aesthetic is absolutized and made the focal point. [. . .] Neither religious nor moral nor political decisions, nor scientific concepts are possible in the region of the only-aesthetic. However, all objective oppositions and differences, good and evil, friend and enemy, Christ and Antichrist, can become aesthetic contrasts and the means of intrigue within a novel and can fit aesthetically into the total effect of a work of art." *PR*, 21.

39. *GLP*, 68; cf. *PT*, 49 (70).

40. In a letter to Alexandre Kojève, Schmitt writes more than thirty years later: "In general the question is—similar to the question of the possibility of a 'dictatorship' in the system of Hegelian philosophy—whether there can be an 'enemy' in Hegel at all. For: either he is only a necessary intermediate stage of negation or null [*nichtig*] and insubstantial" (December 14, 1955).

41. *GLP*, 68. Schmitt continues: "Hegel's philosophy has no ethics that could found an absolute scission between good and evil. For it, good is what in each particular stage of the dialectical process is the rational and thus the real. Good is . . . 'the timely' in the sense of correct, dialectical knowledge and deliberateness. If the history of the world is the world's court of judgment, then it is a process without a final instance and without a definitive disjunctive judgment. Evil is unreal and is conceivable only insofar as something untimely is conceivable, thus perhaps explainable as a false abstraction of the understanding, a passing confusion of a particularity that is limited in itself."

42. *GLP*, 69 and 76. Nor does the "general double-sidedness" of Hegel's philosophy (70), the fact that it can be "taken seriously by active men," historically implemented, and thus practically can become extremely momentous (69), or the consideration that it "harbors enough possibilities of attaining the genuine uniqueness of the historical event," change anything in this regard ("Die geschichtliche Struktur des heutigen Welt-Gegensatzes von Ost und West" [The Historical Structure of the Contemporary Global Opposition of East and West], in *Freundschaftliche Begegnungen. Festschrift für Ernst Jünger zum 60. Geburtstag* [Frankfurt a. M. 1955], 153). The gulf that separates Schmitt from Hegel becomes visible nowhere more sharply than in Hegel's position on the "God manifested in the

Contemplating is not obeying. With this we come full circle. In following Schmitt's dividing line, we have arrived once again at the central point around which everything turns for political theology. Whoever persists in contemplation does not hear the call that confronts him with the decision between either God or Satan, friend or enemy, good or evil. He does not orient his existence towards the commandment that is given him from outside. Such persistence, not-hearing, and not-obeying, demonstrate more clearly than anything else the morality to which Schmitt aspires: Man finds his salvation only in the obedience of faith. Due to his divine provenance he lives in the state of probation and judgment. He is subject to the commandment of historical action. Man is the creature who must "answer in doing."[43] By emphasizing obedience, political theology places that virtue in the center which is, in the words of one of its greatest teachers, "in the rational creature, as it were, the mother and guardian of *all virtues*."[44] By anchoring them in unconditional obedience, the moral virtues are given a character they would not have otherwise. They do not appear as ways and means to a natural optimum, but rather are transformed into unquestionably valid demands.[45] They are endowed with the binding force that alone the command of the supreme authority is able to confer. For political theology, subordination to obedience means that if it wishes to remain in harmony with its presuppositions, it has to understand itself as "theory" on the basis of obedience. Political theology is not excepted from the commandment of historical action. For political theology it also holds that only obedience to God can guarantee protection from the lord of this world. Should we recognize in the *obedio, ut liber sim* of the political theologian the archetype of the "eternal correla-

midst of those who know themselves in the form of pure knowledge" (*Phänomenologie des Geistes*, chap. VI, last sentence), a statement that is most intimately and extremely connected with Hegel's "remaining in contemplation." Concerning this, note in particular the passages of Alexandre Kojève's *Introduction à la lecture de Hegel* (Paris 1947) to which Schmitt refers in this context: 144–145, 153–154, 163–164, 195, 267, 404–405 ("Clausewitz als politischer Denker. Bemerkungen und Hinweise" [Clausewitz as Political Thinker: Remarks and References], in *Der Staat* 6, no. 4 [1967]: 488 n.; cf. Schmitt's rendering of the Hegel quotation on 488). In addition, see *PR*, 94–95, 117; "Die Einheit der Welt," 7, 10–11, and *G*, 27, 107, 210–211.

43. *ECS*, 53, 68, 75, 78; "Die geschichtliche Struktur," 147–154.

44. "Sed oboedientia commendata est in praecepto, quae virtus in creatura rationali mater quodam modo est omnium custosque virtutum." Augustine, *De civitate dei*, XIV, 12.

45. Cf. Aristotle, *Eudemian Ethics*, VII, 1249 b 6–21; *Nicomachean Ethics*, X, 1177 b 1–8, 1178 b 7–22; Nietzsche, *Zur Genealogie der Moral*, III, aphs. 1, 8, 9 (*KGW* VI.2, 357 l. 2–5; 370 l. 19–21; 371 l. 26–27; 372 l. 15–19; 373 l. 19–23; 374 l. 16–19); Leo Strauss, *Natural Right and History* (Chicago 1953), 151.

tion between protection and obedience," an archetype not distorted by any secularization?[46]

When we look more closely at the moral or political virtues that have obedience as their mother and guardian, then the special status that courage is accorded becomes clear at once. Is not the commandment of historical action also a commandment to be courageous? The life-and-death encounter of the enemy demands courage. Whoever wishes to fulfill his "duty to the State" in times of impending civil war will not manage without it. The wars, crusades, martyrizations, and revolutions that world history has in store, to say nothing of the "bloody battle of decision" that cannot be avoided forever, seem to make courage a compulsory requirement. It may not be sufficient in order to be victorious in the battle against Satan, but is courage not necessary in order to begin it? And what is one to say of courage with regard to the bourgeois: Have not his most severe critics, from Rousseau to Nietzsche, from Hegel to Lenin, from Sorel to Jünger, confronted him with courage, the virtue he negates first of all? Political theology makes courage appear indispensable. The political theologian must prove himself in his courage all the more so since he knows *que le combat spirituel est plus brutal que la bataille des hommes*.[47] But what kind of courage is it? It is not the courage that is demanded of him who wants to understand and seize the "innermost necessity of the freedom of existence" in order to charge himself with "his ownmost burden."[48] Nor is it the courage of those who try their hand at the "dangerous life" in order "to carry heroism into knowledge," nor that

46. *BdP*, 53; *ECS*, 20; *Der Nomos der Erde im Völkerrecht des Jus Publicum Europaeum* [*The Nomos of the Earth in the International Law of the* jus publicum Europaeum] (Cologne 1950), 295. —"'Fac, et tolle; fac opus, et accipe praemium; certa in agone, et coronaberis.' Quod est opus? Oboedientia. Quod est praemium? Resurrectio sine morte." Augustine, *Sermo ad catechumenos de symbolo*, III, 9.

47. "Staatsethik und pluralistischer Staat" [State Ethics and Pluralistic State] (1930), in *Positionen und Begriffe im Kampf mit Weimar–Genf–Versailles 1923–1939* [*Positions and Concepts in the Battle with Weimar–Geneva–Versailles 1923–1939*] (Hamburg 1940), 145; *PT*, 52, 54 (75, 80); "Clausewitz als politischer Denker," 502; *G*, 213; cf. "Totaler Feind, totaler Krieg, totaler Staat" [Total Enemy, Total War, Total State] (1937), in *PuB*, 239 and "Die geschichtliche Struktur," 150, where the Rimbaud passage still appears in each case in its authentic formulation and not yet in Schmitt's sharpened formulation. In its complete form the passage reads: "Le combat spirituel est aussi brutal que la bataille d'hommes; *mais la vision de la justice est le plaisir de Dieu seul*." (Arthur Rimbaud, *Une saison en enfer* [1873], in *Œuvres complètes* [Biblio. de la Pléiade], 117; my emphasis.)

48. Martin Heidegger, *Die Grundbegriffe der Metaphysik. Welt, Endlichkeit, Einsamkeit* (1929–30), *Gesamtausgabe* 29–30 (Frankfurt a. M. 1983), 247–248; see 270–271.

of those other obedient individuals who devote themselves to the "good fight" in order to serve as the precursor of some "Holiness of knowledge" or of some "new nobility."[49] Born of obedience, the courage of the political theologian is least of all to be confounded with the courage that stands alongside the virtues of *wisdom* and *moderation*.[50] Rather, it is most intimately connected and associated with *faith* and *hope*. Its place lies between the latter two. The courage of the Spartan, who finds supreme fulfillment in living and dying for his fatherland, can be understood by Schmitt's political theology as a "historical answer" and affirmed in this relativization. With the obvious qualification required by the historical situation, which from the standpoint of political theology has been fundamentally changed, this holds even for the courage of simply standing firm, the courage that, with nihilism in view, perseveres in "faith without content" and wants to endure extreme pain in order "to participate, despite everything, in the mobilization."[51] But neither the late, devout resolution of "heroic realism" nor the original political virtue of the *andreia*-ideal is identical with the courage of political theology. It attains what is most proper to it only in the courage the believer needs in order to lead his life in this world in the face of the "terrible decision," which awaits believers and unbelievers in the other world and promises them either eternal beatitude or eternal damnation.[52]

The series *faith, hope, courage* is fittingly continued with *humility*. For obedience is the mother and guardian of courage also in the sense that in giving courage humility, it gives it as its companion the biblical virtue that counteracts the burgeoning of pride and teaches the courageous man to accept his victory and reward as a work of grace.[53] Now, one could ask whether humility is not in truth the sole fitting virtue for the man who

49. Nietzsche, *Die fröhliche Wissenschaft*, aph. 186; *Also sprach Zarathustra*, I, "Vom Krieg und Kriegsvolke" (cf. *KGW* VII, 16 [50]), III, "Von alten und neuen Tafeln," 21.

50. Plato, *Republic* 427 e; consider *Laws* 630 e, 631 c-d, 659 a, 963 c-e, 965 c-d, and *Protagoras* 349 d, 359 a-360 e. Cf. Seth Benardete, *Socrates' Second Sailing: On Plato's "Republic"* (Chicago 1989), 83–89, and Joseph Cropsey, "Virtue and Knowledge: On Plato's *Protagoras*," in *Interpretation: A Journal of Political Philosophy* 19 (1991–92): 151–155.

51. Ernst Jünger, "Über den Schmerz," in *Blätter und Steine* (Hamburg 1934), 167, 169, 171, 173, 177, 212–213; *Das Abenteuerliche Herz. Aufzeichnungen bei Tag und Nacht* (Berlin 1929), 24, 51; cf. "Die totale Mobilmachung," in Ernst Jünger, ed., *Krieg und Krieger* (Berlin 1930), 29–30 (= *Blätter und Steine*, 152–153).

52. *PR*, 104. Cf. Niccolò Machiavelli, *Discorsi sopra la prima deca di Tito Livio*, II, 2 and I, 26, *Opere* (Feltrinelli), I, 282–283 and 193–194; Jean-Jacques Rousseau, *Du contrat social*, IV, 8, *Œuvres complètes* (Biblio. de la Pléiade), III, 465–467; Leo Strauss, *Liberalism Ancient and Modern* (New York 1968), 193 and 196.

53. Cf. Aristotle, *Nicomachean Ethics*, IV, 7–9.

lives in the faith that he is the creature of the omnipotent God. Can faith in the face of the omnipotence of him who created the world out of nothing be anything but obedience, and can obedience be practiced other than in humility? But what makes obedience humble and humility into a virtue? Apparently humility can be a "virtue" only so long as it is completely absorbed in obedience or, in other words, so long as it does not know itself to be a virtue.[54] Would humility thus be the most profound obedience because it wants nothing but to obey? Is it to be the supreme virtue in the end because it only believes and knows nothing of itself? Be that as it may. However much humility may otherwise give us to think about,[55] we have to speak about it in yet another regard if we are to pursue the question as to which morality Schmitt's political theology aims at. For humility is the key to the proper understanding of Schmitt's historicism. It completely determines the attitude towards history which Schmitt, following Konrad Weiss's interpretation of history, characterizes as the attitude of a Christian Epimetheus. The Christian Epimetheus believes that history is ruled by divine Providence. It thus appears to him as an "indivisible whole," and to wish any one of its pieces different than it actually occurred would be the expression of human presumptuousness. The attitude in which the Christian Epimetheus encounters history is modeled on Mary's *Behold the handmaid of the Lord; be it unto me according to thy word.* All that matters is to comply with the word the Lord of history speaks in and through history, a word which for the obedience of faith is a call to action. However, the counsel of Providence eludes all reason. Its intentions remain concealed from human foresight. The Christian Epimetheus is thus able to answer in doing only by means of a daring-humble "anticipation of a commandment that has to be obeyed

54. Martin Luther names humility "the supreme virtue." He says of it rightly: "God alone knows humility / he alone judges, too, and reveals it / so that man never knows less about humility / than precisely when he is properly humble." By way of elucidation he adds: "Proper humility never knows that it is humble / for whenever it were to know it / so would it become arrogant by viewing the same beautiful virtue / but rather with heart / mind / and all the senses / it clings to the lesser things / it has them incessantly in view." (*Das Magnificat verdeutschet und ausgelegt*, ed. Clemen, II, 148, 150 [*WA* VII, 560, 562].) Concerning this definition of humility as the "supreme virtue," note Luther's illuminating criticism of Socratic virtue at the outset of his *Vorlesung über den Römerbrief 1515–16*. It has all the more weight as there Luther counts Socrates among the "optimi et syncerissimi" and as he mentions him as the only one "inter Gentes et Judeos" by name (chap. 1, paragraphs 1–5; Latin-German edition in 2 vols. [Darmstadt 1960], 8–12).

55. In addition to the references contained in nn. 45, 50, 52, 53, and 54, see Plato, *Laws* 716 a and Leo Strauss, *The Argument and Action of Plato's "Laws"* (Chicago 1975), 58–61; cf. 27–31.

[*Vorgebot*]."[TN6] In the end his humility is proved insofar as he sees in retrospect just how much he as an agent is struck with blindness.[56] If humility is a virtue, then one may certainly say that here a virtue is made out of necessity. Through humility Schmitt's historicism gains its eschatological foothold. It combines in itself, as it were, obedience, courage, and hope. At the same time it confirms Schmitt in his faith that the moral, "like everything" in the world, is historical and must be understood historically: What is morally imperative for him who acts historically can be only decided based on his concrete situation; it is measured on the basis of the question with which history confronts him. Whoever asks about the morality of political theology is thus referred to history. This holds on closer inspection even for the cardinal virtues of *obedience*, *courage*, *hope*, and *humility*. They are historical "in an eminent sense," because and insofar as they are tied to the Christian eon. One may call them "transhistorical" at best in the sense that they are able to claim validity for the entire Christian eon. That they are tied to history appears to Schmitt to be a confirmation of his political theology and by no means an objection to it. For it is not the concern of political theology to find an answer to the question *What is virtue?* Its goal is not the knowledge of what is always valid but rather the action that obeys the challenge of the historical moment, and above all, what is needed for such action is faith.

Political theology presupposes faith in the truth of revelation. It subordinates everything to revelation and traces everything back to it. Insofar as political theology champions the binding force of revelation, it places itself in the service of obedience. To obey revelation or itself, political theology has to want to be "theory" out of obedience, in support of obedience, and for the sake of obedience. Morality is thus its principle in a twofold sense. It stands at the outset of political theology and remains its determinative ground. This fundamental relationship deserves all the more attention inasmuch as political theology *in concreto* can advocate divergent positions on morality. However, that the tenets and demands that obedience of faith is able to derive from revelation can differ from and even contradict one another does not contradict the principle that

56. *PT*, 49 (70); *ECS*, 12, 53; "Drei Möglichkeiten eines christlichen Geschichtsbildes" [Three Possibilities of a Christian View of History], in *Universitas* 5, no. 8 (August 1950): 930–931. (I cite the essay—which was published with the title "Drei Stufen historischer Sinngebung" [Three Stages of the Attribution of Historical Meaning]—in accordance with the authentic title, which Schmitt wrote on the offprints he mailed. He says that the "title improvised by the editors" is "wholly wrong; neither 'stages' nor 'attribution of meaning' is involved.") "1907 Berlin" (1946–47), in *Schmittiana*-I, ed. Tommissen, Eclectica 71–72 (Brussels 1988), 14; *G*, 33, 314, 316; Konrad Weiss, *Der christliche Epimetheus* (n. p.: Verlag Edwin Runge, 1933), 105, 109–110, 111.

governs political theology. If it is true that the moral cannot continue to exist without the theological, then it is certainly no less true that political theology cannot be thought of and understood without the primacy it grants morality. For Schmitt's political theology, the differences and contradictions of political-theological positions are to be explained on the basis of their historicity. They arise precisely from the fact that the commandment of historical action is recognized as binding and that an attempt is made in time to answer the historically unique call. If it is to explain why the answers—each invested with the same resolution to subject itself to the same authority and to serve it to the best of its ability—can differ from one another so widely, not only in different epochs but also in the same historical moment—this confronts political theology, as we have seen, with a problem that is hardly difficult for it to solve. One might ask oneself whether there might not be a more natural explanation. But if we remain within the horizon of political theology, Schmitt's fundamental position on morality appears to be consistent. Whether it may be called orthodox has to be decided by whoever believes himself called to do so. That the *lex naturalis* has no place in Schmitt's political theology does not speak against its consistency. In any case Schmitt would not be, to say only this much here, the first to deny the knowability of "natural law" by human reason and thus to rely on his faith in revelation, especially in the truth of the doctrine of original sin.[57] That Schmitt enters onto the scene as a "critic of morality" speaks least of all against its internal consistency. Neither in his late confrontation with the "tyranny of values" nor in his lifelong polemic against "humanitarian morality" can the moral impetus be missed. The motives of his attack on the "dominion of normativism" are no more concealed than is the moral interest that on the whole determines his critique of the age.[58] When he denounces the "illusion and deception" of a supposed substitution of politics with morality, with one that serves only the veiling and even more effective achievement of political or economic interests, his moral indignation virtually leaps to the eye. Generally speaking, the unmasking gesture with which Schmitt opposes the deceitfulness of conducting politics under moral pretexts, in the guise of the unpolitical, and with underhanded methods, is so pro-

57. Cf. Blaise Pascal, *Pensées*, ed. Brunschvicg, 294, 434, 222, 92, 93 (ed. Lafuma, 60, 131, 882, 125, 126).

58. Cf. *GLP*, 68–69; *NdE*, 67; "Nomos-Nahme-Name," 96–97; *G*, 169, 179; "Die Tyrannei der Werte" [The Tyranny of Values], in *Säkularisation und Utopie. Ebracher Studien. Ernst Forsthoff zum 65. Geburtstag* (Stuttgart 1967), 42–43, 48, 51, 54–55, 58–59 (this is a greatly expanded version of a text that was first published privately in 1960).

nounced, and moral judgments and viewpoints, the high regard for honesty and visibility, the condemnation of cunning and disguise, permeate his political attitudes and preferences to such an extent,[59] that the opinion that Schmitt sharply distinguished between politics and morality, that he was a theoretician of "pure politics" whose sole concern was to grasp and determine "what is," already for this reason alone can only be met with astonishment. Now, the political advantage that Schmitt gains is obvious when he unmasks the morality of the enemy and when he brings to light the political advantage the enemy derives from his immorality. Yet the moral-political thrust of Schmitt's critique extends further. Beyond every polemical unmasking strategy, his critique of the "flight into normativism" has its moral sense in its aiming at the flight from responsibility. What Schmitt has in view also in this case is the avoidance of the "demanding moral decision" with respect to which only a "concrete historical decision" can be of concern, one which entails the risk of failure and on which the gravity of a future judgment without appeal weighs heavily. Whoever hides behind "normativisms," whoever indulges in what is morally desirable and for this reason misses what is necessary here and now, whoever continually appeals to norms while not wanting to contribute anything to creating the normal situation or maintaining the order that such norms presuppose seeks to avoid that decision.[60] The critique of humanitarianism acts on the same impulse. What is decisive for Schmitt, however, first becomes evident upon the precise identification of its locus: Only against the backdrop of the "historical challenge" that Schmitt believes he answers with his fight against humanitarian morality does the moral decision of the political theologian, which forms the basis of his fight, become discernible. An important hint is given by Schmitt's striking phrase: "Whoever says mankind intends to deceive."[61] First, and in the immediate context of its application, this phrase is intended to strike a blow against a "murderous imperialism" that drives its expansion forward in the name of mankind. Schmitt warns emphatically against the "highly political usefulness of the nonpolitical name mankind," whose final consequence consists in "the enemy's being

59. *BdP* III, 56, 57, 59, 60; "Wesen und Werden des fascistischen Staates" [Essence and Development of the Fascist State] (1929), in *PuB*, 114; *Staat, Bewegung, Volk. Die Dreigliederung der politischen Einheit* [*State, Movement, People: The Tripartite Structure of the Political Unit*] (Hamburg 1933), 28; "Nomos-Nahme-Name," 104.

60. *PT*, 11, 13 (16, 20); *Über die drei Arten des rechtswissenschaftlichen Denkens* [*On the Three Kinds of Jurisprudential Thought*] (Hamburg 1934), 22–23.

61. It is first used by Schmitt in "Staatsethik und pluralistischer Staat," in *Kantstudien* 35, no. 1 (1930): 39 (= *PuB*, 143) and then again in *BdP* in the second edition of 1932 (55) and the third edition of 1933 (37).

denied the quality of being human" and "thereby war's being driven to the point of extreme inhumanity." But when Schmitt, in "adapting a terrible phrase by Proudhon," coins the phrase *Whoever says mankind intends to deceive*, he refers implicitly to a deception even more terrible: Mankind, "in its ethical-humanitarian form," has taken God's place. Schmitt's polemical substitution recalls that the absolutization of mankind is preceded by the fall from God.[62] And, above all: the battle *against God* is also fought in the name of mankind.[63] Schmitt attacks humanitarian morality because he sees in it the "vehicle" of an anti-divine "new faith." He fights in it a "hastener" on the path to man's self-deification. Wherever humanity is held to be the "highest value," the danger is great that "every relativization of man on the basis of a transcendence and an otherworldliness" sinks into oblivion. There are good reasons for saying that the danger that arises from pseudo-religion increases to the extent that it makes itself similar to religion. The "pseudo-religion of absolute humanity"[64] Schmitt opposes would then be so dangerous precisely because it appeals to the "values" of the Christian religion and promises their realization in this world. And in fact "pseudo-religion of absolute humanity" is an enemy that is all the more dangerous the more moral it is, or the more its deception is self-deception. – – – If the ques-

62. "In Ernst Jünger one finds the sentence: 'The opposite of humanity is not barbarism but rather divinity.' Instead of barbarism let us say bestiality since the situation thereby becomes clearer. The humanitarian concept of mankind has emancipated itself insofar as it made the divine and the transhuman, which are superior to it, disappear and distinguished itself all the more purely from a doubtless inferior object of comparison, barbarism or bestiality, as the sole magnitude still to come into consideration. That is a rather simple and cheap way to elevate oneself to the absolute and to disqualify one's opponent." Epilogue to *Disputation über den Rechtsstaat* [*Disputation about the Legal State*] (Hamburg 1935), 87.

63. On Proudhon's "battle against God" in the name of mankind, see the explicit reference in *PT*, 45 (64–65); see also *GLP*, 82–83 and *ECS*, 49–50 and 53. Cf. *RK*, 69–73 (45–58). —"*The* man who appears in France at the end of the eighteenth century in order to demand his human rights, he is only the demonic aping of the Son of Man, who appearing in Judea proclaims the reign of God. *The* man who sends his armies into all the nations of Europe, he is the devilish imitator of him who has sent his apostles into all the nations of the *oikumene* . . . here the man who is of the earth dares to adopt 'mankind.' That which only the second person of the Trinity was permitted, to absorb mankind into the divinity, the Frenchman presumes to do and absorbs 'mankind' into man, knowing well that to him who has adopted mankind will belong all the kingdoms of the world. *The* man who here demands his rights is not only the man who murders king and aristocracy and organizes the *levée en masse* but, what is more, knows himself to be free of all sin in doing so—as only the Son of God ever is, though unlike the latter without taking the sins of the world upon himself—and on the basis of such sinlessness now preaches *liberté*, *égalité*, and *fraternité*; however, each of these words is not only a lie but is covered with tears and blood." Peterson, "Politik und Theologie," transcription by Nichtweiß, 5–6; cf. Nichtweiß, *Erik Peterson*, 807.

64. *DC*, 108, 112.

tion concerning what is morally imperative is to be decided only on the basis of the unique historical situation, then the political-theological position on morality *in concreto* must take its bearings by the enemy. It is thus essentially determined by his nature. If the adversary is a master of cunning and disguise, then the demand for visibility and honesty cannot be the last word; moral appeals will not be much of a match for him who constantly talks about morality; and he is hardly to be stopped by means of unmaskings so long as self-deception opens doors for him. The political theologian seems to reach a certain, no longer circumventable line of resistance only where deception is driven to extremes and the end of all enmity is promised. For how could the Old Enemy prepare his victory more cunningly than by making men forget the enmity that is sown between him and them, and how would such forgetting be brought about with greater prospects of success than through the promotion of the errant faith that they no longer had any enemies or that without exception they are well on their way to getting rid of them? How could he disguise himself more perfectly than by disavowing enmity and proclaiming its conquest? What could he do besides pretend to negate what he is and must be by his very being? In the midst of all historical variability, the invariable essence of the adversary apparently is the infallible point of orientation, and enmity the only firm ground by means of which to escape with human methods the groundlessness of deception and self-deception: whoever wants to withstand Satan must insist on enmity. Enmity proves to be Satan's—*sit venia verbo*—Achilles' heel, because his "nature" sets limits to his art of disguise. The battle "for" or "against" enmity, its affirmation or negation, thereby becomes the political-theological criterion of the first order. As an indispensable touchstone, this criterion appears especially in view of the eschatological confrontation with the Antichrist, whose reign, according to the teaching of the Church Fathers, will precede the return of Christ at the end of time.[65] In his early position on the "moral meaning of the age" cited at length at the outset of this chapter, a position he has culminate in an evocation of the image of the Antichrist, Schmitt answered the question as to what is so "horrifying" about the Antichrist and why one should "fear him more" than a power-

65. "Non veniet ad vivos et mortuos iudicandos Christus, nisi prius venerit ad seducendos in anima mortuos adversarius eius Antichristus; quamvis ad occultum iam iudicium Dei pertineat, quod ab illo seducentur. *Praesentia* quippe *eius erit*, sicut dictum est, *secundum operationem satanae in omni virtute et signis et prodigiis mendacii et in omni seductione iniquitatis his, qui pereunt*. Tunc enim solvetur satanas et per illum Antichristum in omni sua virtute mirabiliter quidem, sed mendaciter operabitur." Augustine, *De civitate dei*, XX, 19.

ful tyrant: "because he knows how to imitate Christ and makes himself so similar to him that he tricks all out of their souls." What is horrible is the cunning and disguise of the Old Enemy, which reach their peak in the seeming "omnipotence" of the Antichrist: the "sinister magician recreates the world, changes the face of the earth, and subdues nature"; it serves him "for some satisfaction of artificial needs, for ease and comfort"; the "men who allow themselves to be deceived by him see only the fabulous effect; nature seems to be overcome, the *age of security* dawns; everything has been taken care of, a clever foresight and planning replace Providence; he 'makes' Providence just like any institution."[66] That the Antichrist can by no means make everything is revealed to him who, without wavering, holds fast to the conviction that the destiny of the Antichrist consists in *being an enemy*. The Antichrist could establish his rule lastingly only if he succeeded in convincing men that the promise of *peace and security* has become reality,[67] that war and politics definitively belong to the past, that men no longer need to distinguish between friend and enemy, and therefore no longer between Christ and Antichrist. What finds its supreme confirmation in light of the final decision between Christ and Antichrist holds no less in the secular world, short of the apocalyptic expectations: whoever wants to obey the commandment of historical action must not allow himself to part with or be talked out of his enemies, whom Providence uses and through whom it raises its questions. For the political theologian, who is aware of the eschatological importance of the battle for or against enmity in an age in which "nothing is more modern than the battle against the political,"[68] the defense of the political becomes a moral duty.

66. *Theodor Däublers "Nordlicht,"* 65–66 (my emphasis).

67. There is a long tradition of assigning the slogan *peace and security* to the Antichrist. Thus the last sentence of the Antichrist in the medieval *Ludus de Antichristo* reads: "Post eorum casum, quos vanitas illusit, pax et securitas universa conclusit" (v. 413–414). The assignment is based on the authority of the Apostle Paul, who writes in 1 Thessalonians 5:3: "For when they shall say, peace and security, then sudden destruction cometh upon them." This is the only passage in the Bible that names *pax et securitas* in one breath. Cf. 2 Thessalonians 2.

68. *PT*, 55 (82); cf. *RK*, 28 (19).

II POLITICS, OR WHAT IS TRUTH?

But my speech denies that eros is of a half or of a whole—unless, comrade, that half or whole can be presumed to be really good; for human beings are willing to have their own feet and hands cut off, if their opinion is that their own are no good. For I suspect that each does not cleave to his own (unless one calls the good one's own and belonging to oneself, and the bad alien to oneself) since there is nothing that human beings love other than the good.

Plato, *Symposium* 205 e-206 a
(trans. Seth Benardete, 1986)

Carl Schmitt's concept of the political presupposes the concept of the enemy. The political can endure only so long as there is an enemy, "at least as a real possibility," and the political is *real* only where the enemy is *known*. Knowledge of the enemy seems to be fundamental in every way. Conversely this knowledge apparently cannot completely cease to exist so long as the political persists. The political is based on knowledge and promotes it at the same time. Could the most profound meaning of the political ultimately be one with the meaning it has for knowledge? At the point in his wide-ranging oeuvre where he comes closest to a "definition" of the political, Schmitt explains that the political lies "in a behavior determined by the real possibility of a war, in the clear knowledge of one's own situation which is determined in this way, and in the task of rightly distinguishing between friend and enemy."[1] Accordingly, the political describes a behavior, consists in a knowledge, and names a task. With good reason Schmitt places knowledge in the center of his tripartite definition. For the behavior that is oriented towards the dire emergency

1. *BdP* III, 16; cf. II, 37. In the first edition the political does not yet lie "in the *task* of *rightly* distinguishing between friend and enemy" but rather "in the capacity of distinguishing between friend and enemy" (I, 10).

of war is just as indisputably bound up with knowledge as the task of distinguishing *rightly* between friend and enemy obviously requires knowledge. The former presupposes the knowledge of enmity, of its reality and indispensability; the latter cannot be grappled with except on the path of self-delimitation, self-definition, and therefore self-knowledge. The political seems not only to be based on knowledge and to promote knowledge, but in a precise sense to *be* knowledge. Could it be that Schmitt's most profound thought lies in his conceiving of the political as essentially *self-knowledge*, as serving self-knowledge and arising from self-knowledge?

Yet let us begin at the beginning. That Schmitt's concept of the political presupposes the concept of the enemy says first of all two things. On the one hand, Schmitt's conception of the political employs the concept of the enemy as an indisputably valid magnitude; on the other hand, the meaning of this conception is disclosed solely within the horizon of what Schmitt considers to be an indubitable truth. If one wishes to penetrate to the core of the enterprise in whose service Schmitt places himself with his theory of the political, one has to go back to the question that decides everything, a question that itself is not raised in Schmitt's "theory" but rather precedes it, because for Schmitt it has been answered authoritatively once and for all. If one wishes to speak of the presuppositions that form the foundation of Schmitt's concept of the political, one cannot remain silent about faith in revelation. One cannot grasp Schmitt's teaching of the political if one does not grasp it as a piece of his political theology. The central meaning that the distinction between friend and enemy is accorded in Schmitt's thought can only be comprehended, the entire weight that Schmitt gives his criterion of the political only appreciated, by one who does not fail to attend to that other criterion which subjects the affirmation or negation of enmity to the political-theological distinction.

At first glance the intention Schmitt pursues with his concept of the political looks rather modest. Schmitt wants the distinction between friend and enemy to be understood as "a specification of a concept in the sense of a criterion, not as an exhaustive definition or summary." He speaks of a "simple criterion of the political."[2] The interest in conceptual clarity and scholarly usefulness seems to be predominant. In retrospect Schmitt stresses the "informative purpose" of *Der Begriff des Politischen*; he even goes so far as to assert the "rigorously didactic character" of his exposition.[3] In addition the distinction between friend and enemy itself

2. *BdP*, 26.

3. *BdP*, 1963 Preface, 13, 16. In the 1932 Epilogue, dated "October 1931," Schmitt writes: "What is said here concerning the 'concept of the political' is intended to 'delimit' an

seems originally to have only a limited scope. Schmitt introduces it in answer to the question as to "whether there is"—comparable to the distinctions between good and evil "in the domain of the moral," between beautiful and ugly "in the aesthetic domain," between useful and harmful or profitable and unprofitable "in the economic domain"—"also in the domain of the political a particular, independent, and readily evident distinction, and in what does it consist."[4] "[F]or the domain of the political" the distinction between friend and enemy is to correspond "to the relatively independent oppositions of other domains." Accordingly it extends no further than the dimensions of the political's "own domain," which in 1927 Schmitt seeks to gain for the political in opposition to the "systematics of liberal thought that still definitely prevail today."[5] Schmitt is still worlds apart from publicly declaring that he has come to "know that the political is the total."[6] As a "theoretician of pure politics," for his "domain" he seemingly lays claim only to what liberal thought grants the other "domains of human life," whereas the political "is robbed, with special pathos, of all independence and subjected to the norms and 'orders' of morality and law." On the defensive and at the price of reducing the political to foreign policy, Schmitt makes every effort to provide proof of the "existential objectivity and independence of the political." Thus he asserts that the distinction between friend and enemy can "exist theoretically and practically without moral, aesthetic, economic, or other distinctions being applied simultaneously." And once again in opposition to liberalism, which "has transformed" the enemy "with regard to economics into a competitor, with regard to ethics into an opponent in a discussion," he emphasizes that the concepts of friend and enemy are "to be taken in their concrete, existential sense, not as metaphors or symbols; they are not to be mingled with and weakened by economic, moral, or other notions, not to be taken psychologically as an expression of private feelings and inclinations." The enemy that

---

immense problem theoretically. The individual sentences are meant as a starting point for an objective debate and are to serve scholarly discussions and exercises which may allow themselves to consider a *res dura* of that kind. The present edition contains . . . a series of new formulations, notes, and examples, but no alteration or extension of the line of thought itself. Before making such changes, I would like to wait and see which trends and viewpoints will emerge as decisive in the new debate, which has been pursued vigorously for about a year now, concerning the political problem" (96). For a detailed account of the alterations that Schmitt did in fact make to his conception between 1927 and 1932, see *Carl Schmitt and Leo Strauss: The Hidden Dialogue*, 17–29.

4. *BdP* I, 4.

5. *BdP* I, 3, 4, 29.

6. *PT*, Preliminary Remark to the second edition of 1934.

Schmitt's criterion of the political addresses is said to be "only, at least potentially, i.e., as a real possibility, a *fighting* totality of men that is confronted by another such totality." In addition we learn that the enemy is "only" the public enemy, "*hostis*, not *inimicus* in the broader sense; πολέμιος, not ἐχθρός."[7]

Does a sufficiently clear picture not arise from this? Apparently Schmitt is concerned with defending the political in its independence and purity against extraneous encumbrances, inadmissible encroachments, or usurpations by the other "domains of human thought and action." The distinction between friend and enemy ensures the necessary, rigorous separation and provides an instrument with which one can work. The enemy presupposed by the concept of the political is a public and collective entity, neither an individual nor exposed to individual hate; the enemy is not defined by means of "normativities," but rather is a fact of the "existential reality"; he is not subject to moral, aesthetic, or any other valuation, but rather has "to be treated objectively"; he is the enemy who "must be fended off" in the existential battle.[8] It is finally the "real possibility of physical killing" to which the concepts of friend, enemy, and battle "must refer and continue to refer,"[9] which guarantees the scholarly implementability of Schmitt's criterion. If one is to believe a widely held opinion, then no change worth mentioning occurs in this picture when in the second edition of *Der Begriff des Politischen* Schmitt moves away from the conception originally presented and expressly denies what he formerly asserted no less expressly, namely, that the political is a domain of its own.[10] According to this opinion, when Schmitt now says that the "point of the political" can be reached "from any 'domain'" and that the distinction between friend and enemy has "the sense of denoting the most extreme degree of intensity of a bond or separation, of an association or dissociation," the scope of the application of his criterion has therefore been merely expanded: scholarship has been put in a position to work with it safely and dependably in all "domains of human life" without restriction.[11]

7. *BdP* I, 4, 5, 6, 26, 30.

8. *BdP* I, 4, 5, 9.

9. "The concepts of friend, enemy, and battle obtain their real meaning particularly by virtue of their having to refer and continuing to refer to the real possibility of physical killing. War arises from enmity, for the latter is the existential negation of another being [*seinsmäßige Negierung eines anderen Seins*]. War is merely the most extreme realization of enmity" (*BdP* I, 6 [II, 33]).

10. The statement is to be taken as contrafactual insofar as those holding this opinion, which prevailed until 1988, in no way noticed Schmitt's move away from the original conception. Cf. *BdP* I, 3–4 with II, 26–27; see also n. 3 above.

11. *BdP*, 27, 38, 62. The sense of Schmitt's concept of the political has been understood

In fact the picture of Schmitt's enterprise just sketched proves to be deceptive. It does not hold up with regard to the particulars and misses what is most important on the whole. In order to see this, an attentive perusal of any one of the three different editions in which Schmitt presented *Der Begriff des Politischen* in 1927, 1932, and 1933 suffices. In the second, Schmitt's decisive intention comes more clearly to the fore than in the first; in the third, more sharply and emphatically than in the second. And all three must be accorded the most meticulous attention if the foundations of Schmitt's conceptual edifice are to be laid bare. The legend of the rigorously scholarly purpose of the text or the *fable convenue* of the purely political meaning of its distinctions cannot, however, stand up in the face of any of those editions. Despite the rhetoric of pure politics that Schmitt first brings to bear and despite the detoxifying self-stylization which he later cultivated,[12] neither the autonomy of a "domain of human thought and action" nor its scholarly assessment or juridical circumscription is at issue here. From start to finish what concerns Schmitt is not the independence of the political but rather its authoritativeness. Put more precisely: from the very beginning what matters to him is to locate *what is authoritative* [das Maßgebende] in the political. The concept of the political is oriented towards the "authoritative grouping." It has the "authoritative unit" in view. Even at a time when Schmitt still allots the political a region within the realm of the provinces of culture, the concept of the political aims at the "authoritative case."[13] It aims at the case that *breaks through* the peaceful coexistence of "autonomous domains" of

by several of his interpreters such that the "simple criterion" named by Schmitt is taken to be a kind of litmus test that shows when something becomes "political."

12. In the Preface to the 1963 reprint (13–16) the emphasis placed on the juridical character of the book, which "in the first place" addresses "experts in the *jus publicum Europaeum*," has its equivalent in Schmitt's later assertion that his *Politische Theologie* of 1922 was a "purely juridical text" and that all his statements on the topic of "political theology" were "the statements of a jurist" which moved in the "sphere of research in the history of law and in sociology" (*PT II*, 30, 101 n.; cf. 22, 98 n., 110). Schmitt does not hesitate to slip in the same passage the statement: "My writing *Politische Theologie* of 1922 bears the subtitle *Vier Kapitel zur Soziologie des Souveränitätsbegriffes* [*Four Chapters on the Sociology of the Concept of Sovereignty*]" (101 n.; the statement is rendered no less false by the fact that in 1923 Schmitt allowed three of the four chapters to appear in a memorial volume for Max Weber and chose for this partial reprint—paying tribute to the occasion—the title "Soziologie des Souveränitätsbegriffes *und* politische Theologie" [Sociology of the Concept of Sovereignty *and* Political Theology] [my emphasis]). The *most obvious* reason for self-stylizations of this kind is alluded to towards the end of the cited note (cf. *G*, 23, 71, 80). Concerning the *most profound* reason for Schmitt's defensive strategy, see *Carl Schmitt and Leo Strauss: The Hidden Dialogue*, 57–60 (notice the especially blatant instance documented on 77 n. 92).

13. *BdP* I, 11; cf. I, 7, 12, 13, 14, 15.

human thought and action, at the point from which the parceling of human life can be stopped. But for Schmitt what is authoritative can be the political only when a reality is achieved in the latter which *of necessity* opposes this parceling. It has not yet been achieved, the foundation for firm guidance and a determinate dispensation would not be assured, so long as the political is conceived merely as *what is superior*. Its claim would remain—like every claim to superiority and obedience—contestable. In order to remove it from the quarrel over high and low, higher and lower, precedence and subordination, from the arbitrariness of opinion, wish, and negation, the political must be grasped by recourse to the "most extreme eventuality" of quarrel itself. The requirement that the political always "must refer and continue to refer to the real possibility of physical killing" assures it the inevitability of a material power which mere "ideas," "rational ends," or "normativities" lack. It is only in light of the dire emergency that the exceptional position of the political becomes visible. Only when it comes into view as the reality which at any time can make a life-and-death claim upon man, does the political appear as what is authoritative in both senses of the term.[TN7]

Just as the interest in scholarly implementability is not decisive for Schmitt's linking the concept of the political to the "real possibility of physical killing," likewise his turning away from his conception of domains is not motivated by didactic considerations. If the political is to be what is authoritative, it cannot be a province in the realm of culture. It cannot be subject to the parceling it is destined to overcome. It has to have the capacity to encompass every region of human life. The political must be in a position to place "everything" at its disposal. Hence Schmitt cannot seriously stop with the claim that the political is to be established "independently as a domain of its own" in the field of the other "domains of human thought and action." Nor can he be satisfied with his initial statement that the political has "to have its own, *relatively* independent, *relatively* ultimate distinctions."[14] The exceptional position of the political arises precisely from the fact that the political does not denote one "domain" among other "domains" and that it does not become absorbed by or lost in the relativism of the liberal "philosophy of culture." Therefore, when Schmitt turns away from the conception of domains regarding the political, he merely attempts to raise his theoretical statements or notions to the level of his intentions. He follows the original thrust of his enterprise. For the dire emergency of violent death towards which Schmitt's concept of the political is oriented is "the dire emergency not merely

14. *BdP* I, 3–4 (my emphasis); cf. the new wording in II, 26.

within an 'autonomous' region—the region of the political—but for man simply."[15]

The thrust brought to bear in this orientation can, of course, be implemented in various ways. It opens up paths that, contrary to initial appearances, diverge widely. The political can be conceived as what is authoritative because and insofar as it is able to lay claim to the individual *on behalf of the whole* or because and insofar as it is able to lay claim to him *wholly*. It can be thought of in terms of the community that has the power to place "everything" at its disposal and that imposes a life-and-death obligation upon its members because it encompasses and makes possible the entire reality of their actions. Or, in terms of the individual, it can be conceived as a state that grasps the whole man because this state faces him with the most important decision, confronts him with the greatest evil, and compels him to make the most extreme identification. Schmitt chooses the second path. It is a choice that carries all the more weight inasmuch as he did not seem to be committed to it from the start.

Might not the nearly exclusive concentration on foreign policy in *Der Begriff des Politischen* of 1927 be understood as the expression of a viewpoint that fixes the political rigorously in its gaze on behalf of the whole? Did not the orientation towards war as the dire emergency for man prove that Schmitt, who defined war as armed conflict between peoples,[16] continuously had *the people*[TN8] in view as the subject of politics? Was the vast majority of readers not supposed to get the impression that for the author of the original treatise the "factually existent" peoples are, if not the sole agents, then at least the decisive units in the "pluriverse" of the political world, the defense of which he had made his cause?[17] Was the reference to the people thus tacitly assumed in Schmitt's conception of the political and consequently always to be thought of in conjunction with the latter? Moreover: could not what Schmitt termed 'the domain' of the political easily be interpreted as the level of the community? A specific magnitude for which Schmitt had sought merely a paraphrase and found a general substitute? The first edition of *Der Begriff des Politischen* did not rule out such an interpretation. Were one to rely on this reading, one could see how Schmitt comes to say that the distinction between friend

15. Leo Strauss, "Notes on Carl Schmitt, *The Concept of the Political*" (1932), in *Carl Schmitt and Leo Strauss: The Hidden Dialogue*, 97.

16. *BdP* I, 6.

17. "Were all the earth's various peoples and human groups unified such that a battle between them became really impossible, that is to say, were the distinction between friend and enemy to cease, even as a mere eventuality, then only economy, morals, law, art, etc., would be left, but no longer politics and no longer the State" (*BdP* I, 19).

and enemy can "exist theoretically and practically without moral, aesthetic, economic, or other distinctions being applied simultaneously." Were one to assume that the talk is of peoples as the subjects of politics—subjects which are naturally given or persist in history, which are substantially different from and actually distinguish themselves from one another—then the laconic remark that the enemy is "plainly the other, the stranger" would make sense. Understood in this way, the rhetoric of "pure politics" would have a solid, namable core. To a certain extent even the following assertion would be comprehensible: "to describe the essence" of the enemy it suffices "that he is in an especially intensive sense existentially something other and strange, so that in the case of conflict he signifies the negation of one's own kind of existence and therefore is fended off or fought against in battle in order to preserve one's own, existential kind of life."[18] Yet such a reading is consistently denied by the more precise formulations Schmitt introduces in the text in 1932 and 1933, and the correction of its content or the further development to which he subjects his conception of the political clearly follows a different tack. Just as Schmitt does not maintain the notion that the political is a domain of its own, likewise the fixation on foreign policy or the supposed orientation towards the people as the assumed subject of politics does not persist. In 1932 civil war makes a powerful appearance alongside war, the internal enemy alongside the external enemy, the hostile individual alongside the hostile collectivity.[19] War itself is in turn no longer defined as "armed conflict between peoples" but rather is ascribed with the greatest generality to "organized political units" regardless of their origin and extent.[20] The holy wars of religious communities and the crusades of the Church henceforth appear as authentic manifestations of the political.[21] The peoples have lost their presumed key position. For the pluriverse of the political world they are, as now proves to be the case, by no means indispensable. In 1932 "*religions, classes*, and *other* human groups" are explicitly named in one breath with them as possible constituents of this world.[22] With his textual interpositions, Schmitt makes it clear that war—in contrast to civil war, crusade, the persecution of heretics, or revolution—does not constitute the necessary, all-governing vanishing point of his conception and that the reference to the people in the latter neither is assumed nor does it need to be considered in conjunction with the lat-

18. *BdP* I, 4.
19. *BdP*, 30, 32, 33, 54.
20. *BdP*, 33.
21. *BdP* II, 48; III, 30.
22. *BdP*, 54 (my emphasis).

ter. The people is one human group among others for this conception or, put more precisely, it is an association made up of a majority of conceivable associations. For an association that encompasses at least two individuals is theoretically all that is required by Schmitt's concept of the political. The political "springs up" wherever two come together and join forces against an enemy.

This is precisely the meaning of that conceptual turn in consequence of which the political is to denote "the most extreme degree of intensity of a bond or a separation, of an association or a dissociation." The political is freed from its fixed reference to the community and, as it were, made fluid. But thereby the decisive step is taken in order to reveal that the political *is the total* for an "ontological-existential" interpretation,[23] as Schmitt has it in mind and as his political theology requires. Released from all natural standards, kept free of every substantial classification, the political is able to penetrate everything and to be present everywhere. It emerges as a power that can break into life anytime and anywhere. Its potential ubiquitousness is accompanied by reality's being altogether subject to its gradualization. Not only can the political ignite everywhere and thus attest its authoritativeness with immediate force. It is also confirmed as what is authoritative insofar as it exerts influence over "everything else": "The political opposition," Schmitt states after having made the transition to the notion of intensity, "is the most intensive and extreme opposition, and every concrete opposition is more political, the more it approaches the most extreme point of a grouping into friends and enemies."[24] *As a possibility* everything is political, and everything is always already *more* or *less* political. The political appears as an unshakable, fixed point from and towards which a network of graded intensity pervades and orders the whole. It seems to be flowing and fluid, comprehensive because incalculable, compelling since it has the power of the unforeseen moment at its disposal. To characterize this view of the political as existential would be insufficient. The political totalism that is founded in the recourse to the conception of intensity is the result of an originally individualistic perspective. The political is indeed grasped by Schmitt as existential. But ultimately not in the sense that the existence of the individual is politically determined because the individual necessarily encounters a community that makes demands on him and with respect to which he himself, whether he wants to or not, has to take a stand, has to determine his position. Rather, the individual is required to make the

23. Cf. *BdP* III, 45.
24. *BdP*, 30.

right distinction between friend and enemy as the absolute decision about his own life. The oppositions with which he sees himself confronted become political oppositions not because the community makes the quarrel about them its cause or because they are recognized with regard to the community to be of importance to the whole, but rather because a given opposition is able "as a real possibility" to become a life-and-death quarrel, which is "more political" the closer it comes to the boiling point of a grouping into friends and enemies. When thought through to its logical conclusion, this grouping is not political because it concerns the community, but rather because it constitutes an association and dissociation that is burdened by the gravity of the dire emergency posed by the most extreme battle. Considered naturally and—in view of the limits of mere reason—expressed in a "this-worldly" manner: the association and dissociation in question is a bond and separation *of men* "whose motives can have a religious, national (in an ethnic or cultural sense), economic, or other character" and which "bring about at different times different bonds and separations."[25]

The political "springs up" wherever two or three have gathered who are bound together by the will to oppose one enemy. A leap into a qualitatively new dimension is made when everything is at stake for the individual. The common "reference" to the dire emergency brings about the *political* alliance. It makes the political association the "strongest and most intensive grouping," for the dire emergency identifies and differentiates to the highest degree. Whatever bonds individuals may otherwise enter into, whatever separations the oppositions among men may otherwise bring about, "at any rate that grouping is always political"—as Schmitt explains in the third and final edition of his *Begriff des Politischen*—"which is determined by the dire emergency."[26] Schmitt now also expressly derives from the decisiveness of the dire emergency for the political, the authoritative meaning of the political association *for the individual*: "The political unit," he continues, "is consequently always, as long as it is at all present, the authoritative unit, total and sovereign. It is '*total*' firstly because every concern potentially can be political and therefore can be affected by the political decision, and secondly because man is wholly and existentially grasped in political participation. Politics is destiny. The great teacher of constitutional law, Maurice Hauriou, rightly also saw the jurisprudential hallmark of a political bond in the fact that it

25. *BdP*, 38–39.

26. *BdP* III, 21. "The political always determines the grouping that takes its bearings by the dire emergency" (I, 11). "The grouping that takes its bearings by the dire emergency is at any rate always political" (II, 39). Cf. II, 28.

grasps man *wholly*. A good touchstone of the political character of a community therefore lies in the practice of the *oath*, the true sense of which consists in man's committing himself *wholly*, or who by an oath of loyalty 'allies himself under oath (and existentially).' The political unit is *sovereign* in the sense that the decision about the authoritative case, even if it is an exceptional case, always lies with it, as is necessitated by the concept."[27] With great clarity, more sharply formulated than in any other passage, Schmitt indicates the extent to which—and under which conditions alone—the political is for him what is authoritative: insofar as it is capable of grasping man *wholly*. This word occurs no less than three times in the four newly inserted sentences of the revised text of 1933, two of those specifically emphasized with italics. What Schmitt expresses in view of the sovereign political unit is said fundamentally of every political association. The decisive quality of the political, the intensity in which the individual is grasped, characterizes all "political groupings," should they at all deserve to be called *political*. Consequently the same would hold for the authoritativeness of the political, were it to involve a community organized as a political unit or a party in a civil war, a sect or a band of guerrillas. For the political unit is *authoritative* not because it would be sovereign "in some absolutist sense"[28] but because it is *political*, and it is revealed as political, according to Schmitt, *by the dire emergency*, not on the basis of substantial characteristics. Seen in this way, the substance of the political unit appears as the respective product of the relative strengths of competing political groupings, as a highly changeable magnitude the ascertainment of which requires the diagnostic probe provided by the dire emergency.[29] The substance permits of no standard-setting [*Maß gebende*] orientation. It is not the "substance" that is authoritative [*maßgebend*], but rather the efficacy of the political association, its efficacy in distinguishing between friend and enemy and in carrying out this distinction in the dire emergency. In this way it proves its power to grasp the members of the association *wholly and existentially*. Schmitt directs our attention all the more emphatically to the individualistic starting point of his political totalism when, as if in passing, he puts the oath in play and remarks that the true meaning of the oath of loyalty consists in

27. *BdP* III, 21–22; cf. II, 39.

28. *BdP* III, 22.

29. "If the opposing economic, cultural, or religious forces are so strong that they themselves determine [how] the dire emergency [is to be decided], then they have become precisely the new substance of the political" (*BdP* II, 39). In 1933 Schmitt qualifies the statement: "If the opposing economic, cultural, or confessional forces are so strong that they themselves determine [how] the dire emergency [is to be decided], then they are absorbed into the new substance of the political unit" (III, 22).

allying oneself *under oath and existentially*. The recollection of this "touchstone of the political character of a community" occurs at the right place.

If man is to be grasped wholly and existentially in political participation, whereas the political association in which he "participates" is for its part to be determined by the dire emergency, then the question about the authoritative meaning of the political comes to a head in the question about the dire emergency. The status that the latter holds in Schmitt's conception and the capacity that on closer inspection it is attributed in this conception become the center of attention. Is the orientation towards the dire emergency to be equated with that "reference to the real possibility of physical killing" by means of which the concepts of friend, enemy, and battle or war[30] gain "their real meaning"? Does everything depend on the eventuality of violent death, without distinction and without qualification? And would such a "reference" be capable of grasping man *wholly*, of determining him *in the core of his being*? Or might the most extreme intensity be reached solely at the point where life-and-death battle has erupted and only as long as it lasts in reality? Schmitt would seem to contradict this latter supposition when he declares that the political lies "not in the battle itself." What is more, in his discussions of definitions Schmitt repeatedly takes the "real *possibility*" of battle, war, and physical killing into account. Their actuality remains secondary with respect to what is most important. However, nothing is yet determined thereby as to just how *real*, how close, how present the possibility of battle and death must be if they are to determine the behavior of men thoroughly. Is the knowledge of the "eventuality" of armed conflict sufficient to found the total character of the political? Or is the "reference to the real possibility of physical killing" merely a necessary presupposition, and what would have to be added in this case in order to reveal that the political is the total? Have we not even reached the "most extreme point"[31] in having

30. *BdP*, 33; in III, 15 'battle' (*Kampf*) is replaced by 'war' (*Krieg*) as in numerous other passages in the third edition.

31. "Der politische Gegensatz ist der intensivste und äußerste Gegensatz und jede konkrete Gegensätzlichkeit ist um so politischer, je mehr sie sich dem äußersten Punkte der Freund-Feindgruppierung, nähert." (*BdP* II, 30 [original pagination: 17].) Does the sentence contain a comma too many [before *nähert*]—or one too few [after *Punkte*]? The 1963 reprint corrects the punctuation: " . . . je mehr sie sich dem äußersten Punkte, der Freund-Feindgruppierung, nähert" (translation: "The political opposition is the most intensive and extreme opposition, and every concrete opposition is more political, the more it approaches the most extreme point, the grouping into friends and enemies"). The first edition of 1927 did not contain the sentence since at that time Schmitt had not thought of the concept of intensity of the political. In the third edition the passage reads: " . . . je mehr sie sich dem äußersten Punkte der Freund-Feind-Gruppierung nähert" (11; translation: " . . . the more

reached the life-and-death battle? Is its intensity capable of being heightened? According to Schmitt's concept of intensity, must not the intensity increase to the extent that the intensity of the enmity, which forms the basis of battle, increases? Could it be dependent upon the aim and purpose for the sake of which the existential confrontation is begun and carried out? The orientation towards the dire emergency of the life-and-death battle calls for additional distinctions. Schmitt introduces the most important one in 1933, precisely at the point when he stresses the authoritativeness of the political most emphatically. In the final edition of *Der Begriff des Politischen*, in which Schmitt makes it clear beyond all doubt that he conceives of the political as a state that grasps man wholly, he distinguishes the political for the first time from the agonal.[32] War is now distinguished from the "unpolitical-agonal contest." What is more, the reader learns that war can by no means be regarded as a *factum brutum* or as the unquestionably fixed point of reference that it may first have appeared to be, but that instead it is the object of fundamentally different attitudes, interpretations, and ends: "He who is nothing but a soldier (in distinction to the warrior) tends more to *make a contest out of war* and move from the political into the agonal attitude."[33] What now seems to be of the greatest import is what will be *made* out of war, in which *attitude* one encounters it, whether one understands it *agonally*, or whether one conceives it *politically*. But that means that the "reference to the real possibility of physical killing" cannot be sufficient for the political. Considered in itself the life-and-death battle is not yet the standard-setting dire emergency for man *qua* man. For the "unpolitical-agonal" contest likewise has "reference to the real possibility of physical killing." The danger of violent death weighs on this contest no less than on war understood politically. It, too, is a "life-and-death battle." Wherein does its deficiency have its roots then? Why does the agonal understanding of the life-and-death battle lack that "most extreme possibility" with respect to which "human life gains its specifically *political* tension"?[34] Schmitt introduces the distinction between "political" and "agonal" in the context of a more precise discussion of the concept of the enemy. In the passage in

---

it approaches the most extreme point of a grouping into friends and enemies"). In this seemingly trivial detail, too, the third proves to be the superior edition since it is the most consistent and consequential version of *Der Begriff des Politischen*. In 1963 Schmitt supposedly just wanted to correct a mere oversight in the 1932 edition that he, however, had already revised in another sense in 1933. The 1963 reprint does not retain the level achieved, if not in 1932, then at least in 1933.

32. *BdP* III, 10, 10 n. 1, 12, 15, 17.

33. *BdP* III, 17 (my emphasis).

34. *BdP* III, 18 (II, 35).

which he explained in 1927 and 1932 that the enemy in the sense of *Der Begriff des Politischen* is "not the rival or the opponent [*Gegner*] in general," he adds in 1933: "nor is the enemy the opposing player [*Gegenspieler*], the 'antagonist' in the bloody contest of the '*agon*.'"[35] So we can say that agonal thought apparently lacks the indispensable knowledge of the enemy. To be sure, the decisive question has thus not yet been answered, but rather raised anew and quite sharply: Why does the bloody contest of the agon not reach the level of enmity proper to political confrontation? To the succinct statement in the main text Schmitt adds a footnote that contains all the clues necessary to point the attentive reader to the desired answer. "The great metaphysical opposition between *agonal* and *political* thought," the center of the note reads, "arises in every more profound discussion of war." This observation, which very succinctly names the fundamental character of the distinction later incorporated into the text—fundamental concerning both the issue treated in *Der Begriff des Politischen* and that text's determinative intention—is followed by an elucidation that is emphatically restricted to current events: "In most recent times I would cite the magnificent debate between Ernst Jünger and Paul Adams ([broadcast on the] Deutschland-Sender, February 1, 1933) which, I hope, will soon also be possible to read in print. Here Ernst Jünger represented the agonal principle ('man is not designed for peace'), whereas Paul Adams saw the meaning of war in the establishment of dominion, order, and peace." The opposition between agonal and political thought bears upon the meaning of war and the destiny of man. On the one hand, war is considered the expression of eternal coming to be and passing away and, since it is regarded as arising from the nature of man, is affirmed as such. On the other hand, it is regarded as a state that does not have its raison d'être within but rather beyond itself. From this standpoint war is not the lord or king who allots each the share he is due as the result of free contest and the measuring of one's strengths against others, but rather the slave in the service of a higher order. Over against the agonal principle, according to which man is not designed for peace, stands the political principle, according to which man cannot achieve his destiny save by committing himself wholly and existentially to the realization of dominion, order, and peace. Schmitt can speak of a "great metaphysical opposition" because he sees in agonal thought man's attempt to give meaning, that is, to join in the cosmic play and, should the greatest succeed, to fight a good fight,[36] whereas he believes he

35. *BdP* III, 10; cf. I, 5; II, 29.

36. "The essential thing is not what we are fighting for but rather how we fight. . . . The

sees the most profound basis of political thought in the dependence of everything on whether one takes up the fight for the sake of the good and withstands it as a divine trial.

The quarrel over the meaning of war has to erupt as soon as the question of the dire emergency becomes central. This situation enables Schmitt to play off the superior power of his political-theological position against every "unpolitical" metaphysics. By means of the distinction between "political" and "agonal" he makes it clear that war can be the dire emergency for man *qua* man only when war bears the weight of the decision about dominion, order, and peace. By quoting his friend Paul Adams[37] in order to introduce the series *dominion, order, peace* into the debate, however, he does not just take a stand in the quarrel over the meaning of war. He also has the Catholic journalist provide the decisive key terms in order to make clear to us the dignity of the political and, along with it, the necessity of this quarrel. That is, the quarrel over the meaning of war is itself not to be understood as an "unpolitical-agonal contest," but on the contrary as part of that struggle for dominion, order, and peace which distinguishes the political and is essentially the struggle for just dominion, for true order, for real peace. Thus the quarrel over the meaning of war, as well as political confrontation in general, are both based on the question of what is right. However, the question of what is right is *the question* that is put to man *qua* man. If he wants to answer it seriously, if he seeks to gain clarity for himself, he sees himself confronted

spirit of a warrior, the commitment of the person, and be it for the smallest idea, carries more weight than any grumbling about good and evil. That gives even the knight of a sorrowful countenance his awe-inspiring halo. In the end the most valuable man, he who has earned the world, becomes its conqueror. The law of the world, the play of forces, or God—however one likes—may decide this matter. But we want to show what we've got in us, so that if we fall, we will have really lived life to the fullest." Ernst Jünger, *Der Kampf als inneres Erlebnis* (Berlin 1922), 76. "The purity of heroic thought can be measured by the extent to which it avoids representing war as a moral [*sittlich*] phenomenon." "Here is a standard that has validity: man's attitude in the battle that is the primal relationship of a fatefully oriented order . . . . There is something wonderful, in a time so well equipped with masks and disguises, about life's showing itself undisguised and naked in all its power and defending itself when it frees itself from all that has been instilled, acquired, cultivated, determined by nothing but the most elementary laws. In the midst of impending danger it gains in confidence, in innocence; whoever understands at all how to find something, finds here a magnificent self-confidence in the midst of decline, a steady feeling of immortality which arouses admiration. Based on everything and nothing, the fighting man provides a splendid image . . . because here it is shown the extent to which he does not suffer want even in moments of impending annihilation." Friedrich Georg Jünger, "Krieg und Krieger," in Ernst Jünger, ed., *Krieg und Krieger*, 63, 64; cf. 58. See Chapter I, 18 with n. 51 above; further, Walter Hof, *Der Weg zum heroischen Realismus* (Bebenhausen 1974), esp. 240 ff.

37. That he counted Paul Adams among those friends who stood closest to his own political-theological enterprise is underscored by Schmitt in his *Glossarium* (165).

with conflicting demands, he is subject to the *nomos* of the community, the commandment of God or of men, he encounters answers that are asserted with authority. The question of what is right is put to him in the "sphere of the political." He must find his way in that sphere. It requires a kind of behavior that is oriented towards the real possibility of the life-and-death battle. It demands the knowledge of one's own situation, which is determined by the confrontation over dominion, order, and peace. And it makes the right distinction between friend and enemy the urgent task. The sphere of the political thereby becomes the place of man's knowledge of himself, of the insight into what he is and what he ought to be, of the decision about what he wants to be and what he does not want to be, what he can become and what remains denied him to become. Therein lies the rank of the political. The political theologian and the political philosopher meet in a shared opposing stance towards every, in the strict sense, *unpolitical* "metaphysics." Schmitt's opposition to "agonal thought" in general and to Heraclitus in particular[38] agrees in an important respect with Socrates' critique of the natural philosophy of the Presocratics, as well as of their most recent descendants.[39] For it is just this that constitutes the Socratic turn: that Socrates—of whom it is said was the first to have called philosophy down from heaven, to have established it in political communities, to have forced it to inquire about life, manners, and the good and bad things[40]—that this philosopher, unlike his predecessors, takes the political-theological critique radically seri-

38. "Now the deepest opposition in the views on the essence of the political does not concern the question as to whether politics can relinquish all fighting or not (politics could not do so at all without ceasing to be politics) but rather the question as to *whence war and battle derive their meaning*. Does war have its meaning in itself or in the peace to be won through war? According to the view of a pure 'nothing [counts] but the spirit of the warrior,' war has its meaning, its right, and its heroism in itself; man is, as Ernst Jünger says, 'not designed for peace.' The same is said in Heraclitus's famous sentence: 'War is the father and king of all things; some it proves to be gods, others to be men; of some it makes free men, of others, slaves.' Such a view is purely *warlike* in opposition to the *political* viewpoint." "Politik" [Politics], in Hermann Franke, ed., *Handbuch der neuzeitlichen Wehrwissenschaften* (Berlin/Leipzig 1936), I, 549. In his *Glossarium* Schmitt sarcastically states this opposition with greater precision: "Perhaps the relationship of cat and mouse is also only the result of a long war and only the establishment of the close of a war. As Heraclitus says: war makes some men free, the others slaves. It discloses nature (φύσις) and at the same time establishes it. That is the justice of war; that is natural law. War between men has its honor, it is not just. Only the war between natural beings is just. It ends such that some prove to be free men, others slaves, some cats, others mice" (204). See also *BdP* III, 42: "The political distinction between friend and enemy is even more profound than every opposition in the animal kingdom, just as man as a spiritually existent being is superior to the animal." Cf. *Carl Schmitt and Leo Strauss: The Hidden Dialogue*, 58–59.

39. Xenophon, *Memorabilia*, I, 1.11–16.

40. Marcus Tullius Cicero, *Tusculanae Disputationes*, V, 10.

ously and raises political philosophy to First Philosophy. The political philosopher and the political theologian are bound together by the critique of the self-forgetting obfuscation or of the intentional exclusion of what is most important. Both are in agreement that the quarrel over what is right is the fundamental quarrel and that the question *How should I live?* is the first question for man. However, with the answer that each gives to this question, they stand in insuperable opposition to one another. Whereas political theology builds unreservedly on the *unum est necessarium* of faith and finds its security in the truth of revelation, political philosophy places the question of what is right entirely on the ground of "human wisdom,"[41] so as to develop the question in the most fundamental and comprehensive way available to man. In the most comprehensive way insofar as all known answers are examined, all conceivable arguments are taken up, all demands and objections that claim to be authoritative are integrated into the philosophical confrontation, including those that political theology advances or can advance. In the most fundamental reflection because the ground on which the confrontation takes place cannot be surpassed or outbid by any argument and because the way of life that the most comprehensive confrontation discloses with the question about what is right is itself made the central object of that confrontation. Philosophy has to become a question before it can give an answer. It requires self-knowledge, it must become *political*, if it is to be placed on a *philosophically* sound foundation. That is the decisive insight contained in the Socratic turn. Accordingly the original meaning of political philosophy consists in the *twofold* task of providing the political defense *and* the rational foundation of the philosophical life.[42] From this twofold task arises a new dividing line which allows unpolitical philosophy and political theology to move closer together in one cardinal point. The former fails to recognize the necessity of the political defense as well as the rational foundation of its own way of life. The latter denies the possibility of such a foundation from the very beginning. *Both* are, in other words, based on *faith*. They presuppose the answer to the question of the proper life in unquestioning trust, be it in the correctness of natural inclination, be it in the validity of traditional valuations adopted from others.

41. Plato, *Apology* 20 d-e.

42. Compare Christopher Bruell, "On the Original Meaning of Political Philosophy," in Thomas Pangle, ed., *The Roots of Political Philosophy* (Ithaca 1987), 105 and 109. In his stimulating discussion "Why *Politikè Philosophia?*" *Man and World* 17 (1984): 431–452, Stewart Umphrey fails to recognize the intrinsic connection between the two parts of the task, which is in fact one task (see esp. 444–446). For this reason he does not succeed in recovering the decisive philosophical insight that proves philosophy's political turn to be necessary.

Political theology knows that it is based on faith, and it wants to be, because it believes it knows that every human life must be based on faith. According to Schmitt's teaching, faith is always opposed to faith, metaphysics to metaphysics, religion to religion, even if the opponent poses as unfaith, antimetaphysics, or irreligion. "Metaphysics is something unavoidable."[43] But unlike the follower of the "agonal principle" who believes he has reached the final reality in the sheer irrationality of the battle of faith and who regards the clash of attitudes of faith, which can no longer be accounted for, as part of the great play of the world, the political theologian insists that the battle between faith and errant faith, between true and heretical metaphysics be fought out. He is not concerned with that faith "without which no life is possible." Political theology wants to be based on faith because it believes in the *truth* of faith. In its light every contrary position becomes an apostasy or deviation from the one faith and precisely on account of this must remain a position of faith. Thus unfaith can appear to it to be merely false or dangerous, misled or proud faith. The Socratic objection to the natural philosophers—who, forgetting themselves, fail to recognize the necessity of founding their enterprise and, instead of developing the question of what is right, take comfort in intuitive convictions of faith which find their expression in assertoric declarations[44]—is mutatis mutandis directed with no less reason at political theology. Socrates' critique affects both sides of the "great metaphysical opposition of agonal and political thought." The "agonal" side insofar as it unpolitically misunderstands itself; the "political" side insofar as it conceives of itself as a metaphysical party in a quarrel of faith.[45]

Schmitt's political thinking does not adopt a position of faith only as a result of the metaphysical reading of the opposition to agonal thinking. The notion that is so decisive for Schmitt's articulation of this opposition is already based on faith, namely, that man is grasped wholly [*ganz*] and existentially in political participation. For it is one thing that in the quarrel in the sphere of the political, properly understood, everything is at stake [*ums Ganze geht*], that in that sphere man is *laid claim to* wholly. Whether he can be wholly *grasped* in political *participation* is another question. And assuming he could be wholly grasped politically, would

43. *PR*, 23.

44. Joseph Cropsey has pointed out in which *form* Socrates' critique comes to bear, i.e., how the difference in content is *expressed*. "On Ancients and Moderns," in *Interpretation* 18, no. 1 (1990): 42.

45. "Alfred Baeumler interprets Nietzsche's and Heraclitus's concept of battle entirely in terms of the agonal. Question: whence come the enemies in Valhalla?" *BdP* III, 10 n. 1.

this hold in all circumstances? Independent of the conditions of that claim? And would it apply to all men? Schmitt's notion presupposes that *in action* man is wholly available or wholly himself. For a theory that defends the absolute primacy of action over knowledge, because it subjects everything to the commandment of obedience, this presupposition may seem to be a matter of course. Beyond the context of faith in which political theology moves, it is not. We encounter the same presupposition when we observe Schmitt's use of the sibylline sentence *The enemy is our own question as a figure.*[46] Penned by his friend Theodor Däubler[47] and highly esteemed by Schmitt, this verse deserves all the more attention inasmuch as Schmitt himself ascribes it a key role in the proper understanding of *Der Begriff des Politischen.*[48] In epigrammatic sharpness this poetic phrase seems to give expression to the insight that the political serves self-knowledge and arises from self-knowledge. We can read it as follows: We know ourselves insofar as we know our enemy and insofar as we define our enemy by defining ourselves. We know him to be our enemy who places us in question or the one whom we place in question insofar as we "know" ourselves, as we make ourselves known to ourselves and to others. The enemy proves to be our friend against his will on the way to self-knowledge, and our self-knowledge is transformed suddenly into a source of enmity when it assumes a visible figure.

Schmitt uses the Däubler verse for the first time towards the end of a reflection entitled "Weisheit der Zelle" [Wisdom from the Cell] and dated "April 1947," one that is expressly concerned with self-knowledge.[49] It

46. "Der Feind ist unsre eigne Frage als Gestalt." Theodor Däubler, "Sang an Palermo," in *Hymne an Italien* (Munich 1916), 58 (2d ed., Leipzig 1919, 65). I have discussed the provenance of this verse in *Carl Schmitt and Leo Strauss: The Hidden Dialogue* and attempted to make it fruitful in my reading of *Der Begriff des Politischen* (4, 27–28, 70–71, 82, 87). (Schmitt never mentioned the source of the verse in any of his writings published during his lifetime.)

47. The friendship between Schmitt and Däubler, which goes back before the First World War, has received increasing attention in the course of growing interest in Schmitt's biography. Not, however, the critique of the friend of his youth, a retrospective critique motivated by Schmitt's Christianity and self-criticism for having earlier misunderstood his friend in Christian terms. See *ECS*, 45–53.

48. In the *Glossarium* we can now read the entry from December 25, 1948: "'The enemy is our own question as a figure. / And he will hunt us, and we him, to the same end' (Sang an Palermo). What do these verses mean and where do they come from? An intelligence test for every reader of my little writing: *Begriff des Politischen*. Whoever cannot answer the question from out of his own spirit and knowledge should take care not to enter into the discussion about the difficult topic of that little writing" (213).

49. "You would like to know yourself and (perhaps even more) your real situation?" reads the opening sentence (*ECS*, 79). The immediately preceding text concludes with the statement of faith: "We are all bound by the silence of keeping quiet and the everlasting mystery of the divine provenance of man" (78). Cf. 66 and 75.

culminates in a meditation on *self-deception*, and it is, put more precisely, in this connection that Schmitt raises the question of the enemy which he finally answers with the verse he himself places in italics. The enemy becomes a theme for Schmitt the moment the political theologian addresses the danger of deception and self-deception.[50] "Self-deception is part of solitude."[51] In order to escape it, Schmitt is on the lookout for the "objective power" which "the enemy is" and which no one can "avoid." For, as we learn, "the genuine enemy does not allow himself to be deceived." Whence does the enemy get the knowledge of our true identity? Or might his power to grasp our essence not be based on knowledge? What protects him then from our deception? What preserves him from self-deception if not we ourselves?[52] Thus how, on the basis of what assistance or by means of what dispensation, can the enemy *be* the objective power that Schmitt finds in him, how can he bear the burden that Schmitt loads on him? And in the course of the meditation it becomes clear *what* Schmitt loads on him: He speaks of the enemy who *forces* us into a confrontation, in which we are grasped *wholly* and *existentially*. "Who then can at all be my enemy?" Schmitt asks. "And in fact in such a way that I recognize him as the enemy and even must recognize that he recognizes me as the enemy. In this mutual recognition of recognition lies the greatness of the concept." Here the concern is apparently more than the battle with the enemy who already meets the "simple criterion" of the political because he has "reference to the real possibility of physical killing." Schmitt does not stop for a minute to deal with the enemy who threatens our existence without recognizing us as the enemy or who places us in question existentially without our having to agree to the recognition of his recognition. Is it necessary to mention expressly that he also does not stop to ask whether the knowledge of the enemy and the recognition of the enemy coincide?[53] Schmitt asks: "Whom can I at all recognize to be my enemy? Apparently only him who can place me in question. Insofar as I recognize him as the enemy, I recognize that he can place me in question. And who can really place me in question? Only I myself." Really, not only existentially but

50. In "Weisheit der Zelle" the talk is of the *enemy* only after Schmitt takes up self-deception (88). Cf. Chapter I, 24 f. above.

51. *ECS*, 87. In what follows the passages cited without page references are to be found on 88–90.

52. "All deception is and remains self-deception" (*ECS*, 88). See *G*, 27, 63, 89.

53. In this connection see Schmitt's statement: "Thus be careful and do not speak thoughtlessly of the enemy. One classifies oneself by means of one's enemy. One categorizes oneself by what one recognizes as enmity. Terrible, however, are the annihilators who justify themselves by stating that one has to annihilate the annihilators. But all annihilation is only self-annihilation. By contrast, the enemy is the other" (*ECS*, 90).

also wholly, only I can place myself in question. Why? Perhaps because only I myself and no one else can succeed in knowing me wholly or with respect to what is most important to me, on the basis of and for which I live? But how would self-deception look then? And how would things stand with the objective power of the enemy? But Schmitt continues: "Only I myself. Or my brother. That is it. The other is my brother." The "objective power" that no man can avoid has returned. My brother will preserve me from self-deception. For "my brother proves to be my enemy." But who is my brother? In his meditation on the enemy and self-deception Schmitt believes he finds refuge in the truth of Genesis: "Adam and Eve had two sons, Cain and Abel. This is how the history of mankind begins. This is how the father of all things looks. That is the dialectical tension that keeps world history in motion, and world history has not yet come to an end."[54]

For Schmitt revelation and history cause the enemy to become the objective power, which he can recognize and by means of which he hopes for a way out of the danger of self-deception. The enemy promises such a way out if we see in him the tool the supreme authority uses in order to place us in an objective event, one that most intimately binds us to the other, one in which we are confronted with "our own question" and must "answer in doing." The enemy then appears to us as the guarantor of our identity. He will encounter us when we seek ourselves. We will find ourselves when we face him. Schmitt's "Weisheit der Zelle" reveals that the encounter with the enemy around which the meditation revolves is politically conceived and is to be understood politically, that Schmitt does not interpret the Däubler verse pre- or unpolitically, "only personally" or "purely spiritually." The political confrontation is fundamental. It is held to have constitutive significance for our identity. Precisely that is intended with his meditative reference to history and revelation. Schmitt's intention is strikingly expressed when he formally declares—something he had never done before—fratricidal or civil war to be the father of all things.[55] In the second passage where Schmitt uses the verse, which in the meantime he has made completely his own,[56] we are dealing with a di-

54. "*Historia in nuce*. Friend and enemy. [. . .] The enemy is our own question as a figure. That means *in concreto*: only my brother can place me in question and only my brother can be my enemy. Adam and Eve had two sons: Cain and Abel" (*G*, 217). See *G*, 238.

55. "Many cite Heraclitus's sentence: War is the father of all things. But few dare to think thereby of civil war" (*ECS*, 26; see 56–57).

56. On March 24, 1949 Schmitt writes to a correspondent, to whom he put the question about the significance and provenance of both Däubler verses (see n. 48 above): "That you considered me capable of those verses from 'Sang an Palermo' pleases me; it is, by the way, by no means 'false' to believe that."

rect, political application. "Every war waged on two fronts"—Schmitt writes in the chapter of his *Theorie des Partisanen* entitled "Der wirkliche Feind" [The Real Enemy], and there the talk is expressly of war as well as of civil war, thus of *every* war waged on two fronts—"raises the question of who the real enemy is then. Is it not a sign of inner division to have more than a single real enemy? The enemy is our own question as a figure. If our own figure is unambiguously defined, whence comes the doubleness of the enemy?"[57] It is difficult to see why one's own figure *cannot* be unambiguously determined when it is *delimited* to the same extent vis-à-vis two enemies. And should one's own figure not be able to *set* several enemies against itself precisely when it is unambiguously defined? To say nothing of the war waged on two fronts, which is based on the fact that the others—or at least one of them—do not know their true enemy, *their* question. Schmitt's reflections are obviously not to be taken phenomenologically. The presuppositions that form the basis of his usage of the Däubler verse come all the more clearly to light: First of all the belief in a kind of prestabilized assignment of the enemy. Then the assumption that our own identity is defined essentially by reference to the enemy, that it is authoritatively defined by what we negate. Finally the certainty that man achieves his destiny by means of action alone.[58] For Schmitt abruptly continues: "The enemy is not something that for some reason must be done away with and annihilated because of its want of value. The enemy is on my own level. For this reason I must confront him in battle in order to gain my own standard, my own limit, my own figure." I must recognize the enemy, I must fight with him so that I may achieve my destiny and he his.

The political battle is constitutive of the formation of my identity. In his account of the war waged on two fronts Schmitt changes to the first person singular just as smoothly as in his meditation on self-deception he made the inverse shift to the plural, from the I to the We of the civil war. If man is to be grasped wholly and existentially in political participation, *our* enemy has to become *my* enemy without qualification, my *own* question must prove to be a *political* question, and fundamentally it has to be *answerable politically*. Otherwise the political would concern me only regarding a particular characteristic; I would be grasped merely in one aspect of my being; there would always be a non-trivial "remainder" that would be politically incommensurable and unattainable. The claim to

57. *Theorie des Partisanen. Zwischenbemerkung zum Begriff des Politischen* [*Theory of the Guerrilla: A New Remark on the Concept of the Political*] (Berlin 1963), 87.

58. Regarding these three presuppositions, compare *Carl Schmitt and Leo Strauss: The Hidden Dialogue*, 87.

have come to "know that the political is the total" has its complementary counterpart in Schmitt's interpretation of the sentence *The enemy is our own question as a figure*. Both statements shed light on one another. Thus the verse can indeed serve as a key to *Der Begriff des Politischen*. The use Schmitt makes of it illuminates in particular his central concern to seek in the political what is authoritative and to bring it to bear. At the same time it brings into view the limits that are set for self-knowledge in Schmitt's conception. The unquestioned presuppositions we have already encountered and shall encounter later on meet in the faith that the question on which everything ultimately depends is a question which does not lie in man's power to raise, but which is sent to him historically. A question that is a call, commandment, task, one that must be answered, obeyed, fulfilled. In the face of such certainty of faith distinctions have to fade in importance that, by the light of human questioning and natural contemplation, are of the greatest significance for the knowledge of ourselves, as well as of our enemy—for example, the distinction between what is most urgent and what is most important, what is most intensive and what is highest, between the good that is to be defended here and now and the simply good, between the most threatening enmity and the most profound confrontation. To the political theologian, holding on to such distinctions may appear to be the result of hubristic "ego-armoring,"[59] which necessarily ends in self-deception: When the call is made, all distinctions dissolve. It cannot be circumscribed, prescribed, grasped in advance, for we have no power over it. To perceive it is a matter of faith, just as the answer that we are to risk remains a matter of faith. We believe that only we know *that* we must risk the answer and that it requires our *whole* commitment. Next to the unreservedness of obedience, the intensity of commitment seems to be the most important criterion and the sole one we can hope will lead us out of the sphere of influence delineated by deception and self-deception. If we achieve our destiny in historical action alone, then we apparently achieve the extreme in the most intensive participation, and the political life that Schmitt defends as the intensive life par excellence[60] is the highest life. To the far-reaching assimilation of what is highest to what is most intensive corresponds the occupation of what is most important by what is historically most urgent. For if we be-

59. Cf. *G*, 111, 192.

60. In addition to the conception in the *BdP* itself, see the explicit equation at the conclusion of his inaugural address held on June 20, 1933 at the University of Cologne: "Reich–Staat–Bund," [Reich–State–Federation], in *PuB*, 198. Cf. "Die Formung des französischen Geistes durch den Legisten" [The Formation of the French Spirit by the Legist], in *Deutschland–Frankreich* 1, no. 2 (1942): 29 and *Verfassungslehre* [*Constitutional Theory*] (Munich/Leipzig 1928), 210, 228.

lieve that our own question faces us in the figure of the enemy, as an objective power that cannot be deceived, then the confrontation with the present enemy is not only what is most urgent, but by all appearances is always already what is most important to us. How else would it be possible to exclude a relapse into "ego-armoring"? The confidence in the enemy, as well as the leap into intensity, is based on the faith in the meaning of what happens to us and is to happen through us, a meaning that is all-decisive, is concealed in its details, but is certain in the most profound respect. Or to borrow another poet's expression which Schmitt esteems extraordinarily highly and of which he informs us that it answers the question about the arcanum in his "*fatum*": *Accomplish what you must; it is always already accomplished and you only answer in doing.*[61]

The same faith explains Schmitt's preoccupation with one's *own*: "one's own question," "one's own level," "one's own standard," "one's own limit," "one's own figure." Although Schmitt's attempt to escape "ego-armoring" by turning wholly to this "own" may at first seem astonishing, this reversal of viewpoint looks much less paradoxical once this "own" is understood as *the task given to us*. The faith that the Lord of history has assigned us *our* historical place and *our* historical task, that we are a part of a providential event which we are unable to comprehend by virtue of human capacities, such a faith lends the ever particular a weight which it is accorded in no other system. The assertion or realization of "one's own" is in itself raised to the rank of a metaphysical mission. Since what is most important is "always already accomplished" and is anchored in "one's own," we insert ourselves into the comprehensive, ego-transcendent whole precisely to the extent that we return to "our own" and insist upon it. We open ourselves to the call issued to us, when we become aware of "our own question"; we do our part when we pursue the confrontation with "the other, the stranger" on "our own level" "so as to gain our own standard, our own limit, our own figure." That is the *most profound* reason for statements that are supposedly so thoroughly "existentialist," such as Schmitt's early assertion that a war does not have "its *meaning* in the fact that it is waged for high ideals or for legal norms but rather against one's *own enemy*,"[62] or the famous remark that those participating in a conflict can only decide for themselves "whether the otherness of the stranger in the concrete, present case of conflict means *the negation of one's own kind of existence* and therefore must be fended off or fought against in battle *in order to save one's own, existential kind of*

61. *ECS*, 53.
62. *BdP* I, 17 (my emphasis); cf. II, 50–51.

life."[63] That which is our own as the task with which we are charged can promise a safe haven in the face of the danger of "ego-armoring," however, only so long as it is taken as a *factum brutum* or equated with its prevailing "historical concretion." Neither may "one's own" itself be subjected to distinction and one's individual nature separated in our "*fatum*" from the historically contingent, nor does there remain any room for the thorniest question of human self-knowledge—how is what is specific to man to be defined and classified?—a question linked most intimately with that other question: what does man have owing to his own stock and what have historical circumstances added to or changed in his natural state?[64] No room remains for the distinction between the natural and the depraved, and the question may not be seriously raised as to whether we are capable of attaining what is our own to the greatest extent and in the most excellent sense, insofar as we insist on what is "our own," or whether we instead develop it when we take our bearings by what precedes what is specific to us and points beyond what is our own.[65] Questions and distinctions of this kind are out of place wherever the avoidance of self-deception has become the prevailing viewpoint and all striving for self-knowledge has been left behind. For they would shake precisely that security which "one's own" promises so long as one believes one is able to refer readily back to one's own and lay claim to it as a matter of course. Taken to their logical conclusion, they would destroy the certainty that the good is to be presupposed without question, that there is no need of an examination, that in fact it would not tolerate an examination.[66] In view of Schmitt's awed reluctance about undertaking such an examination, it can also be explained why the friend and friendship remain so conspicuously bland in his conception and pale completely in comparison with the enemy and enmity. In the first two editions of *Der Begriff des Politischen* Schmitt has literally nothing to say about the friend and friendship; the third edition explains parenthetically that friends are those who are "of the same kind and allies";[67] from a "Corollarium" dated 1937 we learn that "according to the German meaning of the word (as in many other

63. *BdP* III, 8 (my emphasis); cf. I, 4; II, 27.

64. Jean-Jacques Rousseau, *Discours sur l'origine et les fondemens de l'inégalité parmi les hommes*, critical edition (Paderborn 1984; 3d ed., 1993), Préface, 42.

65. On this point see the "Einführender Essay über die Rhetorik und die Intention des Werkes," in ibid., lx–lxxvii. [Cf. Heinrich Meier, "The *Discourse on the Origin and the Foundations of Inequality Among Men*: On the Intention of Rousseau's Most Philosophical Work," trans. J. Harvey Lomax, in *Interpretation* 16, no. 2 (Winter 1988–89): 216–227.]

66. Cf. *PR*, 137; *DA*, 25–26; *PT II*, 115; *PT*, 52 (74).

67. *BdP* III, 8.

languages)" the friend is "originally only a member of the clan";[68] in a posthumously published note we come upon the definition characteristic of Schmitt's thought: "A friend is whoever affirms and confirms me."[69] The pivotal issue remains "one's own"; ultimately everything is reduced to its unquestioning, non-distinguishing affirmation and confirmation. But then how could it be possible to say anything more or anything else about the friend and friendship, how could we possibly determine the friend actively when we do not want to expose ourselves to the question of what the good is for us?[70]

The enemy for Schmitt has the advantage of being able to define *himself*, as it were, as the enemy. At least this is the impression that Schmitt gives, for in his oeuvre the enemy comes into view almost exclusively as the attacker, never as the one attacked:[71] Inasmuch as the enemy attacks me or places me in question, he reveals himself as my enemy. The rhetorical advantages of such a perspective are obvious, but the "theoretical" advantages are even more significant to Schmitt. When the attacker demands all one's attention, it seems all the more self-evident that what must be defended can be presupposed. In addition, with his real or impending attack the enemy urgently directs us to "our own." In the end, the "objective power" of the enemy and "one's own" originate from one authority, and, bound together as the call and answer to one event, they move in one direction. Of course, the "friend" who "affirms and confirms

68. Schmitt continues: "Thus the friend is originally only a friend by blood, a blood relative, or he who is 'made into a relative' through marriage, brotherhood by oath, the adoption of a child, or through analogous arrangements. Supposedly it is first through Pietism and similar movements, which found the 'soul mate' [*Seelenfreund*] on the path to the 'friend in God' [*Gottesfreund*], that the privatization and psychologization of the concept of the friend took place, both of which were typical of the nineteenth century but are still widely in effect today. Friendship thereby became a matter of private, sympathetic feelings, ultimately even with erotic overtones in a Maupassant-atmosphere" (*BdP*, Corollarium 2, 104). This is the most extensive discussion of the friend and friendship in Schmitt.

69. The note dated February 13, 1949, in which Schmitt refers back to the meditation on self-deception published one year later in *Ex Captivitate Salus*, reads: "*Historia in nuce*. Friend and enemy. A friend is whoever affirms and confirms me. An enemy is whoever places me in question (Nuremberg 1947). Who then can place me in question? Basically only I myself. The enemy is our own question as a figure." (*G*, 217; the second part of the note is given in n. 54 above.)

70. In this connection see David Bolotin, *Plato's Dialogue on Friendship: An Interpretation of the "Lysis" with a New Translation* (Ithaca 1979; 2d ed., 1988), 85, 117, 127, 134, 158–159, 174–176, 193. Cf. Seth Benardete, *The Tragedy and Comedy of Life: Plato's "Philebus"* (Chicago 1993), 88–91, 128–129, 186, 202–203, 225.

71. The following marks an exception: "Woe to him who has no friend, for his enemy will sit in judgment of him. Woe to him who has no *enemy*, for *I* shall be his enemy on Judgment Day" (*ECS*, 90).

me" also determines himself to be a friend in the sense of Schmitt's definition of the friend. But what do I learn from that about myself? And above all (from Schmitt's viewpoint): does he induce me to act? Does he challenge me "to answer in doing"? Does he compel me to bring what is "my own" to bear? Or even just to recognize him as my friend? Is he able to jettison the "ego-armoring"? Does he point a way out of that state "without a last judgment," which Schmitt abhors as a state of arbitrariness and subjectivism? The friend is ascribed no significant function in Schmitt's conception. Wholly unlike the enemy, who is simply indispensable to Schmitt's theoretical enterprise.[72] To this extent one can justifiably speak of a primacy of the enemy.[73] This holds especially of the question of our identity. It is not the choice of the friend but the battle with the enemy that is to provide information about who we are. If we do not exactly have to love our enemy, we are at least referred to and need him in order to achieve what is "our own": "The enemy is not something that for some reason must be done away with and annihilated because of his want of value. The enemy is on my own level. For this reason I must confront him in battle in order to gain my own standard, my own limit, my own figure." The enemy is so little to be "done away with," we need him so much, that Schmitt can shout to himself elsewhere: "Eureka, I've found him, namely, the enemy! It is not good that man be without an enemy."[74]

72. Compare the foregoing paragraph with the corresponding section of Chapter I, 23–25, esp. 24 above.

73. In the most important respect, which first makes Schmitt's political theology at all possible, this primacy clearly does *not* hold (cf. for now nn. 66 and 71 above). It comes to bear all the more decisively in Schmitt's conceptional action. It seems odd when Schmitt defends himself against the "reproach" of a primacy of the enemy in his conception of the political, and in the 1963 Preface to *Der Begriff des Politischen*—wholly the legal scholar and nothing but the jurist—advances the argument "that every movement of a legal concept emerges with dialectical necessity from negation. In the life, as in the theory, of the law, the incorporation of negation is anything but a 'primacy' of what is negated. A trial as legal action only becomes at all conceivable when a law is negated. Punishment and criminal law posit at their beginning not a deed but a criminal misdeed. Does such a positing perhaps reflect a 'positive' attitude towards criminal misdeeds and towards a 'primacy' of crime?" (14–15). In the same period and on the last page of the same text (124) Schmitt relays new reflections on the "linguistic problem 'enemy-friend'" that once again revolve around the precedence of the enemy: "Today I consider it conceivable that the letter 'r' in friend [*Freund*] is an infix, although such infixes are rare in Indo-Germanic languages. Perhaps they are more frequent than previously suspected. The 'r' in *Freund* [friend] could be an infix (in *Feind* [enemy]) as in the case of *Frater* [brother] (in *Vater* [father]) or in the number *drei* [three] (in *zwei* [two])." The reader will gauge just *how* odd this self-stylization by the nothing-but-jurist Schmitt is when in reading the 1963 Preface he recalls that the "juridical" defense against the "reproach" of a primacy of the enemy stems from the same author who, among other things, informed us: "Woe to him who has no *enemy*, for *I* shall be his enemy on Judgment Day."

74. *G*, 146. Compare once again: "Self-deception is part of solitude" (*ECS*, 87).

In both passages of self-reassurance concerning the enemy in *Ex Captivitate Salus* and *Theorie des Partisanen*, passages in which Schmitt makes the verse *The enemy is our own question as a figure* his key phrase, he seems to come closer to the "agonal" standpoint than "the great metaphysical opposition" may first lead one to expect, namely, the opposition by means of which the author of *Der Begriff des Politischen* sees himself separated from that standpoint. And yet in point of fact the contours of the difference become sharper in those very passages in which he supposedly comes closest to it. It was noted earlier that the enemy, unlike the opponent in the *agon*, compels us to enter into a confrontation in which we are said to be grasped wholly and existentially. And the providential destiny of the enemy and the political battle's constitutive significance for our identity was also noted. The agonal contest is incapable of coming close to any of that. The sentence *It is not good that man be without an enemy* could also be written from the agonal standpoint. Yet this holds only so long as we disregard the context that Schmitt establishes with the chosen formulation. And it no longer holds for the consecutive clause, which is intimately connected with both Schmitt's own message and his interpretation of the Däubler verse: *Tell me who your enemy is, and I will tell you who you are.*[75] The enemy who "is on my own level" is neither a mere comrade-in-arms in the struggle for the comprehensive development of one's personality, nor the opposing wrestler in that battle for power in which the innocence of becoming takes place, the battle that gives rise to orders and shatters them. He is not the opposing player whom has been given the choice of a "free decision-maker," against whom the self-certain man takes up the fight in order to intensify himself and to get beyond what is "his own."[76] Nor is he equivalent for Schmitt to the antagonist in the serious competition for the maximum development of human capacity or natural insight.[77] The enemy is on my own level because he is *assigned* to me. And I must fight with him because he *negates* me or because I must negate him in order to be able *to be* what I *am*. For enmity is the "existential negation of another being."[78] In spite of all the rhetoric about restraint and acceptance, this determination, which is fundamental to Schmitt, should not be allowed to fall into oblivion. True, the enemy does not have to be annihilated *because of his want of value*. He does not have to be *annihilated* in any way since it is not up to man to annihilate

75. *G*, 243.

76. Cf. Nietzsche, *Ecce homo*, "Warum ich so weise bin," aphs. 7 and 8 (*KGW* VI.3, 272–273 and 274 l. 5–10).

77. See 40 ff. above.

78. *BdP*, 33.

what he himself has not created.[79] But if the enemy may neither be annihilated nor done away with, it is no less true that one's ever concrete, *real* or *own* enemy must be killed in the dire emergency. In the life-and-death battle, more is at stake for Schmitt than sheer self-assertion or human recognition. Not even the rather Hegelian-sounding phrases Schmitt employs in his meditation can hide this fact—his talk of the "mutual recognition of recognition" in which lies "the greatness of the concept," of the "relation in the other to oneself" which is said to be "the truly infinite," or of the "negation of negation" on which "the truly infinite" is said to depend. The central paradigm by means of which Schmitt reassures himself of his enemy and gains clarity on the "nature" of enmity, the story of Cain and Abel, speaks another language. The "history of mankind" begins neither with an open duel nor with a battle for human recognition. Cain killed Abel. Nothing is known of Abel's defense of himself. Nothing of *agon* and symmetry. Not to mention of the "mutual recognition of recognition." Schmitt's "beginning" attests fratricide. *This* is how the *father of all things* looks. He attests the *evil* which men have to withstand and which nevertheless bears its *good* within itself—for could it happen otherwise? *That* is the *dialectical tension* that keeps world history in motion.

Only in comparatively brief periods of human history—and even then by no means everywhere—has there been any success in limiting enmity, subjecting it to binding rules, forcing it onto an orderly course. One can read *Der Begriff des Politischen* of 1927 as a plea for the recognition of the *just enemy*. A plea that takes a stand in the form of a theoretical discussion for the moral position according to which the enemy must be granted the same right to seek to defend his "own, existential kind of life" that we claim for the defense of our way of life and the assertion of our being. Schmitt knows of the rarity of such an effort to fence in enmity: "It is really something rare, indeed improbably humane, to get men to renounce the discrimination against and defamation of their enemies."[80] He sees himself as the advocate of the progress of civilization achieved in the *ius publicum Europaeum* when in the thirties and

79. Cf. *BdP* III, 19; "Die Tyrannei der Werte," 61; *G*, 8.

80. *TdP*, 92. Schmitt continues: "That very renunciation now seems to be placed in question once again by the guerrilla. After all, *the most extreme intensity of political engagement* is one of his criteria. When Guevara says: 'The guerrilla is the Jesuit of war,' he is thinking of the *absoluteness of political commitment*" (my emphasis). In the *Glossarium* Schmitt calls the "crimes of conviction on the negative side" committed by him "who has been declared to be the enemy of mankind," *political in the most extreme and intensive sense of the word* (145). So much for the claim that Schmitt considers *absolute* enmity and the criminalization of the enemy or his criminal resistance to be something that "goes beyond the political" and consequently is no longer to be conceived as *political*.

forties he attacks the "turn to the discriminating concept of war," a turn that threatens to annul the "renunciation of criminalizing the opponent in war." He understands himself as the defender of one of the greatest achievements of "European mankind" when in the sixties he wants to counteract the substitution of the "real" enemy with the "absolute enemy" by distinguishing between the *conventional*, *real*, and *absolute enemy*, and wants to provide categories by which to expose the logic of annihilation precipitated by the proscription of the enemy as the "enemy of mankind" or his condemnation as a "want of value."[81] None of this contradicts the insight that the *just enemy* is not identical with the *enemy tout court*. On the contrary, it confirms it emphatically. The "humanization" supported and desired by Schmitt can be achieved in various ways. The enemy may be recognized as a just enemy since he satisfies a moral code or insofar as he uses exclusively "just weapons," but especially because and so long as he renounces discriminating against his enemy as a criminal or a monster. In any case the recognition of the just enemy seems to be bound to a minimum of moral requirements or to a stock of common features that make it possible to distinguish him. Or could it be possible for discrimination against the enemy to cease because the enemy is conceived as an opponent in a game of chance and necessity in which all participants bring forward their moral interpretation of the phenomena in order to strengthen their own positions and choose *the* weapons that correspond to their being, in a game therefore in which "just enemies" alone clash? However this may be, Schmitt's recognition of the just enemy gains its sustenance from another source. It is an expression of the faith that the enemy is part of the divine world order and that war has the character of a divine trial by ordeal[82]—at least when-

81. *Die Wendung zum diskriminierenden Kriegsbegriff* [*The Turn to the Discriminating Concept of War*] (Munich 1938), 1–2, 47, 48–49; *NdE*, 5, 112–115, 298–299; *TdP*, 92, 94–96; "Die Tyrannei der Werte," 46, 58–59.

82. *ECS*, 58; "Nehmen/Teilen/Weiden," 494. In 1937 Schmitt ends the lecture "Totaler Feind, totaler Krieg, totaler Staat" with the words: "War and enmity belong to the history of peoples. The most terrible disaster only occurs, however, when enmity develops out of war, as in the war of 1914–18, instead of a previously existing, unalterable, genuine, and total enmity leading to the *divine trial by ordeal* of a total war, *as is right and sensible*" (*PuB*, 239; my emphasis). What Schmitt here still calls *genuine and total enmity*, corresponds in the later nomenclature to *real enmity*, which is delimited from the *conventional enmity* of the mere duel or "game" on the one hand and from *absolute enmity*, which wants to "do away with" enmity itself, on the other hand as the *right* and *sensible* enmity: "In 1914 Europe's peoples and governments stumbled into the first world war without real enmity. Real enmity arose only out of the war itself, which began as a conventional war between States regulated by European international law and ended with a global civil war of revolutionary class enmity" (*TdP*, 96).

ever war is waged between "just enemies."[83] So long as both antagonists understand war as a divine trial by ordeal, such a war—if we disregard its purpose for a moment—seems to be interchangeable with the agonal contest. What is most important is presupposed; the meaning of the order in which each fights for the preservation or development of his own, is itself not the object of the quarrel. The situation changes considerably as soon as the enemy leaves the common ground, places the binding order in question, and finally wants to "do away with" or "annihilate" the enemy as such. In the war waged for the "abolition of war," in the "global civil war" in which the "absolute enemy" is passed off as the allegedly final obstacle on the path to overcoming all enmity, enmity gains an intensity far removed from the "fenced in" war between States. Thus it is once again confirmed that the decisive quarrel Schmitt has in view—the quarrel in which for him everything, meaning, and order, are at stake—is the quarrel over the enemy. The affirmation and the negation of enmity oppose one another irreconcilably. It is only fitting that Schmitt, in illustrating what the enemy and enmity mean to him, does not choose an example from the epoch in which wars between States were regulated by the *ius publicum Europaeum*. How could "something so rare, indeed improbably humane," which was achieved so late and lasted only a few centuries, be suitable to shed light on the primordial and universal phenomenon of enmity? In keeping with his "ontological-existential way of thinking," Schmitt begins far more fundamentally. In taking up the paradigm of Cain and Abel, he goes back to the first fratricidal or civil war. The civil war is free of the efforts to fence in war. It knows no just enemy. Only in it does "what one says of war" attain "its final and bitter meaning."[84] Only in the civil war does the whole truth about enmity reveal itself. But something else is expressed in Schmitt's paradigm. When Schmitt calls Cain's fratricide to mind, he reminds us that the enemy who is my brother is bound to me by a common link that transcends all human recognition: the enemy becomes the *just enemy* by means of my recognition, but he is my *brother* by virtue of his and my being, thanks to a destiny of which we are not master. At the same time Schmitt reminds us that, regarding the enmity between the brothers, it concerns no mere domestic relationship, no "purely human matter." He calls to mind the rebellion on which fratricide is based[85] and thereby

83. The qualification holds for the theoretician of international law. As we shall see, for the political theologian it cannot be maintained in the strict sense.

84. *ECS*, 26; cf. 56–57 and 89.

85. Compare Calvin's commentary on Genesis 4:2, 5, and 7; in addition Umberto Cas-

refers to a king who is by no means the *basileus* of Heraclitus. Just as little as war is the father and king of all things, likewise world history, which Schmitt says has not yet come to an end, is not the world history of Hegel. For the "Christian Epimetheus" the history of mankind begins with disobedience towards God and ends with God's Last Judgment. *Adam and Eve* and *Judgment Day* mark out the horizon of the history of salvation, a horizon in which Schmitt's meditation on the enemy moves.[86] By referring to the story of Cain and Abel, Schmitt opposes the truth of the Bible to Heraclitus and the "Heraclitean Epimetheus Hegel."[87]

For Schmitt the defense of enmity has a theological foundation, the battle with the enemy follows a providential destiny:[88] The decree *I shall put enmity between your seed and her seed* precedes Cain's fratricide. With that decree we have returned to the principle of faith on which Schmitt erected his political-theological edifice and which occupies a decisive place in *Der Begriff des Politischen* from 1932 on.[89] At this time—at the latest—Schmitt leaves no doubt that the battle with one's *own, real, total* enemy only approaches the most extreme degree of intensity where it is a question of the battle against an adversary whose moral dignity is contested, whose historical legitimacy is disputed, whose religious orthodoxy is negated, or the battle against an enemy who for his part attacks his opponent as the *absolute enemy*. The most extreme stage of enmity begins where the enemies face one another in an *asymmetrical* re-

suto, *A Commentary on the Book of Genesis. Part I: From Adam to Noah* (Jerusalem 1978), 205–207 and 212.

86. *ECS*, 89 and 90.

87. In the *Glossarium* Schmitt speaks of the "great task" of "making visible the Christian Epimetheus from which the Heraclitean Epimetheus Hegel [represents] only an apostasy. Clearly this apostasy is still a thousand times greater than that UN-Toynbee and the positivists of the West" (212). See 40 f. and Chapter I, 15 with nn. 40, 41, 42 above. Against the backdrop of Schmitt's determination of his position on Hegel's philosophy as cited above—in particular of the "question" directed to Kojève as to whether there can at all be an *enemy* in Hegel—compare Hegel's "definition of the enemy" which Schmitt relays in *Der Begriff des Politischen* (62).

88. With the story of Cain and Abel, Schmitt does not call to mind a myth that sums up in a catchy way an insight that could just as easily be grounded anthropologically and derived from other sources; rather, he refers to a truth of faith that for Christians—and for Jews—possesses binding force.

89. *BdP*, 67, as well as III, 49. Although explicity formulated only in 1932, the substance of the sentence already stands, from the first edition of *Der Begriff des Politischen* on, in the center of the seventh chapter, which is devoted to the "anthropological confession of faith" or, put more precisely, the "connection of political theories with theological dogmas of sin," the chapter in which Schmitt inserts it in 1932.

lationship. The most extreme stage, however, is the decisive stage. This lies in the logic of the conception of the intensity of the political, which equates what is authoritative with the greatest intensity, immediately giving rise to the questions: which enmity does Schmitt consider the most intensive, towards which enemy are his statements on the "essence" of the enemy oriented, and at which degree of intensity does he begin to accept politics as political "in the eminent sense"? For just as war can "be more or less war according to the degree of enmity,"[90] likewise, due to the revised concept of the political, politics must be able to be *more* or *less* political, more or less *politics* according to the intensity of the enmity. As for when Schmitt sees the most extreme point of the political reached, two paragraphs of *Der Begriff des Politischen*, which are concerned with the "peaks of great politics," shed light on it. Inserted in the text after his abandonment of the conception of domains, they show quite clearly that the most intensive, decisive enmity presupposes an asymmetrical relationship. The first paragraph reads: "Political thought and political instinct thus prove themselves theoretically and practically in the capacity of distinguishing between friend and enemy. The peaks of great politics are simultaneously the moments in which the enemy is discerned in concrete clarity as the enemy." By way of four examples, the second paragraph illustrates what for Schmitt appears as *great politics*. Whereas the first paragraph concludes with one of Schmitt's central statements, in which the Däubler verse resounds for the first time, at the end of the second stands the fundamental Bible verse from Genesis 3:15. Oliver Cromwell brings it to bear in a speech made on September 17, 1656, a speech Schmitt uses at this key point in *Der Begriff des Politischen* as a medium for self-explication.[91] Schmitt informs us that for the modern era he sees "in Cromwell's battle against papist Spain" "the most power-

90. "Clausewitz (*Vom Kriege* [Berlin 1834], III, 140) says: 'War is nothing but a continuation of political intercourse with the intervention of other expedients.' War is for him a 'mere instrument of politics.' It is that as well, of course, but that does not exhaust its significance for the *knowledge of the essence of politics*. Considered precisely, incidentally, in Clausewitz war is not one of many instruments but rather the '*ultima ratio*' of the grouping into friends and enemies. War has its own 'grammar' (i.e., a special military-technical lawfulness), but politics remains its 'brain,' war has no 'logic of its own.' It can attain the latter only from the concepts of friend and enemy, and this core of all things political is revealed by the sentence (141): 'If war belongs to politics, it will take on the character of the latter. As soon as politics becomes greater and more powerful, so too will war, and that can climb to the heights where war achieves its absolute form.' War can be more or less war according to the degree of enmity." *BdP* III, 16 n. 1 (my emphasis).

91. Only in its light does Schmitt's later statement—"In the meantime we have come to know that the political is the total"—gain its full meaning.

ful eruption of such an enmity" as it becomes manifest at the peaks of great politics. Schmitt says Cromwell's enmity was stronger "than the *écrasez l'infâme* of the eighteenth century, which is certainly not to be underestimated, stronger than Baron vom Stein's hatred of the French and Kleist's 'Strike them dead; no one will ask you for your reasons at the Last Judgment,' stronger even than Lenin's annihilating sentences against the bourgeois and Western capitalism." Stronger than the *battle cry* that the Enlightenment thinker Voltaire hurls against the Catholic Church in the name of morality and mankind, stronger than the guerrilla-poet Kleist's *demand* for absolute national revolt, stronger even than the *sentences* of the propagandist of absolute enmity Lenin, which claim the philosophy of history and science as their own—stronger than all these, it should be noted, is Cromwell's *speech*, in which he expressly claims that his enmity for papist Spain is grounded in the truth of revelation. Schmitt's pointed summary of Cromwell's political-theological justification of his enmity culminates in the sentences: "The Spaniard is your enemy, his enmity is put into him by God; he is 'the natural enemy, the providential enemy'; he who considers him to be an accidental enemy, does not know Scripture and the things of God, who said, I shall put enmity between your seed and her seed (Gen. 3:15); one can make peace with France, not with Spain, for it is a papist State, and the Pope maintains peace only as long as it suits him."[92] The providential enemy, whom the Protestant statesman and dictator discerns in concrete clarity as his enemy, is the truly sovereign Pope.

The peaks of great politics are simultaneously the moments in which the providential enemy is known, in which one's own destiny is fulfilled. What appears to Schmitt as great politics stands in obvious contrast to the "great politics" that Nietzsche had postulated in *Jenseits von Gut und Böse* half a century before him. The "long, terrible will of its own" for which, according to Nietzsche, Europe should decide, the aristocratic will "that could set goals for itself over millennia," the will of the "great risks" which puts "an end to that gruesome dominion of nonsense

92. The quotations, which Schmitt chooses and orders in a sequence such that Cromwell's justification of enmity reaches its peak in Genesis 3:15, are found in ed. Carlyle, vol. III (1902), 269, 270–271, 272, 274–275. The entire speech spans more than 40 pages. Schmitt added the reference *Gen. 3:15*. —In his lecture "Totaler Feind, totaler Krieg, totaler Staat" Schmitt says five years later: "The English naval war against Spain was a world battle between Germanic and Romance peoples, between Protestantism and Catholicism, Calvinism and Jesuitism, and there are few examples of such eruptions of the most profound and ultimate enmity such as one finds it in Cromwell's attitude towards the Spaniard" (*PuB*, 238).

and accident that has so far been called 'history,'" this human will must in Schmitt's eyes appear to be a heretofore unknown monstrosity of Promethean hubris. Schmitt's great politics has something to do with Nietzsche's "battle for the dominion of the earth" only insofar—but, to be sure, insofar—as it decisively opposes the "compulsion to great politics" foreseen by Nietzsche in the form of *this* battle. Is it not the providential enemy of the political theologian who announces his claim in the proclamation of the dominion of the earth?[93] Schmitt's great politics also has to be distinguished from what, before and since Nietzsche, has been conventionally regarded as "great politics." None of the four historical examples that Schmitt advances is taken from the classical power politics between States. None calls to mind the enmity of the "fenced-in war" under modern international law. Nor does any stand for the separation of "outside" and "inside," for the scission of politics and economy, politics and morality, politics and religion. He who here deals with the "peaks of great politics" no longer poses as the "theoretician of pure politics." Rather, he makes it clear that politics—to speak in Clausewitz's terms[94]—"achieves its absolute form" only when it reaches the intensity of the battle of faith. At the peak of great politics, *faith* fights *errant faith*. In light of both new paragraphs on "great politics,"[95] the most profound sense of Schmitt's turn to the concept of intensity becomes evident, along with all that accompanies this turn in particular and in which this turn is reflected: From the silent abandonment of the fiction of "pure politics"[96] via his textual interposition, as inconspicuous as it is characteristic, in the new edition of *Der Begriff des Politischen*—according to which the distinction between friend and enemy can "exist theoretically and practically without *all those* moral, aesthetic, economic, or other distinctions being applied simultaneously," distinctions which Schmitt had assigned in 1927, still without any qualification, to the "*other*, relatively independent domains of human thought and action"[97]—down to the observation made by way of commentary in the

93. Nietzsche, *Jenseits von Gut und Böse*, aphs. 208 and 203; cf. *Also sprach Zarathustra*, "Von tausend und Einem Ziele" (*KGW* VI.1, 70–72) and Nachlaß, *KGW* VII.3, 350 l. 26.

94. See n. 90 above.

95. The concept 'great politics' occurs only in this passage of the *BdP*. In this connection, compare the essay "Der unbekannte Donoso Cortés" [The Unknown Donoso Cortés] from 1929 in *DC*, 75–76, 78.

96. *BdP* I, 25–26. In 1932 Schmitt deletes throughout the phrases "theoretician of pure politics," "pure political concept," and "pure political thinker."

97. *BdP*, 27 (my emphasis). In 1927 Schmitt writes: "The distinction between friend

1933 edition that war can be *more* or *less* war depending on the degree of enmity; from the new discovery of the "internal enemy," of civil war, and of revolution, via the express mention of "dissenters and heretics,"[98] down to the appreciation for the "holy wars and crusades" of the Church as "actions that can be based on an *especially genuine and profound decision about the enemy*."[99] In Schmitt's reference to the most extreme degree of intensity of "great politics" the complete gradualization of the political has its vanishing point. The wresting of the political from its fixed reference to the community, the transformation of the political into, as it were, a fluid, aggregate state that can be reached from anywhere and is capable of encompassing everything, receives its full meaning only in the conceptual orientation towards the battle of faith. As a consequence of such an orientation the *politiké koinonía* is itself ultimately conceived of essentially or in its supreme perfection as a *community of faith*. Schmitt does not delay in drawing this conclusion when he explains in 1933: "For political decisions even the mere possibility of rightly knowing and understanding, and therewith the entitlement to participate in discussion and to make judgments, is based only on existential *sharing* and participating, only on the genuine *participatio*." For this statement—by means of which Schmitt places himself in sharp opposition to all great political philosophers, none of whom, from Plato to Rousseau, would have even thought of denying the stranger "the *mere possibility* of rightly knowing and understanding" for political decisions[100]—obviously has the particularity of a community of faith in view. If it holds anywhere, then nowhere more than in the case of the community of faith that leads itself back to a truth beyond all human reason, a truth with which it believes itself to be blessed, and that sees itself inextricably bound in existential participation in the one truth par-

---

and enemy can exist theoretically and practically without moral, aesthetic, economic, or other distinctions being applied simultaneously" (I, 4).

98. *BdP*, 46–48; cf. 29, 30–32, 42, 43, 47, 53, 54.

99. *BdP* III, 30 (my emphasis). In 1927 there was still no room for the holy wars and crusades of the Church; in 1932 it is said of them for the first time that they are "actions that are based on a decision about the enemy like other wars" (II, 48). Compare the noteworthy interpositions in the immediately preceding sentence (I, 17; II, 48; III, 30).

100. In Plato's case it suffices to recall the *Laws* and the unique role that the Athenian stranger is given in the Platonic corpus. For Rousseau we refer to the chapter "Du Législateur" of the *Contrat social* (II, 7). Moreover, both philosophers have made it abundantly clear through their actions that they saw themselves in a position as philosophers to know rightly the requirements of concrete communities of which they were not citizens and to exert a formative influence on the political decisions of those communities, not only despite but by virtue of the fact that they participated in the discussion, and judged, as strangers.

ticular to it, in the perfected *participatio*.[101] That Schmitt ultimately has *Der Begriff des Politischen* peak in a sharp attack on the "new faith" rounds out the picture. The polemic of the final version's concluding chapter against the "complete inventory" of the "liberal catechism," against the "metaphysics, disguised as 'science,' of the liberal nineteenth century," and against its "Church Father," Benjamin Constant, contains more than a simple reversal of the polemical opposition of the new faith to the old faith that David Friedrich Strauß had made popular.[102] With his attack, Schmitt does not take a stand for the old but for the right faith. From this position he believes he can strike liberalism and Marxism with one blow and even identify the latter as a mere "case of the application of the liberal way of thinking proper to the nineteenth century." Insofar as he fights against the heretical dogma of the final victory of economic, industrial, and technological progress over the political, he aims at the center of faith for both,[103] true to the principle that

101. *BdP* III, 8; cf. II, 27; see "Die Sichtbarkeit der Kirche. Eine scholastische Erwägung" [The Visibility of the Church: A Scholastic Consideration], *Summa*, 2d Quarter (1917): 71, 75, 79. The sentence cited in the text above from the 1933 edition precedes the following insertion, which has no counterpart in the 1927 and 1932 editions: "Neither the question as to whether the 'most extreme case' is given nor the further question as to what becomes vitally necessary as 'the most extreme means' in order to defend one's own existence and to preserve one's own being—*in suo esse perseverare*—could be decided by a stranger. The stranger and the man who is of a different type [*der Andersgeartete*] may behave strictly 'critically,' 'objectively,' 'neutrally,' 'purely scientifically' and, by means of similar obfuscations, intrude with his foreign judgment. His 'objectivity' is either merely a political *obfuscation* or a complete *unrelatedness* that misses everything essential." Concerning the anti-Semitic insinuations of this and other passages of the third edition of *Der Begriff des Politischen*, see *Carl Schmitt and Leo Strauss: The Hidden Dialogue*, 6–8 nn. 5 and 6; cf. Schmitt's lead article "Die deutschen Intellektuellen" [The German Intellectuals], in *Westdeutscher Beobachter*, no. 126 from May 31, 1933 and *SBV*, 45. What Schmitt frames in general statements and more alludes to than openly expresses with his ironic reference to Spinoza's *in suo esse perseverare*, as well as the veiled criticism of Georg Simmel (*Soziologie. Untersuchungen über die Formen der Vergesellschaftung* [Leipzig 1908], 687 on the objectivity and participation of the stranger; cf. 686 and 690), is given a completely anti-Semitic turn a short time later and developed in the crudest way by Schmitt's student and friend Ernst Forsthoff (*Der totale Staat* [Hamburg 1933], 38 ff.; cf. 48). The interpretation of the paragraph as being directed against "the Jew" as the incarnation of the "stranger and man of a different type" was under the prevailing circumstances the most obvious "historical-concrete" application. Nevertheless, the concern is only *one* interpretation, and yet one that suddenly sheds light on what it means—or can mean under certain historical conditions—when the *politikḗ koinonía* is to be understood as a *community of faith*.

102. *BdP* III, 54 ff., chapter 10. The passages cited in the text above are taken from 55–56, 57, and 58.

103. As a "characteristic series of political-polemical oppositions" of the new faith,

"every utterance on the spiritual level has, consciously or unconsciously, a dogma—orthodox or heretical—as its premise."[104]

The battle of faith which Schmitt's concept formation takes as its standard is the battle in which true faith confronts heretical faith. In this battle the *most extreme degree of the intensity of association and dissociation* is reached. The *most intensive* enmity proves to be the *authoritative* enmity. Here the concern is *dominion, order*, and *peace* "in the eminent sense." We are dealing with the *only case that matters*. That everyday politics presents merely a pale reflection of this case, that, measured by the latter, politics appears to be only more or less political, even works against this case frequently and has to prevent it as far as is possible, says nothing against its prevailing centrality. Just as the exceptional character of the "peaks of great politics" says little against the decisive significance of politics for the proper understanding of Schmitt's conception. Likewise, the fact that past expectations of the impending rule of the Antichrist remained unfulfilled time after time does not in the least excuse the believer from directing his attention to the satanic threat that can descend upon him today or tomorrow and from focusing all his energies on an event for which there is no precedent. The "only case that matters" is the point from and towards which Schmitt's thought moves. Whoever wishes to comprehend Schmitt's conceptional action must ask about this case. For it, and not the great majority of what normally "is the case," is what Schmitt has in view with his concept formation. What appears disconcerting as long as one applies the standard of "scholarly implementability," shows itself in another light as soon as the case to which Schmitt's definitions apply to the greatest extent becomes apparent, as soon as the point is seen with respect to which the individual statements, the scattered examples and references, the clarifications communicated either indirectly or as if in passing, can be fit together. The fact that Schmitt's concepts are phenomenologically so "inappropriate" is explained by this orientation towards that which decides everything, towards that alone which for Schmitt in the end has any weight.[105] For example, when Schmitt observes in the most ap-

Schmitt cites the following schematically: "Freedom, progress, and reason linked with economy, industry, and technology conquer feudalism, reaction, and violence linked with State, war, and politics—domestically active as parliamentarianism and discussion, they conquer absolutism and dictatorship" (*BdP* III, 56–57; cf. II, 74.)

104. *PR*, 5.

105. See 45 and 47 above. Schmitt seeks to counter the obvious phenomenological weaknesses of his concept in the second edition by means of the ancillary construction that

palling paragraph of *Der Begriff des Politischen* that only those participating in the conflict can decide "whether the otherness of the stranger in the concrete, present case of conflict means the negation of one's own kind of existence and therefore must be fended off or fought against in order to save one's own, existential kind of life," this statement neither takes its bearings by the political reality in its phenomenal multifariousness nor stops with what Schmitt characterizes as a "simple criterion of the political." Who could not think of dozens of examples of political conflicts straight-away that escalated into warlike or revolutionary confrontations and thus incontestably "refer to the real possibility of physical killing" without the enemies' being determined by a decision that would even remotely correspond to the insight that "the otherness of the stranger" "signifies the negation of one's own kind of existence"? Given that Schmitt rephrased the statement twice in order to intensify it twice, we have every reason to take it literally. Particularly as it comes from the sole passage of *Der Begriff des Politischen* that was explicitly concerned with the "essence of the enemy." If at first the talk was of *the enemy* who "in the case of conflict signifies the negation of one's own kind of existence and therefore is fended off or fought against," afterwards the farthest-reaching decision of concern is whether *the otherness* of the enemy signifies the negation of one's own kind of existence or whether therefore *this otherness* must be fended off or fought against.[106] Which case does Schmitt have in view with the more pre-

within the State and *alongside* the *primarily* political decisions "numerous *secondary* concepts of 'political' arise," or that, as he writes in 1933, "numerous *secondary* concepts of the 'political' are conceivable which are characterized by their reference to an existing State" (II, 30; III, 12; cf. the considerable modifications of the subsequent statements on the "latent civil war"). In spite of this, Schmitt claimed to have proceeded "purely phenomenologically," and many of his followers as well as his opponents have repeated this assertion. *Inter multa alia*: "Mon *Begriff des Politischen* évite toute fondation générale; il est purement phénoménologique (c'est-à-dire: descriptif) . . . ," letter to Julien Freund dated November 10, 1964, in *Schmittiana*-II, Eclectica 79–80 (Brussels 1990), 58.

106. *BdP* III, 8 (see n. 101 above). In 1927 Schmitt writes about the enemy: "He is plainly the other, the stranger, and it is sufficient in order to describe his essence that he is in an especially intensive sense existentially something other and strange, so that in the case of conflict he signifies the negation of one's own kind of existence and therefore is fended off or fought against in order to preserve one's own, existential kind of life" (I, 4). In 1932 this sentence is broken up into several sentences, interrupted by long insertions, and significantly altered in its content, whereby the conclusion reads as follows: "The extreme case of conflict can be settled only by the participants themselves; in particular, each of them can decide only for himself whether the otherness of the stranger in the concrete, present case of conflict signifies the negation of one's own kind of existence and therefore is fended off or fought against in order to preserve one's own, existential kind of life" (II, 27). In the "unaltered" 1963 reprint of the text, Schmitt moved the initial elements of the original statement still further apart by dividing it into *two* paragraphs.

cisely formulated statement? To whom does it most apply? Who negates by virtue of his being? Which being entails such a power of negation that it must be fended off or fought against as otherness? The jurist of the *ius publicum Europaeum* will fail to answer questions of this kind. But not the political theologian.[107]

107. Alexandre Kojève noticed right away the case that matters to Schmitt when Schmitt raises the question as to "whether there can at all be an 'enemy' in Hegel." Schmitt expresses his fundamental doubt to the Hegel-expert in the context of an inquiry concerning "the concept of the enemy in Hegel and in particular the word 'enemy' in the section on the 'unhappy consciousness,' p. 168" of the *Phänomenologie des Geistes*, ed. Hoffmeister. "My concern is the expression: the enemy in his ownmost (several lines later: in his characteristic) figure. Who is this enemy who shows himself in the animal functions? More precisely: how is it possible that he shows himself exactly in the animal functions? What is he after there? In my little book *Ex Captivitate Salus* the following verse (by Theodor Däubler) is cited on pp. 89–90 in a remark on the 'enemy': The enemy is our own question as a figure" (letter dated December 14, 1955). Kojève answers on January 4, 1956: "The 'enemy in his ownmost figure' is most likely the Devil, more precisely: the Christian Devil, who shows himself precisely in 'animal functions.' For Hegel ('for us' or 'in itself') theses functions are 'null' [*nichtig*] because man *negates* them and is man, and not only animal, only as their *negation*. But since the 'unhappy consciousness' (i.e., the religious man, more precisely: the Christian) appears *as a slave* in the face of death and of the risk of his life in the struggle for recognition (of his *human* reality and dignity) and avoids the struggle, 'for *it*' [sc. unhappy consciousness] the animal-character is *not* 'null' but powerful, i.e., precisely 'devilish' . . . . If one . . . has angst in the face of the enemy, the latter becomes 'devilish' and thus 'powerful': he is the 'master' and one is his 'slave' (at least insofar as one does not flee from him, into 'another world'). 'Can there be an enemy at all in Hegel?' you ask. As always: yes and no. *Yes*—insofar and *so long as* there is a struggle for recognition, i.e., *history*. World *history* is the history of *enmity* between men (of which there is none among animals: animals 'fight' *for* something, never *out of* enmity). *No*—insofar and as soon as history (= struggle for recognition) is 'sublated' in absolute knowledge. Thus in the end enmity is only an 'element' of 'logic,' i.e., of human discourse. The fully-concluded [*voll-endet*] discourse of the wise man (absolute knowledge) also talks (in the *Phänomenologie des Geistes*) *about* (past) enmity, but the wise man never speaks *out of* enmity, nor *to* enemies."

III REVELATION, OR HE THAT IS NOT WITH ME IS AGAINST ME

According to the Bible, the beginning of wisdom is fear of the Lord; according to the Greek philosophers, the beginning of wisdom is wonder. We are thus compelled from the very beginning to make a choice, to take a stand. Where then do we stand? We are confronted with the incompatible claims of Jerusalem and Athens to our allegiance.
Leo Strauss, *Jerusalem and Athens*

POLITICAL THEOLOGY stands and falls with faith in revelation. For it presupposes the truth of revelation, which is a truth of faith. Thus it cannot avoid seeing in unfaith its enemy from the very beginning. In opposing it, political theology defends what is most properly its own. Unlike the thousand varieties of errant faith, unfaith in its condensed form is able to place political theology radically in question. It is all the more important for political theology to maintain that this type of unfaith is errant faith and to confront it as the "existential" enemy, regardless of whether it itself remains on the defensive or takes up the offensive. In the battle between faith and errant faith there must be no "neutral": Friend and enemy part ways over the truth of revelation. Whoever denies that truth is a liar. Whoever places it in question obeys the adversary. For the power of the truth to which political theology lays claim, a power that seizes everything, that permeates everything, consists precisely in its compelling us to make a decision, its confronting us with an Either-Or which no one can evade. Enmity is set with the faith in revelation. A theologian who demonstrated the sharpness and clarity of which theological reflection can be capable after centuries of comforting conciliation and blinding "syntheses" put it this way: "Only because there is the revelation of God is there enmity towards God." And further: "Wherever revelation does not awaken faith, it must awaken rebellion."[1]

1. Rudolf Bultmann, *Theologie des Neuen Testaments* (9th ed., Tübingen 1984), 370;

The distinction between friend and enemy thus would not only find its theoretical justification in the faith in revelation, but simultaneously would prove its practical unavoidability in such faith. Schmitt's political theology accounts for this double character when, in view of its teaching as well as in its execution, it conceives of itself determinedly as *political* theology. In view of its teaching, insofar as it does not stop "applying" the truth of revelation to the political or "enlisting" that truth so as to understand the latter, but rather seeks to grasp revelation as inherently political. In its execution, insofar as it understands itself as a historical action in the state of probation and judgment that knows how to distinguish between friend and enemy. Both moments, the mode as well as the doctrine of political theology, meet in the *obedience of faith* in which political theology has its raison d'être.[2] How, incidentally, could it remain concealed from a political theory, which itself claims to be based on revelation, that both this claim and the underlying assertion of a historical event in which the sovereign authority proclaimed its will are faced by numerous competing claims and assertions which make a political distinction inevitable? How, especially, would it be able to close itself to the insight that obedience of faith entails and requires such a distinction from the beginning? And conversely, must not every theology which seriously claims to be based on revelation conceive of itself as political theology? So that any theology of revelation that did not want to understand itself as political theology would not understand itself?

Unlike any other political theoretician of the twentieth century, Schmitt saw revelation and politics together and sought to the best of his ability to combine them. The result will be a source of true outrage for many theologians; the "radicalism" of Schmitt's enterprise may be judged to be politically imprudent and dangerous. But what is politically imprudent and dangerous can promote *insight into the cause* and not infrequently be particularly illuminating to the philosopher. From what could one actually learn more than from the "radicalism" of a thought that is directed towards the "most profound connections"? Than from

cf. 427; *Das Evangelium des Johannes* (Göttingen 1941), 296; see *Die drei Johannesbriefe* (Göttingen 1967), 43.

2. Commenting on Romans 1:5, Calvin says: "Unde colligimus, Dei imperio contumaciter resistere, ac pervertere totum eius ordinem, qui Euangelii praedicationem irreverenter et contemptim respuunt, cuius finis est nos in obsequium Dei cogere. Hic quoque observanda est fidei natura, quae nomine obedientiae ideo insignitur, quod Dominus per Euangelium nos vocat: nos vocanti, per fidem respondemus. Sicuti contra, omnis adversus Deum contumaciae caput, est infidelitas." *Commentarius in Epistolam Pauli ad Romanos*, ed. Parker (Leiden 1981), 16.

the aporias to which it leads, from the fundamental alternatives that—whether deliberately or not—it makes visible, from the questions it no longer allows itself to raise? Schmitt, who conceives of the political theologically, or in constant view of the truth of revelation, and the theological politically, or in light of the distinction between obedience and rebellion, gives us occasion to think of politics and revelation in their relationship to one another and to confront the claims of each. Therein lies the abiding significance of his political theology above and beyond its historical moment. The central element in Schmitt's theoretical edifice which establishes the bond in both directions between revelation and politics is the conceit to reduce the political to a triadic constellation which can set in everywhere and at any time such that two individuals, who unite against one enemy, suffice to constitute a political association, and three persons are enough to establish the political, whether natural, legal, or supernatural persons are involved and whether all three really are present or not. The orientation towards the distinction between friend and enemy makes the political and the theological commensurable. The final step is taken with the turn to the conception of intensity. Once the political has been defined by means of the distinction between friend and enemy as the "most extreme degree of the intensity of a bond or a separation, of an association or a dissociation,"[3] the way is clear for the smooth transition from politics to the theology of revelation. The political necessity of distinguishing between friend and enemy can now be traced back to the friend-enemy constellation of the Fall of Man, whereas on the other hand the political character of the fundamental theological decision between obedience and disobedience, between the reliance on God and the fall from faith, is evident. The battle with the providential enemy can be conceived of as a political battle "in the eminent sense," history in the horizon of the theological teaching of the true friend and enemy of the human race can be understood as a process of salvation. The eschatological confrontation between Christ and Antichrist, in which men must enter into a life-and-death "bond or separation," thus appears simultaneously as the promise of faith and as the completion of great politics.

3. *BdP*, 27, 38, 62; cf. 28, 30, 36, 37, 54, 67. "By the word 'political' no domain of its own and no subject matter of its own is given that could be distinguished from other domains or subject matters, but rather only the *degree of intensity* of an association or a dissociation. Every domain can become political when the object of a grouping into friends and enemies is derived from it. The word 'political' describes *not a new subject matter* but . . . only a '*new turn*.'" *Hugo Preuß. Sein Staatsbegriff und seine Stellung in der deutschen Staatslehre* [*Hugo Preuß: His Concept of the State and His Position in German State Theory*] (Tübingen 1930), 26 n. 1.

Schmitt does not confine himself to keeping open the "gateway to transcendence."[4]

If the political flares up wherever two or three who are united by the will or the commandment to oppose one enemy are gathered, then what was termed 'political' in the exacting sense prior to Schmitt's revision of his concept of the political at the outset of the thirties, now looks to be merely a profane part of a much more comprehensive political-theological reality. Schmitt makes room for political associations of the most diverse kinds: for nations and classes, for polis, Church, and State, for bands of guerrillas, sects, etc. That the operation does not aim at the greatest possible generality or broadest applicability, but rather has the sense of disclosing the political conceptually for, and bringing it to bear on, what Schmitt considers to be that which decides everything—this is confirmed and reinforced by the determinations and references that flank the conceptional expansion, discussed in detail above. For example, the more precisely formulated statements on the "essence of the enemy," the new paragraphs on the "peaks of great politics," the remarks on "genuine *participatio*" on which rest "the mere possibility of rightly knowing and understanding" in making political decisions, or the reminder of the holy wars and crusades of the Church, which can be based on a "particularly genuine and profound decision about the enemy," reveal that in his concept formation Schmitt has both the community of faith in mind as the most perfect or "most intensive" political association and the battle of faith as the most profound or "most extreme" political battle. This orientation is expressed most clearly in the third edition of *Der Begriff des Politischen*, in which Schmitt conducts a hidden dialogue with Leo Strauss. The political philosopher, by whose interpretation and critique the author of *Der Begriff des Politischen* saw himself better understood and more powerfully challenged than by any other confrontation of his thought, causes the political theologian to define his position more sharply in 1933 than he had in 1932 or 1927.[5] Even a contemporary of

4. Cf. *BdP*, 121–123. Concerning the friendship between God and man, Thomas Aquinas writes: "Cum amicitia in quadam aequalitate consistat, ea quae multum inaequalia sunt, in amicitia copulari non posse videntur. Ad hoc igitur *quod familiarior amicitia esset inter hominem et Deum, expediens fuit homini quod Deus fieret homo*, quia etiam naturaliter homo homini amicus est: ut sic, dum visibiliter Deum cognoscimus, in invisibilium amorem rapiamur." *Summa contra gentiles*, IV, 54 (Quod conveniens fuit Deum incarnari): *Opera omnia*, XV, ed. Leonina (Rome 1930), 174 (my emphasis). (Schmitt entered the reference "Summa contra gentiles, IV, 54" in his personal copy of the third edition of *Der Begriff des Politischen*.)

5. Following the publication of my *Hidden Dialogue*, I received two testimonies concerning Schmitt's assessment in 1932–33 of Strauss's "Notes." Piet Tommissen showed me

his, who incidentally formed his judgment in nearly complete ignorance of the underlying state of affairs, did not find it difficult at least to perceive the intensification into the battle of faith and to hit upon, in the decision between God and Satan, that distinction between friend and enemy which in the end matters to Schmitt.[6] Just as the *aim* of his concept formation, or what Schmitt later named by means of the "secret key word" of his "entire spiritual and public existence" as "the struggle for the peculiarly Catholic sharpening,"[7] comes more clearly to the fore in *Der Begriff des Politischen* of 1933,[8] so does the *ground* on which Schmitt stands as a theoretical agent. Strauss has especially this ground in mind

a letter from Werner Becker to Schmitt dated December 15, 1933. Becker was a Catholic priest and one of Schmitt's former students. The letter begins: "I just read Strauss's critique of your *Begriff des Politischen* again. As you said back in Cologne, it is really a good critique." Following his "renewed" reading of Strauss's critique, Becker, whose doctoral dissertation was on Hobbes, expresses "two wishes" he has with regard to Schmitt's text: [that] "it lead up to a political metaphysics—that would be the reference to the fact that the highest concept of the political is positive, thus order, but specifically such an order in which the concept of battle and of the enemy is 'co-posited' (Dirks) and which becomes particularly visible and is even constituted only in the possibility and willingness to distinguish the enemy. And the other wish: [that] it lead up to political theology." In response to Strauss's challenge, both wishes had been fulfilled in the meantime by Schmitt in his own way in the third edition of *Der Begriff des Politischen*, which was published in the summer of 1933. Günther Krauss, who was working on a dissertation on Rudolph Sohm under Schmitt's direction (*Der Rechtsbegriff des Rechts* [Hamburg 1936]), informed me in 1988 that Schmitt referred him to Strauss's essay at that time with the words: "You've got to read that. He saw through me and X-rayed me as nobody else has."

6. "The prototype of the relationship between friend and enemy is the relationship between God and Satan. God and Satan do not face one another as two equally respectable and honorable opponents who in the contest, in the duel must measure their powers against one another in order to fix the hierarchy that is to prevail between them. Between God and Satan rages the *battle of decision* which must end, according to the providential order of things, with God's triumph and Satan's annihilation. From the beginning, God is always the 'friend' and Lucifer the 'enemy.'" "Because God always—and even if in the most inconstant manner—shines forth from behind the friend, and the Devil shines forth from behind the 'enemy,' a *metaphysics* necessarily lies behind the relationship between friend and enemy. The friend is whoever shares the metaphysics; the enemy, whoever denies it faith." Ernst Niekisch, "Zum Begriff des Politischen," in *Widerstand* 8, no. 12 (December 1933): 369.

7. "That is the secret key word of my entire spiritual and public existence: the struggle for the peculiarly Catholic sharpening (against the neutralizers, the aesthetic idlers, against the abortionists, body-burners, and pacifists). Here on this path of Catholic sharpening Theodor Haecker no longer accompanied me; they all kept away from me, even Hugo Ball. The only ones who stayed with me were Konrad Weiß and loyal friends like Paul Adams" (*G*, 165).

8. This holds even of the noteworthy details that do not seem to stand in any direct connection with the main thrust of the book, but which accord exactly with Schmitt's explanation of his "struggle for the peculiarly Catholic sharpening" by means of concretely characterized oppositions. Thus in 1933 Schmitt adds the following, hardly "timely" passage to the text: "A purely 'cultural' or 'civilized' social system will have no lack of 'social grounds' *for aborting unwanted additions and making the unsuitable disappear by means of 'suicide' or 'euthana-*

when he pursues the radical inquiry with which he pushes the interpretation of Schmitt's theory until he reaches the conflict between the fundamental alternatives regarding the political. Schmitt's answer does not leave the attentive reader in the dark about whether he considers the necessity of the political decision to be grounded in the truth of faith. And in this connection, the tracing of the political back to Schmitt's triadic constellation and the turn to the conception of intensity guarantee the constancy of the foundational chain of reasoning: They put Schmitt in a position to seek out the deeper-lying theological or "metaphysical" oppositions within political oppositions and to discern the guarantor for the insuperability of the latter within the inescapability of the former.[9]

There was no question about the "metaphysical core of all politics" for Schmitt already in his *Politische Theologie* of 1922. And yet it is only in the "Preliminary Remark," which he places at the outset of the second edition in November 1933, that Schmitt believes himself able to declare: "In the meantime we have come to know that the political is the total."[10] Both statements, which are separated by 11 years but which collide in the same book, allow one to gauge the significance of the redefinition of the political, which he attempted on three separate occasions, for his political theology; they allow one to gauge how much the redefinition permits him to extend and sharpen the grasp of his political theology. For if one does not wish to fall prey to misinterpretations, such as, for example, that Schmitt entered onto a path after 1922 for the sake of the "comprehensive justification of an independent concept of the political," a path that ultimately led him to a position "equivalent to a thetic cutting of the historical umbilical cord between theology and politics,"[11] or put more sharply: if one does not want to presume to make the assertion that

sia. 'But no program, no ideal, and no purposiveness could justify an open capacity for control over the physical life of other human beings" (III, 31; my emphasis).

9. *BdP* III, 10, 19, 45; cf. *Carl Schmitt and Leo Strauss: The Hidden Dialogue*, 60–62.

10. *PT*, 46, 54 (65, 79). In the "Preliminary Remark to the Second Edition" Schmitt writes: "Among Protestant theologians, especially Heinrich Forsthoff and Friedrich Gogarten have shown that without the concept of secularization a proper understanding of the last centuries of our history is not at all possible. Of course, in Protestant theology another, allegedly unpolitical teaching represents God as the 'Wholly Other' in the same way as the political liberalism that belongs to it considers State and politics to be the 'Wholly Other.' In the meantime we have come to know that the political is the total and as a consequence know also that the decision about whether something is *unpolitical* always signifies a *political* decision, regardless of who makes it and with which arguments it is dressed. That holds also for the question as to whether a particular theology is a political or an unpolitical theology."

11. Hans Barion, "'Weltgeschichtliche Machtform'? Eine Studie zur Politischen Theologie des II. Vatikanischen Konzils" (1968), in *Kirche und Kirchenrecht* (Paderborn 1984), 606.

Schmitt turned his back on political theology, then one will be able to understand the declaration that the political is the total, a declaration made at the beginning of a treatise entitled *Politische Theologie*, which insists strongly on the absolute precedence of the theological only as the proclamation of a political theology which "in the meantime" has assured itself of the means to aim at the whole. As soon as the political is "known to be the total," the whole can be set in relation to the "metaphysical core" inherent in "all politics." Everything moves about one center of gravity, and nothing escapes the fundamental jurisdiction of political theology. The political, however, is not "known to be the total" so long as the "metaphysical core" itself is not capable of being conceived of as political. Schmitt's redefinition of the political provides the necessary presupposition for doing so. The extension and sharpening of the grasp that Schmitt's redefinition initiates could not be greater.

Let us consider the theological implications of Schmitt's political totalism more closely. First of all, two levels may be distinguished on which Schmitt's doctrine is developed: the level of the political-theological confrontation with the opponent and the level of "theory" in the narrower sense. On the level of the political-theological confrontation, the "metaphysical core of all politics" is at first synonymous with the "metaphysics," or more correctly: with the theology that Schmitt discerns as the basis of every political theory, every political teaching, every political attitude. In fact one will have to say that he perceives this theology in every spiritual position. For he knows to identify economic postulates, moral precepts, or aesthetic requirements no less as "derivatives of a metaphysical core." What Schmitt emphasizes about Donoso Cortés applies most to Schmitt himself: He "sees in his radical spirituality always only the theology of the opponent" or, we may add, of the friend, of the "man who is of the same kind and an ally."[12] But if Schmitt's talk of the "metaphysical core of all politics" implied nothing other than that every political or spiritual position must be based on a particular "metaphysics" or theology, would there not then be more reason to believe that Schmitt had come to "know" that the "metaphysical" or the theological "is the total"? How would matters stand in this case with the total character of the political? Could it be known only if beforehand everything had been reduced to the theological and were regarded from that standpoint? Coming to know that "the political is the total" would accordingly be tied to the twofold presupposition: that the theological unlocks the whole and in doing so proves to be political. The same conclusion is

12. *PT* 54 (79); *BdP* III, 8.

reached when one turns immediately to the question as to how the "metaphysical core" in the sense just outlined can be conceived of as political. The fact that there is a plurality of metaphysical or theological positions that deviate from or contradict one another still does not found a political relationship. Taken on its own, their competition for the truth does not compel the distinction between friend and enemy. The situation changes radically as soon as a theology claims to be blessed with the revelation of a sovereign authority that demands obedience. From the standpoint of this theology, everything undergoes a "new turn." It does not regard itself as being faced with any inadequate or untenable metaphysics. It need not assert its insight against errors. In the world in which it orients itself, knowledge and ignorance are not decisive, but rather sin and redemption. That theology must discover whether a spiritual position is premised upon an orthodox or heretical dogma. In its obedience of faith it regards itself as being confronted with disobedience. The "metaphysical core" therefore appears to it to be political, not merely potentially but actually, and from the very beginning: One does not have to wait until metaphysical and theological positions are subjected to the distinction between friend and enemy. Whether "consciously or unconsciously,"[13] these positions are always already a taking of sides in accordance with a firm dividing line between friend and enemy. Since that line is absolute, one cannot avoid taking sides. Even one who is determined not to advocate a metaphysical or theological position, who disclaims knowledge or competence in the quarrel of faith, cannot evade the obligation to take sides. Whoever does not decide for the truth of faith, decides against it. On such a theological basis, the claim to have come to "know that the political is the total" finds its corroboration in the "metaphysical core." Supported by that basis, Schmitt believes himself able to compel every opponent to participate in the political-theological battle in which "metaphysics" can always meet only "metaphysics," theology always only theology, faith always only faith.[14] The political-theological battle is so total, it is so comprehensive and usurping of everything, that even the sworn enemy of every political theology, even Bakunin, whose claim it was to overcome theology and politics, had no choice but to attest the truth of political theology and in fact so much so that he "had to become the theologian of the antitheological" and "the dictator of an antidictatorship"—he *had* to become such, for Satan has no power over God.[15]

13. Cf. *PR*, 5 and *BdP*, 59.

14. On this point see in particular and for extensive proof *Carl Schmitt and Leo Strauss: The Hidden Dialogue*, 72–79.

15. *PT*, 84. In the first edition of 1922, the last two words of the sentence and of the en-

The way a theoretician interprets other thinkers throws light on his own thought. How one reads is usually how one writes. That to which he gives his undivided attention regarding friend and enemy, that is especially to be attended to regarding himself. What suggests itself more therefore than the question of Schmitt's central statements on the level of "theory" about their theological meaning? And what would be more central than his claim to have come to "know that the political is the total"? A political theologian who, following Bonald and Donoso, does not lose sight of the "immeasurably fruitful parallel" between theology and political theory, will hardly miss the opportunity to raise and to answer to his satisfaction the question as to which theological position "agrees" with his knowledge, as to whether—speaking with Bonald, Donoso, and Schmitt—it has its "equivalent" in theism, deism, or atheism, in monotheism, polytheism, or pantheism.[16] An author who informs his readers that the dictum *Power is in itself evil* "means the same thing" as *God is dead*—one can assume about such an author that he is clear on what his assertion *The political is the total* "basically means."[17] Its theological significance becomes obvious as soon as one takes Schmitt at his word: The political can be the total only when there is a god or are gods, and in fact a god—at least one god—who actively intervenes in world events and who as a person makes demands on men. Only then can everything be related to a *person*, to his *will* and to the *adversary* born of that will. For there can be politics only between persons, in the force field of their volition, their action, their insight, never between ideas, laws, or random series. No one knew that better than Schmitt.[18] Neither the self-thinking god of Aristotle nor the gods of Epicurus who adorn the cosmos are sufficient to confer truth on the sentence *The political is the total.* Matters are different with the God of Abraham, Isaac, and Jacob, with the Triune God, with the God of Marcion,[19] or with the God of Mohammed. If there is a God who demands obedience, then the world is not merely "politomorphic"[20] but rather political as a whole: Everything is accessible to the distinction between friend and enemy because everything is subject to dominion. Nothing is conceivable that could be excluded from the supreme sovereign.

---

tire treatise read: 'has become' [*geworden ist*]. After Schmitt had come to "know that the political is the total," he replaced them in 1933–34 with: 'had to become' [*werden mußte*].

16. Cf. *PT*, 52 (76); *GLP*, 89.

17. *Gespräch über die Macht*, 23; *G*, 201; cf. 139, 157–158, 169, and *BdP*, 60.

18. *PT*, 11, 32–33, 46, 56, (16, 44–45, 65–66, 83); *RK*, 35–36, 39–40, 56 (23, 26, 37); *BdP*, 28–29, 37, 39; *G*, 202, 203.

19. *PT II*, 116–123; cf. *Theodor Däublers "Nordlicht,"* 68; *RK*, 16 (11).

20. Cf. *PT II*, 119.

In the most important respect, then, Schmitt's political totalism does not presuppose the primacy of the enemy; rather, it hinges on the primacy of God, of the God who compels the decision, on the primacy of the God against whom disobedience rebels. The rebellion of disobedience, however, has always been regarded as the definition of the essence of the Old Enemy.[21] By binding the political to the distinction between friend and enemy, Schmitt opens the "metaphysical core" to the political. By freeing that distinction from its reference to the community, he makes it, starting from the "metaphysical core," potentially ubiquitous: the constellation of friend and enemy can apply to *everything* and turn up literally *everywhere*. Taken together, both of these movements find their expression in the sentence *The political is the total*. Even if Schmitt had not uttered it, it would still mark one of the load-bearing "axes" of his teaching.[22] For the sense and achievement that the redefinition of the political has for Schmitt's ownmost enterprise cannot be more precisely condensed than in that sentence. It has several valences and can serve as an abbreviation for the designation of various functions. *Theologically* it says within the framework of Schmitt's political theology as much as *The God who demands obedience is the Lord of the whole, of the world and of history*. *Historically* it answers to the challenge of an age in which "nothing is more modern than the battle against the political."[23] *Polemically* it opposes the liberal "philosophy of culture," which at best accords the political its "own domain" in the broad field of that philosophy's autonomous "provinces of culture."[24] *Morally* it pits the severity of the claim made on men against the "illusion" that they could escape the political, and pits veracity against the "deceit" of him who furthers his political intentions behind the "mask," behind the facade of the unpolitical; the sentence

21. Neil Forsyth provides a wealth of information on this point in his *The Old Enemy: Satan and the Combat Myth* (Princeton 1987).

22. Besides the "Preliminary Remark" to the *Politische Theologie* of 1934, see, among other things, "Weiterentwicklung des totalen Staats in Deutschland" [The Further Development of the Total State in Germany] (1933), in *PuB*, 186, *VA*, 361; *Staatsgefüge und Zusammenbruch des zweiten Reiches. Der Sieg des Bürgers über den Soldaten* [*The Structure of the State and the Collapse of the Second Reich: The Victory of the Bourgeois over the Soldier*] (Hamburg 1934), 29; "Was bedeutet der Streit um den 'Rechtsstaat'?" [What is the Significance of the Quarrel over the "Legal State"?], in *Zeitschrift für die gesamte Staatswissenschaft* 95, no. 2 (1935): 197. —Regarding the "axes," cf. *BdP*, 122.

23. *PT*, 55 (82); see Chapter I, 25 above and cf. *Carl Schmitt and Leo Strauss: The Hidden Dialogue*, 23–24.

24. One of the most widespread errors in the literature on Schmitt is the supposition that Schmitt's concern is the defense of the "autonomy of the political." One could not possibly miss the thrust of Schmitt's conception of the political more fundamentally than this supposition does, and in particular it ignores the significance of the sentence *The political is the total*.

stands in the service of "political honesty and upstandingness" when it, for example, helps one attain the insight that "depoliticization [represents] only a particularly useful weapon in the political battle."[25] *Strategically* it has the advantage both of making the believer as well as the unbeliever aware of the unavoidability of an Either-Or that is a matter of life-and-death and of building up a wide front for the "affirmation of enmity" and against the loss of vital seriousness. Finally, *anthropologically* it means the same as *Man can be wholly grasped politically*.

The anthropological translation of the dictum should make it clear that we have not left the consideration of the theological implications of Schmitt's political totalism nor for a moment lost sight of the "most profound connections." Man can be wholly grasped *politically* only because and insofar as the political obeys a *theological* determination; such is the position of political theology. That Schmitt did not "forget" this premise when he expressly stated in the final revision of *Der Begriff des Politischen* that man is "grasped wholly and existentially in political participation," this, among other things, follows, as we have seen, from the fact that he simultaneously introduces the "metaphysical opposition" into the debate, an opposition existing between political and agonal thought, and that he gives voice no less expressly to the series *dominion, order, peace*, which is the object and aim of the political quarrel. The quarrel over just dominion, the best order, and real peace, concerns man *wholly* because in it the question *How should I live?* is raised imperatively for him. That man is wholly *grasped* in political *participation*, in political *action*, however, is tied to the assumption of a complete identification or an irresistible authority. How else than by virtue of his love or his obedience could he be *grasped wholly*? The obedience the Leviathan can compel is insufficient in this regard. The Mortal God does not have at his disposal the power of that authority, which penetrates to the innermost core of men, in order to grasp them in their conscience, their virtues, their deepest longing. In 1938 Schmitt will devote one of his most important books to this topic. Yet already in 1933 he distances himself from the author of the *Leviathan* due to the impression made on him by the incisive critique Leo Strauss published a few months earlier. Now for the first time he too notes that author's "extreme individualism."[26] In fact Schmitt's totalism finds itself in a "metaphysical opposition" not only with agonal thought, which conceives of the life-and-death battle as a part of the

25. *BdP* III, 54; cf. 36, 46, 53, 56, 60; *SBV*, 27–28.

26. *BdP* III, 46; this is discussed at length in *Carl Schmitt and Leo Strauss: The Hidden Dialogue*, 33–38.

great play of the world and so misses the seriousness on which everything depends for Schmitt. "Metaphysically" it is no more compatible with that "extreme individualism" which declares violent death to be the *summum malum*. How could one who regards the death another can inflict on him as the greatest evil possibly be *wholly grasped* politically or theologically? Here it should at least be mentioned that one need not subscribe to the agonal faith or share Schmitt's faith in order to reject as an error the opinion that violent death represents the greatest evil for man: the example alone of the friend Socrates which Plato relayed, is sufficient to remind us of this.[27]

In the "only case that matters" the political coincides with the theological. The decision between God and Satan is simultaneously theological and political, the distinction between Christ and the Antichrist no less. At the "peaks of great politics," when the providential enemy is seen in concrete clarity as the enemy, the definition of the theological and of the political meet in *one* determination of the enemy. Schmitt's orientation towards the *exceptional case* allows him to know that the political is the total without therefore having to deny the total claim of the theological. On the contrary, it allows him by means of the political to assert the theological as *what is authoritative*. By linking these two powers, he goes far beyond the mere "correction" of liberal thought, a correction of which he had still said in the first edition of *Der Begriff des Politischen* that it can be effected, "whether from the political or from the religious [side]."[28] In the usual course of things, however, the theological and the political do not coincide. By far, not everything that is theologically of significance must become the object of political attention or political confrontation, and there may be just as many good theological reasons for not gearing every political decision towards theological viewpoints as there are good political reasons for excluding certain regions from political intervention or postponing such intentions temporarily. Nevertheless, there can be no doubt of the fundamental precedence of the theological for Schmitt. That becomes particularly clear when in *Politische Theologie II* Schmitt, following general usage, separates the theological as the "religious side" from the political as the "worldly side" in order to confront, in accordance with this distinction, the "potential ubiquity of the political" with the "ubiquity of the theological."[29] The theological *is* ubiquitous, the po-

27. Plato, *Crito* 44 d; cf. *Apology* 29 a–b.

28. *BdP* I, 30–31. In both of the later editions the passage has been deleted.

29. "From the worldly side the potential ubiquity of the political asserts itself, from the religious side the ubiquity of the theological [asserts itself] again and again in new manifestations" (*PT II*, 73).

litical *can* be. The theological is the total *tout court*, the political *conditionally*.[30] Schmitt's last word in this matter, which for obvious reasons avoids talk of the "total," gives expression with the greatest precision to what had long been certain.[31] The precedence of the theological is the presupposition of Schmitt's totalism. The political as it is usually understood stands for something that it itself is *not*, but that it emphatically calls to mind. It represents an Other that precedes it and forms its basis, an Other which, to be sure, is not the "Wholly Other" because in the case that decides everything the Other erupts, appears, and exists in real presence in the political.[32] The relationship can also be determined as follows: Whereas "the political" can lay claim to man wholly and as a matter of life-and-death, "the theological," the God who demands obedience, lays claim to him always already and eternally in this way. For "God wants and needs nothing less than everything."[33]

Once again we have returned to the "fundamental theological dogma of the sinfulness of the world and of men" that is of decisive importance to Schmitt's political theology.[34] It says precisely this: God wants nothing less than everything, he demands unconditional obedience, and the world does not fulfill this demand. Thus it is not the fundamental dogma of every theology, but rather of those grounded in revelation and those treating a God who commands obedience. In the dogma of sinfulness they seek to capture the relationship of the world to this God. In the doctrine of original sin, the concern therefore is *first of all* God and *then* man. Accordingly the distinction invoked again and again by Schmitt between the man who is "by nature evil" and who is "by nature good"[35] has a political-theological sense. The distinction does not primarily concern anthropological findings or conjectures, but aims at the fundamental question of faith and unfaith: What in the end matters to Schmitt in the quarrel of faith over the "good" or "evil man" is not the recognition of man's "dangerousness" so much as the recognition of God's sovereignty. At first glance a different picture admittedly seems to arise. In *Der Begriff*

30. Consider *PT II*, 118 and 123.

31. Cf. *PT*, 46, 50, 51, 52, 55, 56 (65, 71, 73, 75, 82, 83).

32. Cf. *PT II*, 118 n.

33. "There are no provinces of which we can say that God has no business there—God need not interfere . . . . God wants and needs nothing less than everything!" Karl Barth, *Vom christlichen Leben* (Munich 1926), 22 f.

34. *BdP* III, 45 (II, 64). See Chapter I, 12 ff. and Chapter II, 57 ff. above.

35. Cf. *PT*, 50–52 (70–75); *RK*, 16–17, 67 (11, 44); *PR*, 3 ff.; *Die Diktatur. Von den Anfängen des modernen Souveränitätsgedankens bis zum proletarischen Klassenkampf* [*The Dictatorship: From the Beginnings of the Modern Thought of Sovereignty to the Proletarian Class Struggle*] (Munich/Leipzig 1921), 9, 146–147.

des Politischen Schmitt devotes a separate chapter to the quarrel over "anthropology" which—to judge by the perceptible reactions of the past six decades—left many, if not most, readers with the impression that Schmitt's exclusive concern is man's "dangerousness," that the theoretician of the political expects and requires nothing of his readers save the admission that man is a "problematic" and "risky being." How does Schmitt succeed in giving this impression? One without which his text would hardly have had the political influence that it in fact has had. And how does he know how to lead those readers, whom he believes to be receptive to it, nevertheless to the theological core of the quarrel, so that they are confronted with the "moral disjunction" of *credo* or *non-credo*? The first sentence of the chapter reads: "One could examine all theories of State and all political ideas for their anthropology and divide them according to whether they—consciously or unconsciously—presuppose a man who is 'by nature evil' or one who is 'by nature good.'" Thus right from the beginning, he evokes the doctrine of original sin, a doctrine to which all theories of State and all political ideas are related—consciously or unconsciously—especially since the cue "anthropological confession of faith" falls in the last line of the preceding paragraph. But then Schmitt continues, saying that the distinction is "wholly summary and not to be taken in a specifically moral or ethical sense." "Decisive," he assures the reader, is "whether—as the presupposition of every further political consideration—man *is held to be* a problematic or unproblematic being. Is man a 'dangerous' or a non-dangerous, a risky or a harmlessly non-risky being?"[36] Could it be that the "anthropological confession of faith" has the status only of a more or less plausible supposition after all? At the first level of his ascent to the doctrine of original sin, Schmitt begins so generally that his enterprise looks to be virtually harmless or at least non-risky. On the one hand, the distinction between the man who is "by nature evil" or who is "by nature good" seems to constitute two categories of "theories of State and political ideas" which can be regarded indiscriminately as *theories of State* and *political ideas*, regardless of whether they agree with or contradict the dogma of original sin. On the other hand, the distinction between "by nature evil" and "by nature good" is translated in such a way that Schmitt can be certain of finding the broadest approval for the alternative "by nature evil." For who would think of denying that man *is* a problematic, dangerous, risky being? The anthropological controversy

36. *BdP* III, 41 (my emphasis). I am citing the final edition, which is not only more precise with regard to content, but is also linguistically superior to the first and second editions (cf. II, 59).

is sparked off, as Schmitt knew of course, by the question as to whether man always *was* and always *will be* such a being. Let us disregard here for a moment the fact that this question also does not yet touch the core of the quarrel over whether man is to be considered a being which is by nature *good* or *evil*. At the second level Schmitt takes the offensive. He now denies that the liberal or anarchic "theories and constructions which presuppose that man is 'good'" are at all theories of State and political ideas. Namely, according to Schmitt, the "faith in 'natural goodness'" can serve as a foundation of neither a *positive* theory of State nor an *affirmation* of the political. The result of his critique of anarchism and liberalism is "the odd and *for many certainly disquieting* statement that all genuine political theories presuppose man to be 'evil,' that is, to be not at all an unproblematic but rather 'dangerous' and 'dynamic' being. For every political thinker in the proper sense, that is easy to prove."[37] Genuine political theories are those which affirm the political. And such theories agree completely with the truth of the doctrine of original sin: that man is evil. Schmitt does not yet go so far as to stipulate the recognition of original sin. He instead presents its truth in a formulation that is immediately plausible to common sense and has to appear all the more familiar to it since common sense has always been inclined to see in the insight that man is *"evil," that is, a being that is by no means unproblematic but rather "dangerous,"* the "proper meaning" of the myth of the Fall of Man, the quintessence of the doctrine of original sin. Schmitt chooses the lowest common denominator acceptable to all those who can be brought into position in the "anthropological" quarrel with the "faith in 'natural goodness'" and won in the political battle as allies against liberalism and anarchism. A brief aside, in which the notion of man's sinfulness and need of redemption is introduced into the line of thought for the first time, prepares the final and decisive step. Schmitt opposes the "anthropological" intellectual presuppositions of the pedagogue, the jurist of private law, and the moralist on the one hand with the "methodological intellectual presuppositions" of the political thinker and the theologian on the other hand, which similarly contradict anthropological "optimism." On the third level, the "connection between political theories and theological dogmas of sin" is voiced openly. The talk is no longer of man's "dangerousness," of his "dynamic," "risky," or "problematic" character. The "connection" that mattered to Schmitt from the first sentence of the chapter on "emerges," we now learn, "only in authors such as Bossuet, Maistre, Bonald, and Donoso Cortés particularly conspicuously; in nu-

37. *BdP* III, 43 (my emphasis); II, 61.

merous others it is just as intensely effective. It is explained first in terms of the ontological-existential way of thinking, which conforms to the essence of a theological, as well as a political, line of thought. But then [the connection is explained] also in terms of the kinship of these methodological intellectual presuppositions." Just as a theologian ceases "to be a theologian when he no longer considers men to be sinful or in need of redemption and no longer distinguishes the redeemed from the unredeemed, the chosen from the unchosen," likewise the political thinker ceases to be a political thinker when he no longer distinguishes between friend and enemy. The political theologian, however, only becomes a political theologian once he discerns the connection between both distinctions and establishes the bond between the theological and the political "line of thought" himself, elaborates it theoretically, and develops it practically. That is just what "authors such as Bossuet, Maistre, Bonald, and Donoso Cortés" have done. For anyone who has not yet become clear on the significance of the "methodological connection" between the theological and political intellectual presuppositions, both of which lead "to a distinction between and a division of men, to a 'distancing,'" Schmitt points out that the Protestant theologian Ernst Troeltsch and the Catholic writer Ernest de Seillière have "shown by the example of numerous sects, heretics, romantics, and anarchists, that the denial of original sin destroys all social order. The methodological connection between theological and political intellectual presuppositions is thus obvious."[38] Step by step Schmitt has drawn our attention to a *foundational chain of reasoning*, and in the end, in the sole passage in which original sin is mentioned in *Der Begriff des Politischen*, he confronts us with an apodictic Either-Or: faith or disorder.

What is in question in the "anthropological confession of faith" in *Der Begriff des Politischen* is not a more or less plausible supposition regarding "anthropology." Nor does Schmitt invoke the dogma of original sin in order to provide an axiom of his "conception of man" with an effective justification. On the contrary, he uses the anthropological quarrel to bring the doctrine of original sin into play. And he does this in turn not solely or first of all in order to assert its political indispensability. What concerns Schmitt above all in the doctrine of original sin is the defense of the center of the theology of revelation and the presupposition of every—as he understands it—genuine morality.[39] In question is the *truth of his*

38. *BdP* III, 44, 45–46; II, 63, 64.

39. See Chapter I, 10 f. and 20–23. In his letter of December 15, 1933 Werner Becker writes to Schmitt: "It is not right to say that you 'bind' yourself to the 'the opponent's conception of morality'—but you do bind yourself . . . to his moral terminology. You refuse to

confession of faith. The widespread opinion that Schmitt could have just as easily substituted his "reference to original sin" with the "reference to contemporary philosophical anthropology," or that he could have achieved the "same result," as it is occasionally expressed, by referring readers who do not give credence to the dogma to evolutionary biology—such interpretations misjudge and miss what is most important.[40] The "fundamental theological dogma of the *sinfulness of the world* and of man" cannot be "substituted" with any insight nor with any result of anthropology. With its "distancing," it is infallibly bound to the recognition of the sovereignty of God. The sovereignty of God, "who said, I shall put enmity between your seed and her seed," is the point in which the three distinctions between *redeemed and unredeemed, chosen and unchosen, friend and enemy* converge. In that sovereignty, the "distinction and division of men"—by means of which "the indiscriminate optimism of a general concept of man becomes impossible"—has its ultimate determinative ground. To anyone who wishes to "disregard" the sovereignty of God, the meaning of the doctrine of original sin and of grace has to remain closed, just as does the thrust of Schmitt's attack on "natural goodness" and the "general concept of man." This "disregard" is exactly the target of Schmitt's critique. His attack is directed at a world that denies or has forgotten its "sinfulness": "In a good world, among good men, of course, only the freedom, security, and harmony among all prevail; here the priests and theologians are just as disturbing as the politicians and statesmen."[41] The politicians and theologians are *disturbing*—and not *superfluous*, as Schmitt first wrote—because they call to mind the sovereignty of God, his dispositions and commandments, the necessity of the decision between obedience and disobedience, which negates such a world. The "indiscriminate optimism of a general concept of man" is the

characterize man as morally evil because the word 'morally' would be immediately misunderstood in a humanitarian manner. The difficulty probably lies in the impossibility of speaking of the nature of man, of his endangeredness and dangerousness and of his neediness, without mentioning original sin. But for the Christian, that has a moral quality which one must accept and apply with devout realism, without a moral reproach of the individual being able to arise from it. Man is precisely not a benignly evil animal (as he is for Hobbes, in whose work 'guidance by the understanding' is equated completely with concepts such as conditioning and habituation), but rather . . . a well-meaning originally sinful man, in this tension between freedom and finitude which is difficult to penetrate and which arises from the fact of redemption."

40. Cf. Heinrich Meier, ed., *Die Herausforderung der Evolutionsbiologie* (Munich 1988), 8–11. Schmitt objects to Arnold Gehlen, the leading representative of "philosophical anthropology" after the Second World War, that his anthropology is ultimately grounded on the "Darwinistic faith" that man has descended from animal ancestors.

41. *BdP* III, 45; cf. II, 64.

expression of and cipher for what Schmitt will not tire of attacking even in his last writings as the *self-authorization* [Selbstermächtigung] *of man*. Friedrich Gogarten defined this concept, which is pitted against the *sovereignty of God* (Gogarten speaks of the "self-authority [*Selbstmächtigkeit*] and autonomy of man"), in a talk published under the title "Secularized Theology in the Theory of State" as the rebellion against "the *fundamental order of the world on which all other orders are based, namely, that of creator and creature*."[42] He thereby strikes the core of the cause that unites him with Schmitt. The lecture, which explicitly mentions Schmitt's *Politische Theologie* and to which Schmitt himself refers several months later in his "Preliminary Remark to the Second Edition" of that treatise,[43] is both a historically and systematically remarkable testimony of political theology. In the present context it deserves special attention because it contains the most revealing commentary submitted from the theological side on Schmitt's "anthropological" distinction between man as "by nature good" and as "by nature evil." "Today," says Gogarten in elucidating the meaning of Schmitt's opposition,[44] since "the idea of the moral-religious autonomy of the individual completely dominates our usual way of thinking, there is the danger that both sentences—man is by nature good or he is by nature evil—will be understood as an opposition within this morally-religiously autonomous thinking. In truth, however, the statement that man is by nature evil, says . . . something completely different from what a thinking dominated by the idea of man's moral-religious autonomy is capable of grasping. The statement stands in radical opposition to that thinking and every statement made by this moral thinking about the characteristics of man." According to Gogarten, this thinking takes "the self-authority and autonomy of man" as its starting point. "[Self-authority] is man's being good, which for that reason can never be abolished, not even by all of man's potential—and certainly never denied—evil . . . . By contrast, the statement that man is

42. The talk, which was held in the Leopoldina Auditorium of the University of Breslau on January 18, 1933 at the annual celebration of the founding of the Reich [by Bismarck in 1871], was printed in an abbreviated form on March 2 and 3, 1933 in the newspaper *Münchner Neueste Nachrichten*. A critical edition of "Säkularisierte Theologie in der Staatslehre" may now be found in Friedrich Gogarten, *Gehören und Verantworten. Ausgewählte Aufsätze* (Tübingen 1988), 126–141; see 126 and 132.

43. See n. 10 above. In the case of Heinrich Forsthoff, the second Protestant theologian whom Schmitt mentions by name, the reference is to the book, also published in 1933, *Das Ende der humanistischen Illusion. Eine Untersuchung über die Voraussetzungen von Philosophie und Theologie* (Berlin 1933).

44. Gogarten's interpretation takes the following sentence from *Politische Theologie* as its starting point: "Every political idea somehow takes a stand on the 'nature' of man and presupposes that he is either 'by nature good' or 'by nature evil'" (50/72).

'by nature evil' precisely does not take the self-authority of man as its starting point but, on the contrary, a power to which man is subject. A power in and through whose opposite position—put more clearly and more definitely: in bondage to it—man is himself. And before this power and before its claim on him, he is evil. He is evil—that means here: he does not want to be himself, as he is in the bondage to this power, but rather in his being free to decide for himself, so that he is responsible to himself alone." Gogarten underscores the sovereignty of God by placing emphasis on two points of view: First, "that man is seen here such that his being a person is not grounded in himself but rather in the responsible opposite position to a power from which he therefore has his life and which therefore also has the power to annihilate him, that is, to plunge him into eternal destruction." Second, it should be noted "that the origin of being by nature evil which is expressed here cannot be demonstrated in the recorded history of a man. It thus does not arise through a singular, particular fact in the history of a man but rather always already determines his entire history. His total person, his total being a person, as it is represented in his history, is always already evil. It is always already caught up in the rebellion against that power . . . . Wherever the knowledge of good and evil descends on man . . . there he always already comes from evil; there he himself is already evil; there he has already ceased to be good in the simple, non-contradictory, childlike-obedient bondage to a power in the face of which he is himself."[45]

From the standpoint of faith in revelation, man is "by nature" evil because he naturally frees himself from the "childlike-obedient bondage" to that power to which he is held to be subject. His *being evil* is synonymous with disdain for the sovereignty of God. It is essentially disobedience. On this point there is general agreement despite all theological differences of opinion on the interpretation of the Fall of Man and original sin.[46] Thus there is general agreement that man's endeavor to live his

45. Gogarten, "Säkularisierte Theologie in der Staatslehre," 137–138. Consider 132 and 139–141; see further "Der doppelte Sinn von Gut und Böse" (1937), esp. 202 ff., in *Gehören und Verantworten*. In light of Gogarten's commentary, compare Schmitt's dissociation of himself from the "moralist," who "presupposes a freedom of choice between good and evil," and Schmitt's reservation regarding a "theological support" which "*usually* shifts the distinction into the *moral theological* sphere or at least confounds it with the latter." *BdP* III, 45–46 (my emphasis); II, 63–64 with n. 24.

46. Cf. *PT*, 51 (73–74); *RK*, 17 (11). Leo Scheffczyk and Heinrich Köster provide a survey of the history of dogma in their *Urstand, Fall und Erbsünde. Handbuch der Dogmengeschichte*, vol. II, fascicles 3 a, b, c (Freiburg i. Br. 1979–1982), as does Julius Gross in his *Geschichte des Erbsündendogmas. Ein Beitrag zur Geschichte des Problems vom Ursprung des Übels* (Munich/Basel 1960–1972), 4 vols.

life based on his own resources, following natural reason and his own judgment alone, *is* the original sin. Theology cannot help but see in the philosophical life a persistent repetition and renewal of the Fall of Man. In view of the unbridgeable gulf by which it knows itself to be separated from philosophy, the distinctions that exist between the positions of individual philosophers on, for example, anthropology fade:[47] what do all the differences in the assessment of human nature mean compared to the fundamental agreement that this nature makes possible the philosophical life and therein reveals its *being good*? Measured by the standard of faith in revelation, philosophers not only move closer together; in light of the criteria of authority and obedience, it becomes obvious that what in truth unifies them and what divides them, proves to be of subordinate rank. Great theologians have always known this truth and insisted on the dividing line again and again. In 1933 Rudolf Bultmann fixes it—with Martin Heidegger in view, whose proximity caused him to be all the more aware of the decisive difference[48]—in the sentence: "Faith can judge the choice of the philosophical existence only as an act of the self-founding freedom of the man who denies his subordination to God."[49] From the

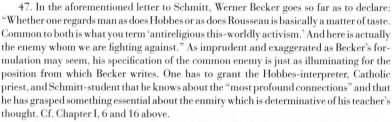

47. In the aforementioned letter to Schmitt, Werner Becker goes so far as to declare: "Whether one regards man as does Hobbes or as does Rousseau is basically a matter of taste. Common to both is what you term 'antireligious this-worldly activism.' And here is actually the enemy whom we are fighting against." As imprudent and exaggerated as Becker's formulation may seem, his specification of the common enemy is just as illuminating for the position from which Becker writes. One has to grant the Hobbes-interpreter, Catholic priest, and Schmitt-student that he knows about the "most profound connections" and that he has grasped something essential about the enmity which is determinative of his teacher's thought. Cf. Chapter I, 6 and 16 above.

48. In his writing *Phänomenologie und Theologie*, Heidegger drew the limit no less sharply from the other side. Held as a lecture in 1927–28 in Tübingen and Marburg and published in 1970 with a dedication to Bultmann, Heidegger observes in it "that *faith* in its innermost core remains as a specific possibility of existence the mortal enemy of the *form of existence* which belongs essentially to *philosophy* and which is factually quite alterable. So absolutely that philosophy does not even begin to want to fight that mortal enemy in any way! This *existential opposition* between faithfulness and one's freely taking one's entire existence upon oneself . . . must bear within itself precisely the *possible community* of theology and philosophy *as sciences* if this communication is to be able to remain a genuine communication, free of every illusion and frail attempt at mediation. Thus there is no such thing as a Christian philosophy, that is a 'wooden iron' pure and simple." ([Frankfurt a. M. 1970], 32; cf. 18–20, 26–27; *GA* 9, pp. 66, 52–54, 60–61; in addition *Nietzsche* [Pfullingen 1961], I, 14.) Compare the paragraph on the original meaning of political philosophy in Chapter II, 40 ff. above with Heidegger's sentence: "So absolutely that philosophy does not even begin to want to fight that mortal enemy in any way!"

49. Bultmann, *Theologische Enzyklopädie* (Tübingen 1984), 89. Consider 93, 131, 143, 201 and cf. 69–70, 108, 165. Eberhard Jüngel and Klaus W. Müller have made available an edition of Bultmann's Marburg lecture course, the care of which corresponds to the significance of this theological self-reflection.

standpoint of faith in revelation, the choice of the philosophical life rests on an act of disobedience. Or as St. Bonaventure and the author of *Der Antichrist* have asserted in virtually the same words: philosophy itself appears to be the tree of the knowledge of good and evil.[50]

You are free to eat of all the trees in the garden, but of the tree of the knowledge of good and evil you are not to eat. Jean-Jacques Rousseau saw the "reason" of this commandment in the intention to "give human actions a morality from the start which they would not have acquired for a long time."[51] Whatever else the Genevan philosopher may have had in view with his interpretation,[52] the anchoring of a primeval moral Either-Or in the faith in revelation could hardly be more precisely expressed. The "commandment, which is in itself indifferent and inexplicable in any other system," the commandment Rousseau seeks to explain, guarantees a moral disjunction that precedes all human knowledge of good and evil. It therefore founds a certainty that radically surpasses human security or insecurity and thereby perfectly satisfies the need of moral man for absolute validity. *Moral man as such is the potential believer.* The first biblical commandment, however, founds not only the certainty of a moral Either-Or, as such. It entails a particular prohibition. It not only makes man aware of the distinction between obedience and disobedience, but simultaneously denies him the means he needs in order to lead a life that positions itself outside of obedience. For it does not forbid man just any tree but rather the one without whose fruit a self-determined life remains denied him. Considered more closely, the commandment denotes nothing less than the biblical alternative to philosophy, and to that extent it is everything but "in itself indifferent." All subsequent commandments and judgments concerning philosophy are anticipated in this first one. Anticipated therein is especially the interdict against the question which is co-original with philosophy and for the sake of which philosophy must become political philosophy: *quid sit deus?*[53] The biblical God reveals

50. " . . . philosophia est lignum scientiae boni et mali, quia veritati permixta est falsitas . . . Cavere debent sibi discentes quae sunt philosophiae; fugiendum est omne illud quod est contrarium doctrinae Christi, sicut interfectivum animae." Bonaventure, *Sermones de tempore*, dominica tertia Adventus, *Opera omnia*, IX, 63 (ed. Quaracchi). Nietzsche, *Der Antichrist*, aph. 48, *KGW* VI.3, 224–225.

51. Rousseau, *Discours sur l'inégalité*, Note IX, critical edition, 320.

52. In addition to the commentary to ibid., 318 ff., cf. xxxi–xxxiv, xli–xliii, lxv with n. 68 and 70–74 with nn. 80, 84, 86, 88, 90.

53. Cicero, *De natura deorum* I, 60. Leo Strauss, *The City and Man* (Chicago 1964), 241. Strauss confronted the biblical alternative unlike any other philosopher of this century. See *Jerusalem and Athens. Some Preliminary Reflections* (1967), in *Studies in Platonic Political Philosophy* (Chicago 1983), 147–173, esp. 155; "On the Interpretation of

himself to whomever he wants, whenever he wants, wherever he wants, and however he wants. The God of revelation indicates to the believer who he is through his action within the bounds his will establishes and for the purposes his judgment determines. In the question of philosophy, therefore, the obedience of faith is able to perceive rebellion, rejection, hubris. Philosophy appears to such obedience, as in Calvin's case, to be an act of presumptuous curiosity[54] or, as in Luther's case, to be the beginning of a path at the end of which stands the forlornness of nothingness.[55] In this way the question "Obedience or disobedience?" is transformed into the answer "Faith in revelation or nihilism." If the *quid*

Genesis" (1957) in *L'Homme. Revue française d'anthropologie* XXI, no. 1 (1981): 6–20, esp. 18–19; consider *Persecution and the Art of Writing* (Glencoe, Ill. 1952), 107; "On the *Euthyphron*," in *The Rebirth of Classical Political Rationalism* (Chicago 1989), 202–203; and compare "Farabi's 'Plato'," in *Louis Ginzberg Jubilee Volume* (New York 1945), 376–377, 393 as well as *Socrates and Aristophanes* (New York 1966), 33, 45, 52–53.

54. "Unde intelligimus hanc esse rectissimam Dei quaerendi viam et aptissimum ordinem: non ut audaci curiositate penetrare tentemus ad excutiendam eius essentiam, quae adoranda potius est, quam scrupulosius disquirenda." Calvin, *Institutio christianae religionis* (1559), ed. Barth/Niesel, I, 5, 9. Cf. I, 6, 2: "omnis recta Dei cognitio ab obedientia nascitur"; and III, 7, 1: "O quantum ille profecit qui se non suum esse edoctus, dominium regimenque sui propriae rationi abrogavit, ut Deo asserat! Nam ut haec ad perdendos homines efficacissima est pestis, ubi sibiipsis obtemperant, ita unicus est salutis portus, nihil nec sapere, nec velle per seipsum, sed Dominum praeeuntem duntaxat sequi." See, in addition, Calvin's commentary on Genesis 2:16–17. An interesting "contribution to the comparison of reformatory and patristic thought" with regard to the question of how far concessions may be made to the *quid sit deus?* of the philosophers is provided by E. P. Meijering under the title *Calvin wider die Neugierde* (Nieuwkoop 1980).

55. "Hoc fit, quando ratione speculatur de deo, he is forlorn, quia [he] becomes confused in ascending and climbing et fit certus, ut dicat non esse deum . . . Quem satan brings to the point that he leads him with thoughts absque verbo, no one can help him." Luther's sermon on John 17:1–3 from August 15, 1528 (ed. Clemen/Hirsch VII, 217, *WA* XXVIII, 92) deals with such a central passage of the Gospel and provides such an important commentary on the *quid sit deus?* from the standpoint of Christian faith, a commentary unequaled in its rigor and clarity, that we shall relay the decisive passage here not simply in the brief excerpt from Rörer's transcript but rather unabridged in the version published by Caspar Cruciger during Luther's lifetime. It is reported that Luther called that edition "his best book" and said: "After the Holy Bible this book is dearest to me" (*WA* XXVIII, 34). Luther comes to speak of the Hiero-Simonides episode from *De natura deorum* in the context of his interpretation of the verse *And this is life eternal, that they might know thee the only true God, and Jesus Christ, whom thou hast sent* from Jesus's prayer: " . . . whoever here wishes to be on the safe side must by all means be on guard against everything that reason and human thought [seek to] master in this article, and know that there is no help for withstanding the temptation of the Devil but that one keep to the bare lucid word of the Scriptures and neither think further nor speculate but rather simply keep his eyes closed and say: What Christ says, that shall and must be true, whether or not I or any other human being can understand and grasp or know how it could be true. He knows well what he is and what he shall say of or how he shall talk of himself. Whoever does not do that must run into [an impasse] and become confused and fall. For indeed it is not possible to grasp the slightest article of faith by human reason or the senses, thus that no human being on earth has ever been able

sit deus? of disobedience has to end in nothingness because God is the Lord of all knowledge of God, but without this knowledge all knowledge remains uncertain and every commandment questionable, then by contrast the obedience of faith seems to be permitted to hope for everything. That knowledge of God is left to him which in the language of the Bible is called eternal life and which alone *revelation* grants: a transhuman event that conquers all human uncertainty. Faith in revelation promises effective protection from the danger of nihilism. It is oriented towards a particular event over which no power of the world has any control; in the case of Christianity it is oriented centrally and decisively towards the incarnation of God in Jesus, the Christ. Carl Schmitt stresses this event's unavailability, which is earth-shattering and which eludes all human endeavor and reflection, when he calls it "a historical event of infinite, unpossessable, unoccupiable uniqueness," and he goes further by adding that his statement about the "essential core" of Christendom "should stave off all philosophical, ethical, and other neutralizations." The *factum brutum* of revelation permits neither subsumption nor indifference. The "historical event" of the "incarnation in the virgin" which breaks through the natural order of things tolerates no other approach than in the humility of faith.[56] *For whatsoever is not of faith is sin.*

Revelation points the solely permissible path to the "knowledge of God." In it divine omnipotence manifests itself without suffering the slightest restriction. As its premise and its content it has the certainty of the faith that nothing is impossible for God. Revelation discloses in everything it commands of and promises men the unfathomability of the divine will and thereby preserves the "fundamental order of the world": the

---

to have a right thought and to hit upon and seize a certain knowledge of God without God's Word, even the pagans had to bear witness to this. For they write of a learned poet named Simonides that he was once asked to say what in fact God was or what he thought of and believed about God; he requested a postponement and delay of three days to think about the question. After those days had passed and he was to answer, he asked for three more days so as better to reflect [on the question], and after they had passed, again three, until he could no longer delay nor wanted to do so, and he said: what should I say? the longer I think about it, the less I know about it. *That shows that human reason, the higher it seeks to climb to fathom and ascertain God's essence, work, will, and decision, the farther it moves away from* [its goal] *and ultimately it reaches the point where it considers God to be nothing and believes nothing at all*" (*WA* XXVIII, 91–92; my emphasis).

56. "Drei Möglichkeiten," 930. "Je n'ai pas changé, il est vrai. Ma liberté vis-à-vis des idées est sans bornes parceque je reste en contact avec mon centre inoccupable qui n'est pas une 'idée' mais un événement historique: l'incarnation du Fils de Dieu. Pour moi le christianisme n'est pas en premier lieu une doctrine, ni une morale, ni même (excusez) une religion; il est un événement historique. Summa contra Gentiles III 93" (*G*, 283). Cf. "Die Sichtbarkeit der Kirche," 75–76; "Die geschichtliche Struktur," 153; further, Chapter I, 10 f. and 18–20.

infinite superiority of the creator over his creation, the unrestricted sovereignty of the omnipotent God. For only the incomprehensible God is omnipotent. Thus Schmitt has good reason for insisting on the "unoccupiable uniqueness" of the "historical event" which Christendom is for him, and for emphasizing that *in its essential core* it is not what it—considered in human terms—may appear to be: "no morality and no doctrine, no penitential sermon and no religion in the sense of comparative religious studies." Christendom must be part of that history which is ruled by Providence and which Schmitt calls "an implantation of the eternal into the course of the ages—an implantation which roars in grand testimonies and grows in powerful creaturings." A "testimony" and a "creaturing," of course, whose uniqueness prohibits every comparison and which is based on a core- or founding-event whose incomprehensibility can only be accepted in faith or rejected in unfaith. Schmitt regards the *Ecce, ancilla Domini, fiat mihi secundum verbum tuum* as the "total ground and total image" of man's answer, which is demanded by the omnipotence of God.[57] The political theologian is conscious of the inseparable connection between omnipotence and unfathomability, a connection we encounter ultimately in all facets of the faith in revelation. We encounter this inseparable connection between omnipotence and unfathomability not only in view of the facts of salvation and their proclamation in particular, but also in the faith in miracles altogether and in divine Providence as a whole, in the doctrine of original sin and in the notion of the election to grace, in the promise of eternal life, as well as in the punishment of eternal damnation. Schmitt strikes the nerve of the question when, concerning the greatest of all miracles, the *creatio ex nihilo*, he stresses that the talk of the "creation out of nothing" has "no other sense than to make the world's provenance from God incomprehensible and to leave it in the incomprehensible."[58] He explicitly makes himself the advocate of divine omnipotence when he adopts Léon Bloy's *Tout ce qui arrive est adorable* and repeats it as a Christian Epimetheus.[59] And we see him take a stand for divine unfathomability when he praises Calvin's doctrine of grace because it has restored "the unpredictability and immeasurability" to the concept of grace "that it is due in the right order": "[Calvin's doctrine] moves [the concept of grace] from a humanized, normativistic order back into the divine order due to it, an order above

57. "Drei Möglichkeiten," 930–931; *G*, 30, 269. "Not *humanitas* but rather *humilitas*" (274).

58. *G*, 212; cf. Schmitt's own talk of the *creatio ex nihilo* on 60; *PT II*, 125.

59. "*Tout ce qui arrive est adorable*. Whoever is not capable of praising the omnipotence of God should at least fall silent before it." "1907 Berlin," 14; see *G*, 8.

human normativizations."[60] In the same sense Schmitt defends theology against its "evaporation" into "merely normative morals"; he recalls the "ontological-existential" character of the distinction between friend and enemy, redeemed and unredeemed, chosen and unchosen; he opposes the "sinfulness of the world and of men" to the "viewpoint of the freedom of choice."[61]

In fact in its defense, should it require defense, omnipotence is nowhere more dependent upon unfathomability than in the doctrine of sin and grace. For how else could the Fall of Man be compatible with the omnipotence of God without God's infinite goodness being harmed? And how could the faith in his infinite goodness be saved without the notion of omnipotence having to be abandoned? How could this succeed if not with reference to the unfathomability of the divine will? "God has allowed what has happened and not allowed what has not happened."[62] All questions about the meaning of, the necessity of, the ultimate reason for the Fall of Man must end in the unfathomability of the divine will and fall silent before it if the omnipotence of God is not to be placed in question. Matters are no different regarding questions about the election to grace. Why did God love Jacob, but hate Esau "before the children were born and had done neither good nor evil?" How is such an election to be brought into harmony with divine justice? Regardless of whether one answers that "because of the sin of the first progenitor all men were born as those who are due damnation," so that God is merciful to those whom he frees by his grace, "by contrast, just to those whom he does not free, but unjust to no one,"[63] or whether one refrains from every dilatory intermediate step in order to reply straight-away that the reason God is not unjust is because "*he* wanted it that way and it has pleased *him* that way for all eternity," for there is "absolutely no law and no obligation" that con-

60. *DA*, 26.

61. *BdP* III, 45. "To the extent that theology becomes moral theology, this viewpoint of the freedom of choice emerges and the doctrine of the radical sinfulness of man fades. 'Homines liberos esse et eligendi facultate praeditos; nec proinde quosdam natura bonos, quosdam natura malos,' Irenaeus, *Contra haereses* (L. IV, c. 37, Migne VII, p. 1099)" (*BdP* II, 63 n. 24).

62. "1907 Berlin," 14.

63. "Cum enim omnes homines propter peccatum primi parentis damnationi nascantur obnoxii, quos Deus per suam gratiam liberat, sola misericordia liberat: et sic quibusdam est misericors, quos liberat, quibusdam autem justus, quos non liberat, neutris autem iniquus." Thomas Aquinas, *In omnes S. Pauli Apostoli Epistolas Commentaria* (Turin: Marietti, 1902), *Ad Romanos*, caput IX, lectio 3, p. 136. Cf. lectio 3 in fine, lectio 4, p. 139. Likewise Augustine, *De diversis quaestionibus ad Simplicianum*, I, 2, no. 16, ed. Flasch (*Logik des Schreckens. Die Gnadenlehre von 397*, Latin/German [Mainz 1990]), pp. 200–202; cf. 20, p. 226.

strains his will[64]—in both cases the human justification of the election to grace finds its ultimate support in the unfathomability of the divine will. No creature is capable of asserting its rights against the will of an omnipotent creator. Thus in one of the most influential works of political theology of all times, the question about the justice of God is dismissed with the counterquestion: "Shall the thing formed say to him that formed it, Why hast thou made me thus? Hath not the potter power over the clay, of the same lump to make one vessel unto honour, and another unto dishonour?" Yet the appeal to the absolute right of the omnipotent creator remains, if it is to be an appeal to his right,[65] no less bound up with the presupposition of the unfathomability of the divine will. Only on this presupposition, namely, will the creatures be able to affirm the will of the creator in loving obedience and to perceive in the "vessels of wrath" and the "vessels of mercy" testimonies of what, with Paul, is called the *glory*, *gloria*, *doxa* of God.[66]

The unfathomability of the divine will is enough to defend all divine

64. "Ratio itaque, quod non ideo est iniustus Deus, est, quia sic voluit ac placuit ab eterno, et voluntatis eius nulla est lex nullumque debitum omnino. Voluntas libera, que nulli subiacet, non potest iniusta esse, cum sit impossibile eam esse iniustam, nisi contra legem aliquam faciat." Luther, *Vorlesung über den Römerbrief 1515–1516*, 156. "Hoc enim vult efficere apud nos, ut in ea quae apparet inter electos et reprobos diversitate, mens nostra contenta sit, quod ita visum fuerit Deo, alios illuminare in salutem, alios in mortem excaecare: neque superiorem causam eius voluntate inquirat. Insistere enim debemus in istas particulas, Cuius vult, et Quem vult: ultra quas procedere nobis non permittit . . . Satan autem ipse, qui intus efficaciter agit, ita est eius minister, ut non nisi eius imperio agat." Calvin, *Commentarius in Epistolam Pauli ad Romanos*, 209.

65. Calvin's commentary is especially clear: "Ratio cur non debeat figmentum cum fictore suo contendere: quia fictor nihil facit nisi ex iure suo. Per vocem Potestatis non intelligit suppetere virtutem ac robur figulo ut pro libidine agat: sed optimo iure hanc facultatem ei competere. Neque enim vult Deo asserere potestatem aliquam inordinatam: sed quae merito illi sit deferenda" (212). Consider Luther, 154.

66. Paul, Romans 9:11–23. "Atque ita tenacissime firmissimeque credatur id ipsum, quod deus cuius vult miseretur et quem vult obdurat, hoc est cuius vult miseretur et cuius non vult non miseretur, esse alicuius occultae atque ab humano modulo investigabilis aequitatis." Augustine, *De diversis quaestionibus ad Simplicianum*, I, 2, 16, p. 198; cf. p. 202 (aequitate occultissima et ab humanis sensibus remotissima iudicat), 212, 232 (ita occulta est haec electio, ut in eadem consparsione nobis prorsus apparere non possit), 238. Compare Thomas Aquinas: "In quo datur intelligi quod homo non debet scrutari rationem divinorum judiciorum cum intentione comprehendendi, eo quod excedant rationem humanam" (caput IX, lectio 4, p. 139). Calvin: "ac non potius suo silentio moneat, mysterium quod non capiunt mentes nostrae, reverenter adorandum, atque ita curiositatis humanae proterviam compescat. Sciamus itaque Deum a loquendo non alium in finem supersedere, nisi quia immensam sapientiam suam modulo nostro comprehendi non posse videt" (211; cf. 204–205 and 212). Luther, 168–170; compare Luther's commentary on Romans 9:16: "Hic tamen moneo, ut in istis speculandis nullus irruat, qui nondum est purgate mentis, *ne cadat in barathrum horroris et desperationis*, sed prius purget oculos cordis in meditatione vulnerum Jhesu Christi" (160; my emphasis).

attributes: mercifulness, wrath, and glory, God's omnipotence and omniscience, his goodness and justice. Yet are not all the attributes abolished at the same time in that unfathomability? The omnipotence of God suffices to dispose of every contradiction and to admit of every miracle. But what may still be regarded as a miracle where there is no longer anything that appears impossible? The unfathomability of the omnipotence of God is the sole presupposition needed to found the possibility of revelation as a whole. But *what* must be presupposed in this case?[67]

It is not only for Carl Schmitt that in the end everything depends on the question before which he stops himself. Tertullian's guiding principle *We are obliged to something not because it is good but because God commands it* accompanies Schmitt through all the turns and vicissitudes of his long life.[68] A thought whose center is the sovereignty of God finds its concise expression in what "the jurist and theologian Tertullian says," a thought that takes the sovereignty of God as its starting point, only to return to it again and again.[69] Tertullian's famous saying calls to mind the no less famous question: does God want the good because it is good or is the good good because God wants it? thus: does the good have a being that is independent of God's will or not? and further: is there a standard, an order, a necessity by means of which God's will is limited, or is there no

67. "I shall be what I shall be." Exodus 3:14; cf. 33:19 and Paul, Romans 9:15.

68. *PR*, first edition (1919), 84; second edition (1925), 136; *DA* (1934), 25–26; *PT II* (1970), 115. In 1919 and 1925 Schmitt quoted Tertullian in the original wording: audacium existimo de bono divi praecepti disputare, neque enim quia bonum est, idcirco auscultare debemus, sed quia deus praecipit. In 1934 he translates the guiding principle himself into German: "Wir sind zu etwas verpflichtet, nicht, weil es gut ist, sondern weil Gott es befiehlt" [We are obliged to something not because it is good but because God commands it] and appends the correspondingly abridged Latin text in parentheses. In none of these passages, however, does Schmitt reveal the source. The quotation stems from Tertullian's *De poenitentia*, IV (*Opera Omnia*, ed. Migne [Paris 1866], I, 1344A) and is continued with a statement that can serve as the motto of Schmitt's political theology *in toto*: "Ad exhibitionem obsequii, prior est majestas divinae potestatis: prior est auctoritas imperantis, quam utilitas servientis."

69. The Protestant theologian Alfred de Quervain observed this with greater matter-of-factness than the Catholic writer Hugo Ball, who did not go the whole way but contended that Schmitt's thought takes its bearings by the sovereignty of the Pope. "The inclination to the absolute that characterizes him," Ball writes about Schmitt, leads "in its final consequence not to an abstraction that conditions everything, whether it is called God, form, authority, or something else, but rather to the Pope as the absolute person." "Carl Schmitts Politische Theologie," in *Hochland* (June 1924): 264; cf. 277, 278, 279, 284. For Schmitt, however, God is not an abstraction. He shares Hamann's critique of Kant (*BdP*, 89). For de Quervain "what is decisive" is "that Schmitt sees through the high-handedness of morality and of the weltanschauung and of the power relations which are consolidated in themselves and assert themselves. Here the knowledge of God's sovereignty is not pushed aside. It is the presupposition." *Die theologischen Voraussetzungen der Politik. Grundlinien einer politischen Theologie* (Berlin 1931), 168; consider 43, 63, 64, 70.

such thing? Schmitt's answer leaves no room for doubt. Indeed, he originally introduces Tertullian's "classical phrase" in order to oppose it to every attempt that aims at or could have as its result the limitation of God's sovereignty in any way: God's will may be neither limited by the order of nature, nor "compelled with the aid of logical rigor," nor "be subjugated to a law such as the political revolutionaries wanted to subjugate the monarch to the *volonté générale*." That is the "opposition" that Tertullian had "formulated classically."[70] One and a half decades later Schmitt endeavors to clarify the presupposition with which Tertullian's dictum is bound up: "The ever so unsearchable counsel of a personal God is, *so long as one believes in God*, always already 'in order' and not a pure decision." Only if God were not God, omnipotent, infinitely good, unfathomable could it not be always already "in order." Faith in God, in the God of Christian revelation, decides everything and nothing.[71]

Faith puts an end to uncertainty. For faith the *source* of certainty, the *provenance* of truth, is alone decisive.[72] Revelation promises such unshakeable protection from human arbitrariness that compared to it ignorance appears to be of subordinate significance. For that, too, Tertullian, with whom Schmitt has so much in common,[73] coined the classical

70. *PR* (1919), 84. In the second edition Schmitt alters the passage and adds two sentences which fix his position still more sharply: "*How does philosophy, Fénelon asked, come to want to limit God's authority? It is right that God is subjugated to a general order in such a way and that the authoritarian command and every activity becomes impossible.* Here lies an analogy to the way of thinking proper to the political revolutionaries who sought to subjugate the monarch to the *volonté générale*. It is the old opposition for which Tertullian found the classic formulation: audaciam . . . " (*PR* [1925], 137; my emphasis). Regarding the *locus classicus* of the opposition in Plato's *Euthyphron*, see from the philosophical standpoint the essay mentioned above which Thomas L. Pangle published from the papers of Leo Strauss in 1989 under the title "On the *Euthyphron*" (n. 53 above).

71. *DA*, 26 (my emphasis).

72. "Dieu d'Abraham, Dieu d'Isaac, Dieu de Jacob, non des philosophes et des savants. Certitude, certitude, sentiment, joie, paix. Dieu de Jésus-Christ." Pascal, *Le Mémorial du 23 novembre 1654* (*Œuvres complètes*, ed. Mesnard [Paris 1991], III, 50.) Cf. Tertullian, *De carne Christi*, V (Migne, II, 805B–807B).

73. The points they have in common—if we disregard what is most important and also leave aside what is most obvious, to which Schmitt himself refers—extend to the particulars of their rhetoric and style of thinking, which—mutatis mutandis—has been noticed by the interpreters of the one as well as of the other. Jan H. Waszink writes in his edition of Tertullian's *Über die Seele* (Zurich/Munich 1980), 316: "Since Tertullian changes his opinions continually in his largely polemical writings and allows them to be determined by the prevailing situation, there are few 'fixed points' in his doctrine of faith. That places certain limits on a systematic development of his intellectual world." The few "fixed points" are no less "fixed" for that reason but, on the contrary, decide everything. Thus another Tertullian expert can explain: "That with respect to dogmatic questions Tertullian's view remained in its core the same is not surprising. Since his concern was not to deepen once-gained findings in quiet work but he instead wanted to intervene with his work immediately in life and in the

phrase: *Praestat per Deum nescire, quia non revelaverit, quam per hominem scire, quia ipse praesumpserit.*[74] The commandment of the absolutely ruling God puts an end to human discretion. Not in the way that knowledge which is binding for all who have acquired it puts an end to arbitrariness. Rather, in such a way that the revealed or transmitted commandment confronts one with the decision between obedience and disobedience. The "authoritarian command" of the divine sovereign brings about a "division of men," a "distancing." It creates order through distinction, mutuality through separation. Schmitt's Roman witness had a clear notion of the division of men which arises from the divine command. He knows to distinguish between Christians and rebels against Christ,[75] between the orthodox and the dissenters, he knows to distinguish between the friends of God[76] and the enemies of God.[77] He especially knows about the deep opposition that separates him, as well as his descendants, from the philosophers. The political theologian who pits obedience against the question of the good, "formulated" the "old opposition" "classically" not only de facto but, what is more, gave it immediate expression with notable laconism: "What then does Athens have to do with Jerusalem? What does the Academy have to do with the Church? What do the heretics have to do with the Christians?" reads the beginning of the equally famous, even if not the most famous, phrase penned by Tertullian.[78] The sharp division between "the philosopher and the Christian, between the disciple of Greece and the one of Heaven," is

---

spiritual battles of his age, he did indeed build further onto the intellectual edifice he once drafted, but redesigned it only in a few points . . . there was no break in Tertullian's development." Carl Becker in his introduction to Tertullian's *Apologeticum* (3d ed., Darmstadt 1984), 20. Compare the characterization of Tertullian in Hans Blumenberg, *Die Legitimität der Neuzeit* (Frankfurt a. M. 1966), 283 (new edition: 1988, 345), which Schmitt counts among "the passages of [Blumenberg's] book that are most important to me" (*PT II*, 115).

74. *De anima*, I, 6 (Migne, II, 689B). Cf. Hans Blumenberg, *Die Legitimität der Neuzeit*, new edition, 349.

75. Christi rebelles. *De praescriptione haereticorum*, IV, 4 (ed. Preuschen, 4; Migne, II, 18B).

76. In this connection see Peterson, "Der Gottesfreund. Beiträge zur Geschichte eines religiösen Terminus," *Zeitschrift für Kirchengeschichte* (n. s.) IV (1922): 161–202, esp. 180 ff., 194, 198; and see 68 f. with n. 4 above.

77. Dei hostes. *Apologeticum*, XLVIII, 15 (ed. Becker, 216; Migne, I, 595B).

78. "Quid ergo Athenis et Hierosolymis? Quid academiae et ecclesiae? Quid haereticis et Christianis? Nostra institutio de porticu Salomonis est, qui et ipse tradiderat dominum in simplicitate cordis esse quaerendum. Viderint qui Stoicum et Platonicum et dialecticum Christianismum protulerunt. Nobis curiositate opus non est post Christum Iesum, nec inquisitione post Evangelium. Cum credimus, nihil desideramus ultra credere. Hoc enim prius credimus, non esse, quod ultra credere debeamus." *De praescriptione haereticorum*, VII, 9–13 (ed. Preuschen, 7; Migne, II, 23B–24A).

characteristic of Tertullian's thought. The opposition to the "patriarchs of the heretics" is the direct result of his creed.[79]

In Schmitt's case matters are no different. True, the pre-Constantine Doctor of the Church from North Africa and the Christian Epimetheus in post-Reformation Central Europe are separated by seventeen centuries of an eventful history of the relationship between theology and philosophy, a history of resistance and exchange, of dominion and servitude, of rebellion and conformity. Yet no historical event is able to annul the order of things, nor would any more successful historical accommodation be in a position to abolish a principial opposition. A political theologian who as a historical agent intervenes in the political-theological battles of the present and who wants to bring his concepts, theories, and conceptions "with full awareness to bear on the age,"[80] must conform his strategy and rhetoric to the changing historical conditions. But if he wants to conceive of himself as a political theologian, he will not be able to avoid taking aim at the "old opposition" and reassuring himself, regardless of all historical change, of his own position. Schmitt's opposition to the philosophers and the philosophical life does not just come to light indirectly or in a disguised form. Schmitt is not content to speak with Tertullian's voice or to ask with Bishop Fénelon how philosophy came to want to limit God's authority. Nor does he attack the philosophers merely furtively by seemingly taking aim at other opponents. For example, when he remarks of Donoso Cortés, once again a close kindred spirit, that no "Russian anarchist" has "made the assertion 'Man is good' with such elementary conviction as the Spanish Catholic [has expressed] the answer: Whence does he know that he is good if God has not told him?"[81] In his own name Schmitt explains in a prominent place: "The strongest and most consequential of all spiritual turns of European history I consider to be the step taken by the seventeenth century in moving from received Christian theology to the system of a 'natural' scientificity." And he leaves no uncer-

79. "Adeo quid simile philosophus et Christianus, Graeciae discipulus et caeli, famae negotiator et salutis (vitae), verborum et factorum operator, et rerum aedificator et destructor, amicus et inimicus erroris, veritatis interpolator et integrator et expressor, et furator eius et custos?" *Apologeticum*, XLVI, 18 (ed. Becker, 206; Migne, I, 580A–581A). Haereticorum patriarchae philosophi: *Adversus Hermogenem*, VIII; *De anima*, III, 1 (Migne, II, 223C; II, 692A). Tertullian's judgment of Socrates reads: "Adeo omnis illa tunc sapientia Socratis de industria venerat consultae aequanimitatis, non de fiducia compertae veritatis. Cui enim veritas comperta sine Deo? cui Deus cognitus sine Christo? cui Christus exploratus sine Spriritu sancto? cui Spiritus sanctus accomodatus sine fidei sacramento? Sane Socrates facilius diverso spiritu agebatur." *De anima*, I, 4 (Migne, II, 688A).

80. *VA*, 8.

81. *PT*, 52 (74).

tainty about what he especially counts among the consequences of this step: "The concepts that were developed over many centuries of theological thought are now becoming uninteresting and are turning into a private affair. God himself is evicted from the world in the metaphysics of deism in the eighteenth century and becomes a neutral instance vis-à-vis the battles and oppositions of real life; as Hamann said against Kant, he becomes a concept and ceases to be a being."[82] The "strongest and most consequential of all spiritual turns of European history" with which Schmitt has the "sequence of the stages" of modern neutralizations and depoliticizations begin, is marked for him by the turn away from faith in particular Providence, in the absolutely ruling God.[83] Whatever may be said specifically about the "historically concrete situation" to which this turn gave rise, Providence can be led back to the opposition "for which Tertullian found the classical phrase." The unobstructed view of the fundamental opposition from which everything else follows, protects one from the spurious opinion that Schmitt's opposition is "epochally bound," that it is linked to the historical development that begins with the seventeenth century,[84] that it is merely directed against modern philosophy. There is even less room in Schmitt's thought for Socrates than for Nietzsche. Plato or Xenophon, Aristotle or Cicero are at best considered "teachers of law" of an era long since past or as the authors of historically illustrative material by which the "development of concrete concepts out of the immanence of a concrete legal and social order" can be exemplified.[85] As representatives of the philosophical life, they are passed over in eloquent silence. Nor does Schmitt in the least allow himself to get involved in a confrontation with their own claims to truth. To be sure, only modern and medieval philosophers can be reproached for having fallen

82. "Das Zeitalter der Neutralisierungen und Entpolitisierungen" [The Age of Neutralizations and Depoliticizations], in *BdP*, 88–89. Cf. the wording of the first edition "Die europäische Kultur in Zwischenstadien der Neutralisierung" [European Culture in the Intermediate Stages of Neutralization], in *Europäische Revue* 5, no. 8 (November 1929): 524–525.

83. *PT*, 37, 44 (49, 62). Schmitt says of Joseph de Maistre that, "still completely [filled] with the notions of the theology of the classical age, [he] sees the individual man in his insignificance before the transcendent providential power that rules us." In another passage we learn about the theology from which Maistre gains support: "over a millennium of spiritual work in the Catholic Church and its theology, all human problems were discussed in the highest form that they can have, that is, theologically" (*PR*, 154, 182).

84. In *Nomos der Erde* the gradual decline of the "knowledge of the meaning of Christian history" begins in the thirteenth century. "Here, too, the great philosophical systems have abolished concrete historical meaning and dissolved the historical creaturings of battle against pagans and unbelievers into neutral generalizations" (33).

85. *NdE*, 37; *VA*, 427, 502.

away from the revealed truth of faith. With this reproach Schmitt's attack on the "atheism" and "nihilism" of the philosophers takes on another quality, and the same holds of his objection that they are guilty of "ego-armoring" and "neutralization"—in a word: that they closed their hearts to the call of the Lord of history. Correspondingly the tone in which he addresses the philosophers of the "Christian eon" is sharpened. It is unmistakable, for example, in the outbursts against Nietzsche, who was outlawed already quite early as a "high priest" and "sacrificial lamb" of the "private priesthood," but is by no means confined to them.[86] In his posthumous work *Glossarium*, Schmitt dispenses completely with the restraint he still practices in his published writings. Here the attack on philosophy and philosophers becomes a leitmotif, ranging from condescending mockery to brusque rejection.[87] It peaks in the condemnation of Spinoza: "The most audacious insult ever to be inflicted upon God and man, and which justifies all the synagogue's curses, lies in the '*sive*' of the formula: *Deus sive Natura*."[88] The equation of God and nature seems to surpass by far the monstrousness of the "opposition of *nomos* and *physis*," in which Schmitt already sees a work of "destruction."[89] And yet in that equation something that begins in the latter opposition merely comes to an end. It is the principle of natural goodness that holds the middle ground, as it were, between the identification of *Deus sive Natura* and the distinction between *physis* and *nomos* with which philosophy begins.[90] Schmitt fights against that principle, as even the most superficial reader can see, with special persistence. It has to appear all the more remarkable that at the most important point of his attack on the "faith in 'natural goodness'" Schmitt does not once mention the name of the philosopher with whom, more than any other, the notion of man's being naturally good is linked. Jean-Jacques Rousseau goes unnamed in the chapter on "anthropology" in *Der Begriff des Politischen*. And with good reason, for Rousseau is in no way suited as a witness in Schmitt's attempt to raise the—conscious or unconscious—agreement with the dogma of original sin to the necessary presupposition "of all genuine political theories." How could Schmitt possibly contest with any seriousness that the

86. *PR*, 27. On Nietzsche see *DC*, 107, 109; "Drei Möglichkeiten," 930; *VA*, 428, 429; *G*, 87, 91, 163.

87. "Cogito ergo sum—sum, sum, sum, Bienchen summ herum [little bee buzz about]" (*G*, 58). "A philosophy of the will to power, however, is the peak of the most wretched tastelessness and existential stupidity" (49). Cf. *G*, 46, 89, 165, 210–212.

88. *G*, 28; see 60, 84, 86, 141, 276.

89. *NdE*, 38, 40.

90. On the discovery of nature as the beginning of philosophy, see Strauss, *Natural Right and History*, 81–95, esp. 90–91.

Genevan was the author of a "genuine political theory"?[91] On the other hand, Rousseau is Schmitt's true antipode in the chapter on "anthropology," for Rousseau pits man's being naturally good *en pleine connaissance de cause* against the doctrine of the Fall of Man and original sin. The being good in question here, of course, has nothing to do with either the Romantic sentimentality of a lost paradise nor the self-forgetful phantasmagoria of a future idyll of general peaceableness and philanthropy. Its hard core is the natural capacity of being self-sufficient: What allows man to be *good* is the preservation of his fundamental independence, the realization of his being himself in a self-centered whole [*Beisichselbstsein*], which his nature in principle permits him to achieve. This being good—and not some diffuse "faith" in "natural goodness"—is the true counterconcept of and firm point of resistance to the "fundamental theological dogma of the sinfulness of the world and of men."[92] But Rousseau does not only speak of man's being naturally good. He also coined the expression 'natural goodness', and in fact in that text in which in Rousseau's own judgment the principles of his philosophy "are revealed with the greatest boldness, if not to say audacity."[93] In the *Discours sur l'inégalité*, in which Rousseau subjects the presuppositions of political theology to a far-reaching critique,[94] 'natural goodness' makes its first and most decisive appearance for everything thereafter in the form of the maxim: *Do your good with the least possible harm to others*. Rousseau introduces it as the "*maxime de bonté naturelle*" in order to substitute it for a maxim which he calls "*cette maxime sublime de justice raisonnée*," but which is generally known as one of the central commandments of the Sermon on the Mount: *Do unto others as you would have them do unto you*.[95] As one can see, even natural goodness has a hard core and the concept is applied by Rousseau in a politically purpo-

91. The only alternative would be to twist the facts so that they fit the doctrine. Schmitt took this path in his *Politische Theologie* when he advanced the claim in reference to Baron Seillière that in the *Contrat social* "man is still by no means by nature good; it is only in Rousseau's later novels that, as Seillière has proved so excellently, the famous 'Rousseauian' thesis of the good man is unfolded" (51 [73]). Everything in this statement is false. Beginning already with the chronology of the texts to which Schmitt refers, for both of the only "novels" Rousseau published, the *Nouvelle Heloïse* and *Emile*—should one want to call the latter a "novel"—were published either before or at the same time as the *Contrat social*, that is, in 1761 and 1762, respectively, and the *Discours sur l'inégalité* appeared already in 1755.

92. Rousseau, *Discours sur l'inégalité*, Note IX, critical edition, 300; consider the references and explanations provided on 300–301 n. 368.

93. *Les confessions*, IX, *Œuvres complètes*, I, 407.

94. *Discours sur l'inégalité*, xxxii ff., lxv, 70 ff., 104, 168, 270, 318 ff., 386 ff.

95. *Discours sur l'inégalité*, 150 with nn. 187 and 188.

sive manner. Conversely, one will not be able to deny that Schmitt has a good sense of who his enemies are. Even when he does not really know them.[96]

Schmitt takes a stand against Nietzsche and for the "Protestant theologian" Kierkegaard. He opposes to the avowed anti-Christian, "the most inward of all Christians."[97] Against Heidegger he enlists the Catholic theologian of history Konrad Weiss.[98] In the most fundamental taking of sides, he follows unwaveringly that dividing line that runs between political philosophers from Socrates to Strauss, from Plato to Rousseau, on the one hand, and political theologians from Tertullian to Donoso Cortés, from Augustine to Calvin, on the other. So there is no doubt that in the most important respect, incomparably more separates him from Hegel than from Friedrich Julius Stahl[99] —who later will be re-

96. In the last two decades of his life, Schmitt saw Rousseau in a more favorable light. At that time he was under the influence of the authority of the Catholic historian and literary figure Henri Guillemin, who assured Schmitt that Rousseau had been a Christian and that it was for that reason Voltaire tried to kill the Genevan. On the occasion of Rousseau's 250th birthday, Schmitt publishes an article on the front page of the *Zürcher Woche* (June 29, 1962) with the title "Dem wahren Johann Jacob Rousseau" [To the True Jean-Jacques Rousseau], which expresses his sympathy for the victim of persecution: "When I hear the expression 'last man', I think immediately of Jean-Jacques Rousseau, the despairing solitary person in an overcivilized world, the persecuted individual who ended in persecution mania, who dared resist a brilliant and overpowering civilization, antiprogressive in the middle of the torrent of the Enlightenment and its then still unbroken faith in progress."

97. *PT*, 15 (22); "Die Sichtbarkeit der Kirche," 75. Schmitt concludes the epilogue to his edition of Johann Arnold Kanne, *Aus meinem Leben* (Berlin 1918; reprint, 1940) with a eulogy to Kierkegaard, "who, like a new Church Father, articulated anew the eternally same truth for his age" (68). This is one among several similar characterizations (e.g., *PR*, 97; *DC*, 101–102, 106–107). In the *Glossarium*, Schmitt calls Kierkegaard "un chrétien véritable authentique, un père de l'église invisible, qui reste le père et le grand maître et la source authentique de tout existentialisme; et l'existentialisme de Kierkegaard est encore plus profondément chrétien que celui de Heidegger est athéiste" (80; cf. 22, 71, 151, 158, 179).

98. *G*, 83; cf. 80, 111, 151, 168, 220, 236, 275. Regarding Schmitt's attitude towards the solitary inhabitant of the Black Forest, much more that is of importance is to be gained from the following note by Schmitt dated April 24, 1949 than from the innumerable papers that mention Schmitt and Heidegger in one breath: "I know the Psalm and read in the Bible: 'The Lord is my shepherd, I shall not want.' I know modern philosophy and read in Heidegger: man is the shepherd (of being)" (*G*, 232). Consider Strauss, *Liberalism Ancient and Modern*, 234–235, 236–237, 256.

99. Until 1933 Schmitt still considers the political theologian to be among those who are particularly close to him (*BdP*, 64; cf. *D*, 9; *PT*, 39, 40, 45, 53 [53, 56, 64, 77]), and in direct comparison with Hegel he attributes to Stahl an insight that agrees with his own view in a remarkable way: "<in Hegel and the Hegelians> nothing led back to the old God of Christian metaphysics despite the reactionary elements in and despite the Christological terminology employed by Hegel. And Stahl proved his superiority by recognizing with certainty that Hegelianism is the enemy of the tradition which stands on the Christian foundation and by taking his point of departure from Schelling's philosophy, which since 1809 had re-

viled beyond all measure—or that he has infinitely less in common with a political philosopher of Spinoza's rank than with a political theologian of Joseph de Maistre's caliber. Schmitt's opposition to political philosophers, in the most succinct sense of the term, can be discerned without difficulty in general or in particular.[100] For Thomas Hobbes alone a different picture seems to arise. Schmitt praises the author of the *Leviathan* not only as a "genuine teacher" as which a political theologian can esteem and recognize a political philosopher to be to the same extent as a political philosopher can recognize and esteem a political theologian without either of the two thereby having to lose sight of the difference that separates him in the most important respect from the other. At times he emphatically calls the "solitary philosopher from Malmesbury" a "brother" and, after appealing to the crucified God, his "friend" for whose soul no one can keep him from praying.[101] Friends, students, and admirers of Schmitt have for their part emphasized the common features they believed to perceive in Hobbes and Schmitt. One commentator even went so far as to declare Schmitt to be the "German Hobbes of the twentieth century."[102] Could it be that in Schmitt's relationship to Hobbes we have hit upon the one counterexample of importance for which a careful interpretation has to be on the lookout?[103] Or could it be that we have found an

---

turned to the recognition of a personal God. Stahl was not a Romantic" (*PR*, 95; cf. 89 n., 95 n. 1). On Hegel, see Chapter I, 15 with nn. 40 and 42 above. With the appearance of *Introduction à la lecture de Hegel* Schmitt considers his assessment of Hegel's atheism to have been confirmed by Kojève's authority. On May 1, 1955 he writes to the philosopher in Paris: "Everything that is decisive is on p. 215 of your *Introduction à la lecture de Hegel* . . . Many have characterized Hegel as an 'atheist,' and we all know Bruno Bauer's funny *Posaune des jüngsten Gerichts*. But this passage of yours on p. 215 would have to change all previous philosophy, were the philosophers—who today, as a result of the academic division of labor, administer the legal right to the firm 'philosophy'—really to hear you." Clarifying his reserve regarding the Hegelian-Kojèvean position on the "self-deification of man," Schmitt continues: "I am not of your opinion, however, that 'taking' ['*Nehmen*'] ceased after Napoleon and that today there is only production (grazing [*Weiden*]). All that is left is disemboweling [*Ausweiden*]. The earthly God who only gives and no longer takes because he creates out of nothingness, creates first of all the nothingness out of which he creates, i.e., takes."

100. This is in no way contradicted by the fact that Schmitt has recourse, for example, in his *Verfassungslehre*, to certain of Rousseau's concepts or that he seeks to unfold a paragraph from Hegel's *Grundlinien der Philosophie des Rechts* in the context of his own reflections on the significance of land and sea to the course of world history.

101. *Der Leviathan in der Staatslehre des Thomas Hobbes* (Hamburg 1938), 5, 125, 132; *ECS*, 61, 64, 67; cf. 68, 75, 78, 89.

102. Helmut Schelsky, *Thomas Hobbes. Eine politische Lehre* (Berlin 1981), 5.

103. Niccolò Machiavelli is ruled out as a possible counterexample since Schmitt did not regard him as a philosopher. All that Schmitt has to say about the "poor Florentine humanist" (*L*, 128), after whose estate he will name his house in his seclusion in Plettenberg, remains in every respect within the realm of the conventional. In a newspaper article on the

exception in him, contrary to which the usual views prove nothing, whereas the exception proves everything? And assuming we had found it, what sort of exception would it be exactly? It is certain that no other philosopher is present in a similar way in Schmitt's oeuvre spanning from the first to the second *Politische Theologie*. It is just as certain that there is no other philosopher of whom Schmitt's judgment is subject to comparable vacillations and all in all is marked by such deep-seated ambivalence. These are reasons enough to consider Schmitt's relationship to Hobbes more closely.

Schmitt presented the most important testimony of his critical engagement of Hobbes under the title *Der Leviathan in der Staatslehre des Thomas Hobbes. Sinn und Fehlschlag eines politischen Symbols* [*The Leviathan in the State Theory of Thomas Hobbes: Sense and Failure of a Political Symbol*]. The thin volume occupies in many ways a special place in Schmitt's corpus. Appearing a few weeks after Hobbes's 350th birthday and punctually on Schmitt's fiftieth birthday, for which the Preface is predated "Berlin, July 11, 1938," it is the first and, with the exception of the later essay collection *Donoso Cortés in gesamteuropäischer Interpretation*, sole book that Schmitt published on another political theoretician. At the same time it is a book in which Schmitt speaks essentially of himself, often disguised, full of allusions and encoded references, but granting no less insight for that reason, in the decisive respect arguing *e contrario*, fixing his own position by means of comparison, contrast, and contradiction. Thus a book on Hobbes *and* Schmitt, "in the shadow" of a political symbol and biblical nightmare of sinister actuality to his contemporaries. Above all, however, a treatise in which as nowhere else in Schmitt, politics and religion collide and "cross paths" or, if one is to believe the majority of his interpreters, "cross one another out." Next to *Der Begriff des Politischen*, *Politische Theologie*, and *Politische Theologie II*,

400th anniversary of his death, Schmitt writes that Machiavelli was "neither a great statesman nor a great theoretician." "He spent the last 14 years of his life in exile in the countryside in a small house on the road leading from Florence to Rome, with the pursuits of a retired small farmer, and on the whole as a poor devil who tried in vain to regain his political career. That is the situation in which both of his political texts arose which have made him world-famous" (*Kölnische Volkszeitung*, June 21, 1927). Schmitt sees in Machiavelli the patriot, the moralist, and the technician. He esteems his "honesty" and stresses that the author of the *Principe* was no Machiavellian. He does not even want to grant him a "theory of State," however, and he sees in him even less a political philosopher with whom he would seriously have to enter into a critical discussion (cf. *D*, 6–10; *GLP*, 89; *BdP*, 65; *L*, 78, 128–129; *G*, 49, 55). Leo Strauss showed the level on which such a discussion can best be led with his book *Thoughts on Machiavelli* (Glencoe, Ill. 1958) and with a no less astonishing essay on Machiavelli in *History of Political Philosophy* (2d ed., Chicago 1972, 271–292; 3d ed., 1987, 296–317), which he and Joseph Cropsey edited.

Der Leviathan in der Staatslehre des Thomas Hobbes becomes the touchstone of every confrontation that aims at the center and the context of Schmitt's thought. The book, which begins with the word 'Hobbes' and ends with the word 'Hobbes', revolves around what is literally the central sentence: "But the idea of the State as a technologically perfected *magnum artificium* created by men, as a machine that has its 'right' and its 'truth' only in itself, that is, in performance and function, was first grasped and systematically developed as a clear concept by Hobbes."[104] The sentence marks in a pithy way the key role Schmitt ascribes Hobbes in the "decisive first step" on the way to the "fundamental neutralization of every truth, a neutralization that culminates in technologizing."[105] Its 'but' summarizes the central object of the political-theological critique which Schmitt develops in the first half of the book and after which the critique takes a dramatic turn in the second half that goes far beyond Hobbes. The political-theological critique of Hobbes had been long overdue for Schmitt at least since his dialogue with Strauss about the concept of the political, and the essay "Der Staat als Mechanismus bei Hobbes und Descartes" [The State as Mechanism in Hobbes and Descartes] published in 1937 represents the first attempt to make up for its lack, at least in part. In the first half of his book on the Leviathan, in which the 1937 essay was absorbed for the most part, Schmitt develops his critique in three respects: First it concerns the "wholly individualistically" interpreted construction of the contract on which the State as an "artificial product made by men" is based, a State called a "mortal God" by Hobbes; then it is directed against the "machine that has its 'right' and its 'truth' only in itself," whose final result will be "a gigantic mechanism that serves to secure the this-worldly, physical existence of the men whom it rules and protects"; lastly it is aimed at the symbol Hobbes chose for "the first product of the technological age," at the fatal mistake of the Enlightenment thinker "of giving rise to the great animal" and all the forces that have been bound up with it from time immemorial.[106] It is thus directed against each of the "three different, non-harmonizable notions" of his "God" which, on Schmitt's view, Hobbes uses: "The notorious, mythical image of the *Leviathan* stands conspicuously in the foreground,"

104. *L*, 70. This is the central sentence of the central paragraph of the central chapter of the book.

105. *L*, 64, 65.

106. *L*, 9, 51, 52–53, 54, 123; "Der Staat als Mechanismus bei Hobbes und Descartes," in *Archiv für Rechts- und Sozialphilosophie* 30, no. 4 (1937): 628, 629, 630 (published simultaneously, with an identical layout but different pagination, in *Dem Gedächtnis an René Descartes. 300 Jahre Discours de la Méthode. Erinnerungsband der Internationalen Vereinigung für Rechts- und Sozialphilosophie* [Berlin 1937], 164, 165, 166).

Schmitt writes in the initial exposition of his critique. "At the same time a legal construction of the contract serves to explain how a sovereign *person* comes to be through representation. In addition, Hobbes—and that seems to me to be the core of his philosophy of State—translates the Cartesian notion of man as a *mechanism with a soul* into the 'great man,' the State, which he turns into a machine animated by the sovereign-representative person."[107] In all three respects the thrust of Schmitt's critique is *essentially political-theological*, and in all three he takes aim at Hobbes as a *philosopher*.

At first glance it may seem surprising that Schmitt's political-theological critique concerns not only the notion of the mythical image and the machine, but also that of the legal construction of the contract, which serves Hobbes in explaining how a sovereign person comes to be through representation. Was the orientation of Hobbes's thought towards the decision of the sovereign person, were the personalism and decisionism associated with him not Schmitt's big discovery beginning with his *Politische Theologie* of 1922? Were not Hobbes's personalism and decisionism reason enough to treat the "legal thinker" with such deep respect that the "philosopher and the natural scientific thinker," on the other hand, could be certain of Schmitt's leniency for more than a decade?[108] In fact Hobbes's personalism is not disregarded in 1938, but is placed in a new context and revalued. Schmitt emphasizes that the sovereign-representative person, who for Hobbes is "the sole guarantor of peace," "comes into being not by, but only on the occasion of, a consensus," which is expressed in the social contract. From Hobbes's legal construction of the contract it follows that the sovereign-representative person is "disproportionately more than the strength all the participating individual wills could produce together." The "amassed angst of those individuals who tremble in fear for their life," we learn, "conjures up the new God more than it creates him," and what cannot be *created* but only *conjured up* seems to retain the superiority of transcendence: "To that extent the new God is *transcendent* both to all individual contractual partners and to their sum total, but of course," the political theologian adds, "*only in a legal, not in a metaphysical sense*."[109] However, a merely legal "transcendence" in no way suffices to ensure the fundamental superiority of the sovereign to which on Schmitt's view he must be entitled and to which he alone can be entitled as the representative of a higher authority that

107. "Der Staat als Mechanismus," 624 (160); cf. *L*, 48–49.
108. *PT*, 32–33 (44–46); cf. 43 (61).
109. *L*, 52 (my emphasis).

exceeds man's creativity and capacity for control. Legal transcendence requires metaphysical transcendence. Authoritarian dominion requires a metaphysical foundation.[110] Owing to his "rationalism" and "radical individualism," Hobbes neither wanted, nor was capable of, such a foundation. For that reason his personalism, viewed historically, fought a losing battle from the start. Since the sovereign-representative person could be transcendent "only in a legal, not in a metaphysical sense," it could "not restrain the complete mechanization of the notion of State which took place over the course of the following century."[111] What is more, the "legal thinker" who earlier was praised by Schmitt for his "personalism" now appears in historical retrospect not even to be a failed *restrainer*, but rather a *hastener against his will*: Since for Hobbes the State as a whole is not the person, but rather the sovereign-representative person is merely the soul of the "great man," Schmitt says that the process of mechanization was "only just completed" by Hobbes's personalism. "For this personalistic element, too, is drawn into the process of mechanization and drowns in it." The sovereign-representative person is after all "only a product of human artifice and intelligence." He bears the flaw that stigmatizes the Hobbesian State as a whole, "heart and soul": to be a *homo*

110. Gogarten varies the theme taken from Schmitt's *Politische Theologie* in the following way: "State power and national law . . . are destroyed in their core if they receive their legitimization from the secularized religious-autonomous personality. If they are to be real power and real law vis-à-vis man, they must receive their legitimization from the same power to which man is subject in his innermost being and in his proper being." "The application of secularized theological concepts in the theory of State means that the State is no longer . . . transcended by the sovereign but that *the State itself takes the sovereign's place*. But factually that means that *the people become the sovereign*. Just as in theology itself, regarding the secularization of its concepts, mankind in some form . . . takes the place of God, thus God becomes something in man, precisely in the same way in a theory of State dominated by secularized theological concepts the people take the place of the government appointed by God and responsible to God, the authority of the State no longer comes from God but rather from the people. The century slides, so to speak, into the position the theological concepts have lost the power to occupy precisely because they have been secularized." The State "is deprived of its special sovereignty through the overestimation of the people. For a sovereignty given to me by him with respect to whom I am to have it, is no longer a genuine sovereignty." "Säkularisierte Theologie in der Staatslehre," 131, 132, 135. Cf. Forsthoff, *Der totale Staat*, 30, 31, 42.

111. *L*, 52, 53. In the first version Schmitt makes explicit the causal connection asserted by him: "To that extent the new God is transcendent both to all individual contractual partners and to their sum total, but only in a legal, not in a metaphysical sense. *Therefore* the sovereign-representative person cannot stop the complete mechanization of the notion of the State" ("Der Staat als Mechanismus," 629 [165]; my emphasis). A year later Schmitt leaves it to the reader to relate the "therefore" back to the "of course only in a legal, not in a metaphysical sense." He spreads the two parts of the original statement over two paragraphs and places a safe distance between them by means of a lengthy insertion, a distance for which he has recourse to a passage located elsewhere in the old text (630 [166]).

artificialis, a machine, a *work fabricated* through and through *by men*, a work "with regard to which material and artisan, *materia* and *artifex*, machine and machine-maker, are the same, that is, men."[112] Schmitt's critique of the "legal construction of the contract," which serves Hobbes in "explaining" how the sovereign person comes into being, is therefore part of a far more comprehensive critique that starts with the notion of the social contract as a Promethean invention, one by means of which "atomized individuals" are to work the miracle of an omnipotent, although mortal *New God*. Schmitt sees the "decisive element" of Hobbes's construction in the fact "that, unlike medieval notions, this contract does not concern an existing community *created by God* and a preexistent, natural order, but instead that the State as order and community is *the result of human understanding and human creativity* and arises only through the contract." Schmitt's political-theological opposition becomes perspicuous when he says of the *deus mortalis* thus brought to life: "because State authority is omnipotent, it possesses a divine character. Its omnipotence, however, is of a provenance wholly other than divine: it is the work of man."[113] The distinction between *divine provenance* and the *work of man* proves to be a leitmotif of the entire book. In its light it becomes immediately clear why Schmitt focuses on the idea of the State as a machine created by men that has its "right" and its "truth" only in itself, as well as how this idea is related to the step taken in the seventeenth century away "from received Christian theology towards the system of 'natural' scientificity," a step Schmitt characterized in his "Zeitalter der Neutralisierungen und Entpolitisierungen" as "the strongest and most consequential of all spiritual turns in European history." What Schmitt outlined there "in the broader context of the history of ideas" is shown here *in principio*, at its historical beginning, by means of the State as the "*machina machinarum*." Conversely, that means that Schmitt represents the modern State from the beginning with a view to its historical end and Hobbes's theory from the viewpoint of its most distant consequences, or as an "essential factor in the great, four-century-long process" of progressive "neutralization": the turn away, which Hobbes took in the seventeenth century, from the "medieval notions" of a community of divine institution and of a representative person of divine right as the determinative prelude to a development which "peaks with internal consistency in universal technologizing" and as a result of which the dominant ideologies of the twentieth century unanimously consider the State "to be

112. *L*, 54; "Der Staat als Mechanismus," 629 (165).
113. *L*, 50–51 (my emphasis); cf. 126 and "Die Sichtbarkeit der Kirche," 74.

an apparatus which the most diverse political powers can use as a technological-neutral instrument."[114] In the same sense "Das Zeitalter der Neutralisierungen und Entpolitisierungen" went full circle from the fall "from received Christian theology" in the epoch of Bacon, Galileo, Descartes, Hobbes, and Spinoza, to the "dull religion of technicity" and to the "mass faith of an antireligious this-worldly activism" in the present. In 1938 Schmitt avoids such concepts. Nor is there any more talk of "vulgar mass religions," not even of an "activistic metaphysics."[115] And yet *Der Leviathan in der Staatslehre des Thomas Hobbes* explicitly stresses that the "decisive step" that Hobbes took with the notion of the State "as an artificial product of human calculation" was based on a "metaphysical decision" and that thereafter "nothing else" had any need of "a new metaphysical decision."[116] The turn to modern science and technology is *metaphysically neutral* neither in its origin nor in its result. Was Hobbes aware of which "metaphysical" front he took a stand on and which power he helped to succeed? That he imposes the name of a biblical monster on the State—in which Schmitt sees "a prototypical work of the new, technological age"—has to appear from the perspective of Schmitt's reading to be an anachronism. Schmitt is indeed of the view that for Hobbes's conception the image of the Leviathan is "inadequate," and in fact not only as far as that conception's "core" is concerned. Yet, one might ask, what is the significance of such "inappropriateness" if the image, as Schmitt repeatedly remarks, is nothing but "a half-ironic, literary conceit born of good English humor" anyway, one which furthermore can "be explained in view of the history of the time"?[117] And yet what at first looks like a "defense" contains Schmitt's actual critique: Hobbes's "literary conceit" does justice neither to the seriousness of the cause nor to his own situation. He conjures up a "mythical symbol fraught with enigmatic meaningfulness," a symbol which goes beyond "the scope of

114. *L*, 53, 54, 62, 63–64. Schmitt cites "Western liberal democracy" and "Bolshevist Marxism." The contemporary reader, in whose ears rang slogans such as "The State is a means to an end" or "The Party commands the State" from innumerable mass gatherings and official bulletins, could himself complete Schmitt's list with National Socialism, about which Schmitt is conspicuously silent in his treatise.

115. *BdP*, 92–94.

116. *L*, 59, 64; "Der Staat als Mechanismus," 630 (166).

117. *L*, 48, 53; 31 n., 43 n. "Only the tremendous power of this mythical image led to the error [of supposing that one could] see in it the central notion of the new system of State theory. The sentences and words with which Hobbes introduces the Leviathan, however, leave no doubt about the fact that he himself took this image seriously neither conceptually nor somehow mythically or daimonically . . . . He uses the image without a shudder and without respect." "Der Staat als Mechanismus," 625–626 (161–162).

every merely intellectual theory or construction." Hobbes ventures into a domain and, because it is not his own, misjudges its dangers. The philosopher gets mixed up with powers he cannot master because he does not *believe* in them. The name 'Leviathan', however, "belongs after all," so we learn from Schmitt, "among those mythical names that cannot be cited *without punishment*."[118] Humor and irony are inappropriate where salvation and ruin, disaster and redemption are concerned. The "popular Christian faith of the Middle Ages" still knew that a whale, a snake, or a dragon called the Leviathan could serve as a symbol for the "evil enemy as such," for "the power of the Devil in its various manifestations," or for "Satan himself." It is against the backdrop of this knowledge, which "disappears" with the ancient faith in the sixteenth and seventeenth centuries and which Schmitt revives with his book on the Leviathan, that the weight Schmitt gives to the mythical symbol is to be grasped,[119] even though the image of the Leviathan may have been merely a "literary conceit" for Hobbes.[120] Schmitt later judged Hobbes to be "also an 'Enlightenment thinker' precisely to the extent that he lacks any sense for the mythological."[121] For Schmitt this lack explains why the political symbol chosen by Hobbes had to result in "failure." Yet the sentence passed on Hobbes, on his views and errors, is one thing. Another is the question as to whether the mythical image to which Hobbes "half-ironically" fell prey does not possess a more profound truth. Is the Old Testament symbol for the strongest power on earth, when applied to the "*machina machinarum*," merely an anachronism or does it not instead help to elucidate the theological opposition that in Schmitt's eyes forms the basis of the four-hundred-year-long process of "neutralization"? Is not the hubris of the modern endeavor of "self-authorization" expressed conspicuously enough in the ancient image, which in Hobbes's reformulation seeks to force God, man, animal, and machine together

118. *L*, 9, 79 (my emphasis). In his review of Schmitt's treatise, Ernst Forsthoff accords the assertion that "Hobbes's image of the State . . . ultimately was destroyed by the myth of the Leviathan," the "rank of a paradigmatic lesson." "The overwhelming of Hobbes's conception of the State by irrational powers shows the limited capacity of the *ratio* in the historical sphere; the *ratio*'s reach for the State as the strongest historical-political potency failed and had to fail. In this respect Schmitt's book is conclusive and final." *Zeitschrift für deutsche Kulturphilosophie* (n. s. of *Logos*) 7, no. 2 (1941): 212–213.

119. *L*, 12, 14, 16, 36, 37, 39, 44. In a marginal note on Job 41, Luther explains: "*Leuiathan*, he names the great whale in the sea / yet he thereby characterizes the prince of the world / the Devil with his followers."

120. That it was perhaps more indeed is something Schmitt no longer wants to rule out in 1938 (43–44).

121. "Staatliche Souveränität und freies Meer" [State Sovereignty and the Free Sea], in *Das Reich und Europa* [*The Reich and Europe*] (Leipzig 1941), 98.

into one?[122] And if for "every good Christian" it had to be a "gruesome idea to see a great animal opposed to the *corpus mysticum* of the God incarnate, the great Christ," then did Hobbes's "mistake" not help to open one's eyes? Schmitt himself reminds every good Christian of *who* could sit enthroned on the Leviathan in the future or could use the value- and truth-neutral apparatus of the State in the present, when he poses the question of the identity of the New or Mortal God: "Who is this God who brings peace and security to angst-stricken men?"[123]

The Antichrist's slogan *peace and security* surfaces a second time at the outset of the fifth chapter of Schmitt's book. Before the motto Schmitt states the thesis that sums up the chapter's topic in one sentence; namely, that "the question of faith and of miracles became the undoing" of the Leviathan. The Leviathan, whose "sickness unto death" Schmitt treats in what follows, is not the extremely successful Great Machine which in the three hundred years after Hobbes "becomes separated from all content of political goals and convictions," but rather the Mortal God, "who brings men peace and security and *for that reason*—not by virtue of a 'divine right of kings'—demands *unconditional obedience*." It is the "godlike sovereign person of the State" whom one has "no right to resist, neither with reference to a higher or other right, nor based on reasons and arguments of religion"; the Great Man who "*alone* punishes and rewards," who "*alone* by virtue of his sovereign power" determines by law "what are right and property in questions of justice, and what are *truth and confession* in matters of religious faith."[124] According to Schmitt's thesis, the question of faith and of miracles becomes the undoing of the Leviathan, who seeks to establish the "unity of religion and politics" on the basis of his own absolute power. Or to put it plainly: Schmitt's object is the failure of the attempt *post Christum* to make religion a part of politics. Of course, Schmitt himself by no means speaks plainly. On the contrary, he is so far from doing so that he gives the impression that he speaks from the standpoint of that very position he wants to prove untenable. He uses the rhetorical device of seemingly adopting the perspective of his ad-

122. *L*, 31, 48, 79. Cf. "Der Staat als Mechanismus," 624 (160).

123. *L*, 48, 96. Whereas Schmitt uses *peace and security* only twice, the series *quietude, security, and order* is cited repeatedly as the determinative aim of Hobbes's construction of the State (cf. 47, 64, 71–72, 90). In only one place is the Antichrist himself named explicitly: "In the Gent *Liber floridus* (twelfth century) the Antichrist sits enthroned on the Leviathan, who is described as a *serpens* and represented as a great fish, thus it likely means only the 'world' here, not an apocalyptic figure; cf. the *Reallexikon zur deutschen Kunstgeschichte*, Otto Schmitt, ed. (Stuttgart 1937), I, 716, article 'Antichrist' by Oswald Erich" (13 n. 1).

124. *L*, 63, 79–80, 99 (my emphasis).

versary in order to be able to show all the more effectively how necessary it is that the adversary's cause fail. Everything has been carefully staged, beginning with the drama's initial constellation, which Schmitt lays out towards the end of the first chapter with reference to and in his confrontation with the "Jewish scholar" Leo Strauss. "From the German side" he enlists his critic Helmut Schelsky.[125] Strauss is the author whom Schmitt has introduce into the discussion the distinction between religion and politics. Strauss is said to have remarked in his book *Die Religionskritik Spinozas* [*Spinoza's Critique of Religion*] "that Hobbes regards the Jews as the real authors of the seditious, State-destructive distinction between religion and politics." In order to channel the distinction securely from the start, Schmitt immediately seeks to make a historical "correction": "That is only correct with the qualification that Hobbes fights against the typically Judeo-Christian split of the original political unity." The problem that interests Schmitt first arises with the "Christian eon." In it, too, there is nothing left for Jews and pagans as previously. Following Strauss he continues: "The distinction between worldly and religious power, was foreign to the pagans according to Hobbes because for them religion was a part of politics"; silently "supplementing" Strauss's text, he adds: "the Jews achieved the *unity* from the religious side. Only the Roman papal church and the power-hungry Presbyterian churches or sects live off the State-destructive severance of religious and worldly power." Schmitt then summarizes: "The battle against the 'Kingdom of Darkness' striven for by the Roman papal church, the restoration of the original unity, is, as Leo Strauss observes, the real meaning of Hobbes's political theory. That is right."[126] In the passage to which Schmitt refers, however, Strauss speaks neither of the "Roman papal church," nor of "the real meaning of Hobbes's political theory," nor even of the "original unity," the "restoration" of which was supposedly at issue. In Strauss the talk is not the critique of the "papal church," but of Hobbes's fundamental critique of revealed religion, be it Judaism or Christianity, be it before or after the Christian revolution, be it aimed at Catholicism or Protestantism. Of a correspondingly fundamental type is the alternative which Strauss formulates in view of the determination of the relationship between religion and politics. "For the pagans religion was a part of politics." By contrast, *revelation* "makes politics a part of

125. *L*, 20, 22. Schelsky will likewise refer to the "Jewish scholar" in 1941 (*Thomas Hobbes*, 217), to be sure not by citing *Die Religionskritik Spinozas*, but rather the book *The Political Philosophy of Hobbes: Its Basis and Its Genesis* (Oxford), which appeared in 1936 and which Schmitt does not mention.

126. *L*, 21 (my emphasis).

religion; thus—as we understand Hobbes—it reverses the natural relationship which was realized in paganism."[127] The focus of attention for Hobbes and Strauss is the political consequences of faith in revelation, and the decisive political question for both philosophers reads: Should politics become a part of religion? Schmitt takes up the first of the alternatives, but is careful not to mention the second. A small, shifting movement of thought suffices for Schmitt in order to take the edge off the distinction between religion and politics, an edge it has in those philosophers, and to transform the clear alternative *supremacy of politics or revealed religion* into the ambiguous opposition of *split or unity of religion and politics*. In addition, it allows him to contrast Christianity to Judaism and simultaneously, referring to what the Jews succeeded in doing *ante Christum*, to recall discreetly that "the unity" can also be brought about "from the religious side." Finally, the movement is of use to him in making the "restoration of the original unity" the true test for Hobbes's enterprise, whereby he does not fail to stress at the outset of his argumentation that the attempt, the failure of which is demonstrated *ad oculos* in the fifth chapter, stands in direct opposition to the Pope and the Church.[128]

127. Leo Strauss, *Die Religionskritik Spinozas als Grundlage seiner Bibelwissenschaft. Untersuchungen zu Spinozas Theologisch-politischem Traktat* (Berlin 1930), 75. A quarter of a century later Strauss reaffirms this: "The Old Testament set up the rule of priests, i.e., a form of government which is bound to issue in chaos, as the Old Testament record itself shows. The rule of priests was responsible for the fact that after the anarchy had induced the Jews to set up a king 'after the manner of the nations,' 'generally through the whole history of the kings . . . there were prophets that always controlled the kings.' That is to say, the Old Testament laid the foundation for the dualism of power temporal and power spiritual which is incompatible with peace, the demand par excellence of reason. As regards Christianity, it originated in rebellion against the civil sovereign and therefore was forced eventually to sanction the dualism of the two powers. Holding the view of the Bible which he did, Hobbes was compelled to try his hand at a natural explanation of the Biblical religion. The fundamental difference between paganism and Biblical religion consists in this: that whereas pagan religion was a part of human politics, Biblical religion is divine politics, the politics of the kingdom of God." "On the Basis of Hobbes's Political Philosophy" (1954), in *What Is Political Philosophy?* (Glencoe, Ill. 1959), 188. Cf. *Thoughts on Machiavelli*, 184–185 and 231.

128. *Die Religionskritik Spinozas* is the most important book for grasping the argumentation of the treatise on the Leviathan. That Schmitt develops his interpretation and critique of Hobbes in the confrontation with Strauss will not be surprising to anyone familiar with their hidden dialogue from 1932–33 concerning *Der Begriff des Politischen*. The intensity with which Schmitt engaged Strauss's book on Spinoza is evidenced by Schmitt's copy (now in my possession), by its numerous underlined passages, marginal notes, and other entries. On the second page at the beginning of the book, Schmitt noted in ink under his signature: "1st encounter: Spring 1932; 2nd encounter: Summer 1937; 3rd encounter (1st re-encounter) July 1945 (impetus: the conversation with Eduard Spranger 6-30-45)." (Concerning the conversation with Eduard Spranger, see *ECS*, 9–12.) Karl

The second witness whom Schmitt calls upon fulfills a twofold task. On the one hand, he certifies for everyone that the perspective seemingly advocated by Schmitt may be regarded as timely. On the other hand, he reveals to the attentive reader that with his procedure Schmitt pursues a thoroughly untimely intention. Schmitt brings to bear Helmut Schelsky's 1938 essay "Die Totalität des Staates bei Hobbes" [The Totality of the State in Hobbes], an essay which is in no way guilty of untimeliness. Unlike in the case of Leo Strauss previously, Schmitt lets the author himself speak, which allows him to have, among other things, the concept *political theology* appear in the book without his having to utter it a single time. "With the image of the Leviathan," Schmitt summarizes Schelsky's interpretation, "'Hobbes opposes all religiously determined thought of the State and joins the ranks of the great political thinkers. His fellow travelers on this path are Machiavelli, Vico, and, more recently, Nietzsche and Sorel.' The 'deep significance of his concept of the Leviathan,' however, lies in the fact that this 'earthly' and 'mortal' God, who is merely present here below, depends wholly on the political deed of man which must repeatedly wrest him all over again from the chaos of a 'natural' state. Thus Hobbes 'fought his great contemporary historical battle against political theology in every form.' The Leviathan is the great symbol of this battle." Schmitt makes no mention of the fact that Schelsky's interpretation is essentially directed against *him*, and it goes without saying that he certainly does not address the fact that Schelsky's interpretation has *his* political theology in view.[129] The selection of the three brief quotations from Schelsky speaks for itself. Instead of contradicting the young scholar, who more than four decades later will say of himself in retrospect that he was at that time "more of a supporter" of National Social-

Löwith, who possessed the copy from 1956 until 1973, informs Strauss on June 28, 1956 that he had received the book on Spinoza from a bookseller's catalogue, "and behold: Carl Schmitt's copy along with lots of marginal notes! A stamp shows that it obviously was sequestered with Schmitt's library by U.S. officials in 1945." He then tells of the ink-entries and asks: "How is this so-called 3rd encounter to be understood?" (Department of Special Collections, University of Chicago Library, Leo Strauss Papers, Box 2, Folder 11.) Two decades before, Löwith had already had difficulty understanding the character of the *encounter* between Schmitt and Strauss (see *Carl Schmitt and Leo Strauss: The Hidden Dialogue*, 7–8 n. 6, 61–62 n. 64).

129. On pp. 30–31 and 43 Schmitt does mention one point from Schelsky's critique. The attack, of which Schmitt says it is "not entirely just," immediately precedes the paragraph containing Schelsky's true challenge. "Die Totalität des Staates bei Hobbes," in *Archiv für Rechts- und Sozialphilosophie* 31, no. 2 (1938) is a direct reply to Schmitt's article "Der Staat als Mechanismus bei Hobbes und Descartes," which was published in the same journal only a few months earlier (cf. 177, 181, 189, 190–191; consider 176 and 193).

ism,[130] or instead of even "correcting" him in the least, Schmitt takes up Schelsky's interpretation and uses it for his own ends: "*However, according to this interpretation of Schelsky's*—and in fact precisely in the sense of his thesis of the thinkers of the political deed—*everything must depend decisively* on whether the myth of the Leviathan created by Hobbes was a genuine restoration of the original vital unity, whether or not it proved itself as a political-mythical image in the battle against the Judeo-Christian destruction of the natural unity, and whether [that myth] was up to the severity and malice of such a battle."[131] Here the initial constellation is reached. The endeavor to restore the "original," the "natural," indeed the "original and natural pagan unity of politics and religion" under the sign of the Leviathan is on the test stand and with it every position that finds in the Leviathan the "great symbol" of its battle against political theology. Political theology, which comes to speech only in the mode of negation, has to appear superior to the extent that it is successfully proved that the anti-Christian restoration is doomed to failure.

Schmitt does not spare irony in his argumentation. He has "the question of faith and of miracles" become the undoing of Thomas Hobbes's "new God" and the "miracle"[132] worked by him; he has the great symbol of the battle against political theology smashed to pieces against the latter's ownmost domain; he has the philosopher, whom he certifies to be one "of the first and boldest critics of all faith in miracles,"[133] fall because of the faith in miracles. The irony is intensified to barely concealed scorn when Schmitt discusses the suggestion that miracles be subjected to the capacity for control proper to the State sovereign and thereby make them a part of politics—of politics insofar as it is a work of man. "Hobbes, the great decisionist," ultimately makes "his typically decisionistic turn: *Autoritas, non Veritas*," also in the case of miracles. "Nothing is true here, everything is command here. A miracle is what the sovereign State power commands should be believed to be a miracle; but also—and ridicule suggests itself at this point particularly—the reverse: miracles cease when the State forbids them."[134] For a moment the au-

130. Schelsky, *Thomas Hobbes* (Preface from 1980), 9; cf. 11.

131. *L*, 22–23 (my emphasis).

132. *L*, 48.

133. *L*, 82. "His critique already seems thoroughly in the mode of the Enlightenment. Here he makes his appearance as the true inaugurator of the eighteenth century. Almost reminiscent of Voltaire, he already describes the possibilities of error, of delusion, and of open or secretive deception, the tricks of the forgerers, actors, ventriloquists, and other swindlers so vividly that any claim to faith in this domain seems to be absurd and actually no longer worth any discussion at all."

134. *L*, 82–83.

thor of *Politische Theologie* seems to have trouble containing himself. Yet Schmitt remains true to the self-chosen shift of perspective and hunts his adversary along the predelineated path to the end. He follows the Leviathan to the peak of his power, which the Mortal God achieves as soon as he has "miracles as well as confession" at his command, but only so as now—carrying the irony to extremes—to "demand" for him what has to remain forever unattainable for him. At the climax of the drama, "at the peak of the sovereign power that brings about the unity of religion and politics," Schmitt shows "the point of rupture in the unity which is otherwise so closed, so irresistible"; he uncovers the "seeds of death," which will destroy "the mighty Leviathan from within." For here, "where miracles and faith are at issue, Hobbes evades the decisive point" since he introduces "the distinction between inner faith and outward confession" into the political system of the Leviathan and merely lays claim on behalf of the Mortal God to the dominion of the outward confession of those subject to the State, while he recognizes in principle the freedom of thought and faith. Hobbes, or the person of the same name on whom Schmitt conferred the role of "restoring the original unity," apparently shies away from the ultimate consequence of the restorative endeavor.[135] The "unity of religion and politics" could be realized only if one would succeed in grasping men *wholly*, from within and from without, body and soul, in their acting and in their thinking, with respect to their confession and on the deepest ground of their faith. But for that the "omnipotence" of the Mortal God is insufficient. His compulsory force, which is nothing but the work of man, has no power over thoughts and the conscience. His command fails before faith. Or as Schmitt observes later and at the right place: *Nothing divine can be forced externally*.[136] The attempt to establish the "unity of religion and politics" under the sign and by means of the Leviathan is thereby carried out ad absurdum. The "point of rupture" cannot be closed from the worldly side.[137] Even if the distinction between inside and outside is not recognized, "the ultimate superiority of the internal over the external, of the invisible over the visible, of the quiet over the loud, of the other world over the secular world" asserts itself.[138] In the superiority of the internal

135. *L*, 84–86.

136. *L*, 94.

137. Cf. Fyodor M. Dostoyevsky, *The Grand Inquisitor*, ed. Charles B. Guignon, trans. Constance Garnett (Indianapolis 1993), 31 (*The Brothers Karamazov*, trans. David Magarshack [London 1958; reprint 1982], 302); Flavius Josephus, *Contra Apion*, II, 165–166.

138. *L*, 95 (cf. "Die Sichtbarkeit der Kirche," 75 and 77). In his review from 1941 Forsthoff cites Schmitt's somewhat less "offensive" statement, which is found in the first

and of faith, of the divine and of the beyond, in the superiority of what resists external compulsion and evades human capriciousness, the failure of the Mortal God has its true basis—whereas political theology finds its decisive support therein.[139] It is not only due to disastrous abortive developments or hostile attacks that the Leviathan which Schmitt describes is "an externally omnipotent, internally impotent concentration of power."[140] His principle of construction makes him a colossus with clay feet. He is a God who promises men quietude, security, and order for their "this-worldly, physical existence," but who does not know how to

---

part of the paragraph and does not yet make direct reference to the theological: "The moment in which the distinction between within and without is recognized, the superiority of the internal over the external and thus of the private over the public is in its core an affair that has already been decided." He notes here: "This observation of Schmitt's is of the greatest significance. Only the question could be raised as to whether it depends on the distinction's being recognized <thus likely recognized by the authority of the State itself>, whether it is not sufficient that it is available and exists in the general consciousness" (211). Schmitt's answer to this "question" leaves no doubt. The dramatic staging he uses in his book fulfills not least the aim of bringing the distinction home to "the general consciousness" with the greatest urgency.

139. Jürgen Moltmann is mistaken in wanting to claim Schmitt as State's evidence for just that position the untenability of which Schmitt seeks to demonstrate with his *Leviathan*, and thus in asserting that Schmitt attempted a pagan "remythologization" of the Leviathan ("Covenant oder Leviathan? Zur Politischen Theologie der Neuzeit," in *Zeitschrift für Theologie und Kirche* 90, no. 3 [August 1993]: 311–314, 315). As for how matters stand with "Carl Schmitt's admiration and paganization of the Leviathan," which Moltmann attributes to the author of the 1938 treatise and which he criticizes from the standpoint of political theology, the reader can make up his own mind when he pays attention to the illustration Schmitt chose for the last page of his text and for the dust jacket of the original edition. It deserves all the more consideration inasmuch as Schmitt never before and never again "illustrated" one of his books. Schmitt chooses the not very impressive portrayal of a Leviathan whose peculiar way of holding his head baffles the viewer. (The depiction apparently seemed so little impressive to the editor of the 1982 reprint that he used the "more attractive" etching of "Der angespülte Fisch" [The Beached Fish] for the jacket.) Schmitt's choice, however, was not determined by aesthetic considerations. He had cut "his" Leviathan—without saying a word about it anywhere—out of the "magnificent drawing in the *Hortus deliciarum* by the Abbess Herrad von Landsberg (twelfth century), where God is depicted as the fisherman, Christ on the cross as the bait on the hook, and the Leviathan as the hooked giant fish" (*L*, 15–16). For the viewer of the "magnificent drawing" the riddle of the peculiar way in which the monster holds its head is solved: What on first glance may appear to be the animal's tongue proves to be the tip of the hook. In agony the Leviathan has turned his head upwards, for he finds himself, run through with the cross, in a life-and-death struggle, and his mouth is held wide open by the victorious Christ. That is how Schmitt's "admiration of the Leviathan" looks when put in pictorial terms. (A reproduction of the drawing, from which Schmitt took the picture, may be found in the *Reallexikon zur deutschen Kunstgeschichte* [Stuttgart 1937], I, 695 under the headwords "Angel, Angler" [fishing-rod, fisherman]. Schmitt does not mention the source, yet he refers the reader to the article "Antichrist" in the same volume [*L*, 13 n.], and whoever follows up on the Antichrist will hit upon the fisherman.) See the illustrations on 174 below.

140. *L*, 93–94.

reach their souls and leaves their deepest longing unquenched; a man whose artificial soul is grounded on legal but not on metaphysical transcendence; an animal whose incomparable earthly power is held to be in a position to keep the "children of pride" in line through terror, but cannot do anything against the terror that comes from beyond and that is inherent in the invisible; a machine that represses the idea of representation by means of the "factual, present achievement of real protection" and that demands "unconditional obedience to the laws of its functioning," but allows no identification.[141] The determinations emphasized by Schmitt converge without exception in the "external power" on which the Leviathan is based and in the "pure this-worldliness" in which he arises: his *auctoritas* is nothing but *potestas*.[142] The *summa potestas* of the Leviathan suffices to create a "security State," the "most essential institution" of which is the police. It suffices to have command over a mechanism which has "its value, its truth, and its justice in its technological perfection."[143] But "a mechanism is incapable of any totality." Nor "can the pure this-worldliness of the individual physical existence attain a meaningful totality."[144] Hobbes may declare the *summa potestas* of the State sovereign to be the *summa auctoritas*. He may use "the formula 'God's governor on Earth' received from the Christian Middle Ages" to designate him because the State sovereign "would otherwise become the 'Pope's governor on Earth.'" He may finally give him the authority in the "battle with the Roman Pope" to decide what can and cannot count as a miracle. The authority of Christ's representative—an authority whose power derives from the reference to the divine, which has access to faith, whose effectiveness is unfolded in inwardness, and which knows how to bind and free for the beyond—remains denied to the Mortal God.[145] Just as the distance "that separates a technological-neutral State from a medieval community" looks "worlds apart," likewise the gulf that separates the *auctoritas* of the

141. *L*, 47, 48, 54, 55; 50–51, 52, 126; 32, 35, 96; 53, 69, 71, 72.

142. *L*, 68–69, 86; cf. *DA*, 27–28; *RK*, 34–36 (22–23); *ECS*, 16, 71.

143. *L*, 47, 90; 69.

144. It is not surprising that Schmitt does not include these two statements—with which the last section of the essay "Der Staat als Mechanismus bei Hobbes und Descartes" began (631 [167])—in his book after Schelsky attacked them already with the choice of his title, "Die Totalität des Staates bei Hobbes." The "meaningful totality" goes unmentioned in 1938. Its place is taken by the question of the "restoration of the original unity," and Schelsky is allotted a special role in the demonstration Schmitt now carries out *e contrario*.

145. *L*, 68; 50, 103, 125–126; 80–81, 84; consider 68 n. and 81 n. Cf. *RK*, 30, 35–36, 39–40, 45, 66 (20, 23, 26, 29–30, 43); *G*, 243.

Leviathan from the *auctoritas* of the Pope, and even from the *potestas* of the Emperor within the unity of the *respublica Christiana*, appears worlds apart.[146]

Hobbes obviously has weighty political and philosophical reasons for not striving to secure that authority for the Leviathan which Schmitt "demands" for him in order to demonstrate his failure. The weightiest reason in the present context for why "the inward *thought*, and *belief* of men" remain excluded from every debt to the sovereign[147] is that the defense of the *libertas philosophandi* matters no less to Hobbes than to his successor Spinoza, even if he does not speak of it "straight-away in the subtitle of his book" as does Spinoza in the *Tractatus theologico-politicus*. In Schmitt's dramatic narrative the roles are distributed differently, to be sure. In that narrative it devolves upon the "Jewish philosopher" to recognize "the barely visible point of rupture" in the system of the Leviathan and to use it for unfolding the *libertas philosophandi*. The "individual freedom of thought," which is said to remain open in Hobbes "only as an ultimate, unobtrusive reservation," becomes the "formative principle" in Spinoza, and "the necessities of public peace, as well as the right of sovereign authority of the State, are transformed into mere reservations." What in truth unifies both philosophers is completely obfuscated and the point at which their attitudes towards religion are actually different is

146. *L*, 70; cf. 50–51, 80. "The medieval, Western and Central European unity of *imperium* and *sacerdotium* was never a centralist accumulation of power in the hands of one man. From the beginning it was based on the distinction between *potestas* and *auctoritas* as two different sequences of order of the same comprehensive unity. Thus the oppositions between Emperor and Pope are not absolute oppositions but only '*diversi ordines*' in which the order of the *respublica Christiana* lives. The problem inherent therein of the relationship between Church and Empire is essentially different from the later problem of the relationship between Church and State. For *State* means essentially the overcoming of confessional civil war, which became possible only as of the sixteenth century, and in fact an overcoming brought about by neutralization. In the Middle Ages the changing political and historical situations entail that the Emperor also lays claim to *auctoritas*, the Pope also to *potestas*. But the mishap first occurred when—from the thirteenth century on—the Aristotelian doctrine of the '*societas perfecta*' was used to sever Church and world into two kinds of *societates perfectae* . . . . Neither for the Emperor who had a Pope appointed or deposed in Rome, nor for a Pope in Rome who released the vassals of an Emperor or of a king from their oath of allegiance, was the unity of the *respublica Christiana* thereby placed in question for even a moment" (*NdE*, 30–31). Cf. Rudolph Sohm, *Kirchenrecht* (Munich/Leipzig 1923), II, 244–245.

147. Thomas Hobbes, *Leviathan or the Matter, Forme and Power of a Commonwealth Ecclesiasticall and Civil*, ed. Oakeshott (Oxford n.d.), XL, 307–308. "A private man has always the liberty, *because thought is free*, to believe or not believe in his heart those acts that have been given out for miracles, according as he shall see what benefit can accrue by men's belief, to those that pretend or countenance them, and thereby conjecture whether they be miracles or lies" (XXXVII, 291; my emphasis).

distorted beyond recognition[148] when Schmitt declares that "the Englishman" does not seek "to place himself outside the faith of his people with such a reservation but, on the contrary, to stay within it," whereas "the Jewish philosopher approaches a State religion from without and for that reason brings the reservation with him from without."[149] After this split, which displays masterfully the distinction between within and without, we are prepared to a certain extent for the final turn which awaits us, one that penetrates still deeper into the interior. Not only is Hobbes said to have sought to stay "within the faith of his people," but he was supposedly filled with a "monarchical faith" as well. In the king he saw God's true representative on earth and gave him this title not, as Schmitt lets us assume up to that point, merely because he intended to strengthen the State sovereign's position in the battle against the Pope. To be sure, Hobbes was able "to save his monarchical faith only by retreating into a fundamental agnosticism. That was the abyss from which his piety sprang, for"—Schmitt confesses—"*I believe that in Hobbes there was genuine piety. But his thought was no longer devout.*"[150] After Schmitt had divided Hobbes, as it were, into two persons, he now presents us with a double-being composed of two persons. He shows us a philosopher who is under the influence of other philosophers, such as Bacon and Descartes, and who abides by their "metaphysical decision"; a

148. Schmitt had read and marked in his copy of Strauss's book: "Whereas Spinoza, who in this respect is completely in line with the Averroist tradition, indeed takes the tendency of this tradition to extremes, has to recognize religion as a necessary means for the maintenance of the State, in Hobbes's theory of State there is no starting point for such a defense of religion. That science and religion (the Scriptures) are essentially different, that the association of science and religion (the Scriptures) is harmful to both, is taught by Hobbes just as it is by Spinoza. But Hobbes goes beyond Spinoza in that he believes he is able to anchor the political allegiance of all the subjects of the State in reason alone, without making any claim to revelation. According to Spinoza, the commandment 'Thou shalt love thy neighbor' is binding for the will of the multitude only as 'revealed'; but according to Hobbes this commandment is adequately prescribed for men already by virtue of the fact that God has created them as rational beings: the distinction between wise men and the multitude does not come into consideration; *because* that distinction does not come into consideration, there is no need of recourse to religion" (*Die Religionskritik Spinozas*, 80–81). Schmitt notes in the margin concerning the last sentence: "Spinoza the *foreign* spectator, cf. p. 228." He refers himself to an example which Strauss gives for the pleasure Spinoza took in *contemplation* (228 n. 302).

149. *L*, 86–87, 88. In a letter written on the occasion of Schmitt's fiftieth birthday, the Protestant professor of constitutional law, Rudolf Smend, praises "the brilliant contrast drawn between Hobbes-Spinoza, p. 88" as "for me the most impressive and beautiful" among Schmitt's "ingenious discoveries" [*Columbuseier*], "a number" of which are contained in the book. "And that is just small change for you!" (Letter of July 10, 1938 in *Schmittiana*-III, 140–141.)

150. *L*, 125–126 (my emphasis).

philosopher who is distinguished by "his philosophical-systematic theory of State" from Christian thinkers such as Erastus or Bodin, and "made into a groundbreaker of modern natural scientificity," as well as of "their concomitant ideal of technological neutralization"; a philosopher who is ascribed a main role in the strongest and most consequential upheaval of European history, in the turn away from Christian theology and its faith in particular Providence; a philosopher who is "the first and boldest critic of all faith in miracles" and thereby makes his appearance "as the true inaugurator of the eighteenth century" and its attacks on Christianity; in short, a philosopher whom Schmitt completely contradicts and whom he subjects to a sharp critique from the standpoint of political theology. At the same time he shows us a "*vir probus*" who kept the Christian faith "since he belonged to a Christian people"; a pious man whose innermost core was not touched by his irreligious thought; a Christian with whom Schmitt sees himself bound insofar as, like himself, he held fast to the decisive truth. Because for Hobbes, too, as we learn in the end, "Jesus is the Christ."[151] As for how both persons could be combined in Hobbes, as for how, for example, the philosopher of the state of nature, how the critic of religion and the Bible could be made to agree with the devout Christian, especially as for how the critic of all faith in miracles could have excluded the miracle of the incarnation of God from his thought and evaded his own critique—all that remains Schmitt's secret.[152] But inasmuch as Schmitt refers the reader emphatically to the creed of a "*vir probus*" who belongs to a Christian people, he can at least make that reader aware of his own creed. In fact, the confession that Jesus is the Christ is expressed twice (in the first and seventh chapters) in the book Schmitt publishes on the occasion of his fiftieth birthday, just as the Antichrist's slogan occurs twice (in the third and fifth chapters). Schmitt introduces the "sole principle of faith that is essential" in a footnote, which he adds to the first mention of Leo Strauss. Hobbes presupposes a Christian community, Schmitt asserts, "in which the sovereign does not infringe upon but rather protects the sole principle of faith that is essential—*that Jesus is the Christ.*" It is only the "technologizing of the State" that makes "all distinctions such as Jews, pagans, and Christians groundless" and leads "into a region of total neutrality." How Hobbes "presupposes" a Christian community—whether as a historical given that has to be reckoned with, at least provisionally, or in the sense of his

151. *L*, 48, 59; 65–66; 64, 65, 70, 80; 82; 126.

152. Concerning Hobbes's critique of revealed religion, we refer here once and for all to Strauss's essay "On the Basis of Hobbes's Political Philosophy," esp. 182–191. Cf. *Persecution and the Art of Writing*, 28.

own reservation of faith, or even as a necessary presupposition of his intellectual edifice—is still unclear at this point. In light of the confession from the seventh chapter, it becomes clear to the reader who returns to the beginning of the treatise that Schmitt wants to exempt the Christian Hobbes from the reproach he has to bring against the philosopher Hobbes, namely, that he is the "precursor," even the "revolutionary pioneer" of the "fundamental neutralization of all truth" and of the "scientific-positivistic age." The "*vir probus*" did not mean it that way and wanted something else. He was unable to anticipate the consequences of his endeavor. His concern was not the neutralization, but rather the positivization of the decisive truth, the salvation of the "sole principle of faith that is essential," which is a *principle of distinction*: the distinction between Jews, pagans, and—philosophers.[153] It is along this line of interpretation, which is alluded to in the note on Strauss in the first chapter and in the passage on the *vir probus* in the seventh, that the entire revaluation and appropriation of Thomas Hobbes, which Schmitt attempts in his later work, moves. In his essay "Die vollendete Reformation" [The Completed Reformation] from 1965 the philosopher comes second to the Christian. Schmitt characterizes the question about his "position in the process of so-called secularization, in the progressive dechristianization and dedivination of public life," as the "most important question" which must be clarified for the "the identification of the spiritual locus of Hobbes."[154] To bring about this clarification, Schmitt lets the "critic of all faith in miracles" fall into oblivion. Instead of the designer of the "*machina machinarum*," of the State-machine which has its "right" and its "truth" only in itself, the advocate of the "political unity of a Christian community" moves into the foreground.[155] And the precursor of the "most fundamental neutralization of every truth" is now replaced in

153. *L*, 20–21 n. 1. On November 2, 1976 Schmitt writes in a letter to the author that he would very much like to know if Strauss "knew my book on the Leviathan from 1938 and, especially, if he perceived the challenge of my essay on Hobbes 'Die vollendete Reformation' (that Jesus is the Christ). That is important not just for personal reasons."

154. "Die vollendete Reformation. Bemerkungen und Hinweise zu neuen Leviathan-Interpretationen" [The Completed Reformation: Comments on and References to New Interpretations of the Leviathan], in *Der Staat* 6, no. 4 (1965): 61. Regarding the "new interpretations of the Leviathan" addressed by Schmitt, the concern lies exclusively with theological interpretations of Hobbes. Whereas Schmitt employs the concept 'political theology' just once in his book from 1938, that is "negatively" in his quotation of Schelsky, he expressly makes use of it five times in the 19-page essay. (I am citing the original publication since the 1982 reprint included in the new edition of the book on the Leviathan is unreliable; see *Carl Schmitt and Leo Strauss: The Hidden Dialogue*, 62 n. 64.)

155. "Die vollendete Reformation," 52, 64. The shift in accent becomes especially conspicuous when one places the contrasting comparison of Hobbes and Erastus in the treatise

every form by the defender of the truth—that Jesus is the Christ. Schmitt expressly takes a stand for Hobbes against the suspicion that the confessional formula *that Jesus is the Christ* could itself be at the vanguard of the neutralization of Christian truth.[156] "The effective neutralization looks completely different." Lessing, for example, was guilty of it in his *Nathan der Weise*. Philosophically conceived and used in a politically purposive manner, his parable of the three copied rings "is no longer an intra-Christian affair; rather, it neutralizes Christianity in its entirety—as one of several theistic religions—along with two other theistic book-religions, Judaism and Islam, into a general faith in God. The sentence, that Jesus is the Christ, now becomes interchangeable; now, e.g., it can also read: Allah is great. That can be continued without effort, first to the point of a general faith in God, then to a still more general faith." Hobbes is completely different. Whatever else one can reproach him for, "in any case it did not occur to him to imitate the genuine ring. His sentence, that *Jesus is the Christ*, strikes the core of the apostolic proclamation and fixes both the historical as well as the kerygmatic topic of the entire New Testament. *Quis est mendax nisi is, qui negat quoniam Jesus est Christus?* (1 Jn 2:22)."[157] The second half of the verse, which Schmitt does not relay, reads: *hic est Antichristus, qui negat Patrem et Filium*. The confession that answers the question of who God is includes the answer the question of who God's enemy is.[158] Schmitt believes that in the respect that decides everything, Hobbes has rightly distinguished between friend and enemy. The "sole principle that is essential" takes on such paramount significance for Schmitt's interpretation of Hobbes that in 1965, unlike in 1938, he no longer sees merely an ultimate, unobtrusive reservation of faith on the part of the Englishman, but rather wants to elevate that principle to an "axis of the conceptual system of thought proper to his political theology." Not only the *vir probus*, but now even his thought

on the Leviathan (65–66) alongside the revaluation Schmitt makes in 1965 regarding the same cause, but without relying on new material or new arguments (58–59).

156. "Insofar as he is content to name what Christianity is with the sentence, that Jesus is the Christ, he seems, at least within the Christian domain, to reduce Rome and Geneva and all the many other Christian churches, denominations, and sects, to a common, neutral denominator, 'Jesus Christ.' In reality he does not mean it that way. In Hobbes, religious unity and the particularity of the individual Christian churches are preserved because they are borne by the sovereign decision of the Christian sovereign. That is a *cujus regio, ejus religio*, and precisely for that reason it is not a neutralization but first of all rather the opposite, that is, a dogmatic positivization against the peculiarity of the divergent opinions of the confessional opponent or neighbor" (62).

157. "Die vollendete Reformation," 62–63.

158. Compare Luther's sermon on John 17:3 from August 15, 1528, *WA* XXVIII, 90; ed. Clemen/Hirsch, VII, 216.

is to be rescued for faith.[159] At another point Schmitt goes so far as to declare: "Thomas Hobbes's most important sentence remains: Jesus is the Christ."[160] If a sentence, which is not Thomas Hobbes's sentence, but rather the core statement of the Gospel, could be regarded as the philosopher of Malmesbury's most important sentence, then his thought would indeed be wholly confined to the obedience of faith.

159. "Die vollendete Reformation," 52; *BdP*, 121–123.
160. *G*, 243.

IV HISTORY, OR THE CHRISTIAN EPIMETHEUS

From the Christian standpoint one has been more than victorious already in advance, so that one does not suffer in order to be victorious but rather because one has been victorious, which gives one precisely the pleasure of reconciling oneself to everything and lifts one above all pain; for since one has been victorious, one can already reconcile oneself to a little pain. From the worldly standpoint one must wait to see—anxious in uncertainty—what comes after the suffering, whether the victory will come; from the Christian standpoint there is nothing to wait for, in faith one has long since been handed the victory in advance.

Søren Kierkegaard, "The One Thing Needful"

HISTORY IS the state of probation and judgment for political theology. In it falls the decision between God and Satan, friend and enemy, Christ and Antichrist. In it obedience, courage, and hope must prove themselves. In it, however, sentence is also passed on political theology, since it conceives of itself as an endeavor of historical action or as theory based on obedience. From the standpoint of political theology, morality, politics, and revelation are united in history, just as obedience, courage, and hope are united for political theology in humility. Yet does political theology succeed in combining morality, politics, and revelation such that it is able to give historical action a "concrete" orientation? Does political theology thereby live up to its own claim? Can it ever live up to it? Or should it attest its humility by itself admitting that such a venture cannot be realized? Of what value would it be then? And what would depend on it? To what end would it be "theory"?

In Schmitt the dilemma of political theology emerges particularly acutely since he answers with a forced historicism to the fundamental aporia with which any political theory that wants to be theory based on the obedience of faith sees itself confronted. Everything that appears to him to be essential in this world appears to be essentially historical. And in everything he believes to perceive as the "historically real," he believes to perceive an "infinite uniqueness." He regards the insight that all historical truth is true only once, as the "arcanum of ontology." As a Christian Epimetheus he claims to have been blessed with the truth that "every human word is an answer," and he thinks he knows furthermore that the answer of historical action, which the Lord of history commands through his "call," "can, seen from the perspective of man, be only an anticipation—and even for the most part only a blind one—of a commandment that is to be obeyed."[1] Does Schmitt express a historical truth thereby that is true only once? Or does he seek to gain understanding and leniency by means of "theory" for his, for our blindness? And do men not deserve leniency and pity who are thus stricken with blindness, as Schmitt shows them to us "in [Louis de Bonald's] terrible picture, which is to portray the path mankind takes through history: a herd of blind men, led by a blind man who feels his way forward with a cane"?[2] Could it be that the Christian Epimetheus initiates us into a truth he seeks to conceal to the best of his ability?

For more information we turn to the "infinite uniqueness of the historically real" with the help of two concrete examples. First of all we shall ascertain how the Christian Epimetheus judges historical action in the case of another theoretician. Then we shall consider how Schmitt's own case looks from the perspective of the Christian Epimetheus. In this way we can scrutinize not only the decisions that Schmitt's historicism brings about in history, but simultaneously observe *in vivo* the consequences that arise from the dilemma of political theology. Understood in this way, "history" may be called a test of what can be learned from a theory that, sure of the all-decisive truth, does not seriously take up the questions: What is Virtue? What is God? What is the Good?

The most astonishing, and therefore most illuminating, assessment Schmitt makes of a theoretician of the past is of Thomas Hobbes. Why, of all things, does Schmitt attempt to make the critic of the Bible, of revelation, and of miracles into a witness to Christian truth? Why does he insist upon wanting to save the author of the *Leviathan* for faith at the price of splitting him into a philosopher and a *vir probus*? The most plausible supposition—the one most favorable to Schmitt and most fruitful for us—seems to be that Schmitt wants to show in the figure of the Englishman the paradigmatic case of a man unrecognized in his piety, met with

1. "Die geschichtliche Struktur," 148, 151, 166; cf. *BdP*, 62, 79.
2. *PT*, 49 (70).

hostility on all sides a man who answered to the political-historical challenge of his age with the daring feat of an "anticipation of a commandment that is to be obeyed." Schmitt chooses Hobbes because he attaches paramount historical significance to his answer and deems it worthy of deep Christian faith. Whether Hobbes is suitable as such an example depends alone—and, to be sure, does depend—on whether "in Hobbes there was genuine piety." That he failed to see the political consequences and historical repercussions of his actions, that he became entangled in errors and wrong decisions with far-reaching implications, that good Christians may have even regarded him as a precursor of the Antichrist—none of that speaks against but rather substantiates, the paradigmatic character of his case. Faith, however, is indispensable.

The contours that the case takes on in the retrospect of the Christian Epimetheus are well known. The "call" to which Hobbes answers is the challenge of the schism; his "anticipation of the commandment that is to be obeyed" is his advocacy of the modern State. Haunted by the insecurity and disorder to which the schism gave birth, Hobbes asks about the secular instance who is able to make an unappealable decision. Aware of the bloody turmoil the century of confessional civil wars had brought upon vast parts of Europe, he sees in the State sovereign the sole power that can be enabled to secure peace and guarantee security. Aside from "Thomas Hobbes's most important sentence," all of the Englishman's statements and positions, which Schmitt appreciates and to which he returns again and again, are directly connected with Hobbes's advocacy of the modern State: His insistence on the necessary correspondence of *oboedientia et protectio*; his defense of the *potestas directa*; and his rejection of the political claims raised by the *potestates indirectae*; his decisionist clarification *auctoritas, non veritas, facit legem*; his theoretical implementation of the governmental principle of dominion and pacification *cuius regio, eius religio*; his unwavering adherence to the questions *quis iudicabit? quis interpretabitur? quis interrogabit?* However, on Schmitt's view the decision for the modern State was *in concreto* a decision for "secularization." For the "completely incomparable, unique historical particularity of what one can call 'State' in a specific sense, lies in this State's being the vehicle of secularization." By characterizing it as a "vehicle of secularization," the State, which Schmitt wants to be understood as "a historical, concrete concept that is bound to a particular epoch," is incorporated into the Christian view of history. It is inserted into a course of events possessing transcendent significance and is assigned its place within the history of Christian Europe, which encompasses several epochs. "The new entity 'State' eliminates the sacred Reich and the Empire of the Middle Ages; it also eliminates the Pope's *potestas spiritualis* in international law and seeks to make the Christian churches an instrument of its State police and politics. The Roman church itself retires into a mere '*potestas indirecta*' and, as far as I can tell, does not even speak of an *autoritas directa* anymore." Seen from "the viewpoint of scholarship and sociology, the dethroning of the Emperor and the Pope signifies the de-theologization of argumentation" in law; "practically speaking," the elimination of previous efforts to fence in war, the end of the medieval doctrine of tyranny, "i.e., of the Emperor's and the Pope's possibilities of intervening," the end of the right of feuding and resistance, "but also the end of the old Peace of God." The world-historical extent of the course of events is manifested in the altered situation of Christianity in the battle of faith: "Above all, this kind of State spells the end of the crusades, i.e., of the papal mandates as accepted legal titles for land appropriations from non-Christian princes and peoples."[3]

"Secularization" marks an end and a new beginning. The pluralism of the Behemoths and Leviathans—which face one another as sovereign political units and thus, by virtue of their power of efficient performance and on the basis of principial equality, form a new, profane, and rational order—takes the place of the political-theological order of the *respublica Christiana*, with its hierarchical organization and sacred orientation. Domestically they succeed in keeping down the quarrels between denominations and factions by establishing clear jurisdictions, by means of centralized legislation, administration, and judiciary. Among themselves they achieve a more or less successful fencing in of enmity by means of the mutual recognition of their jurisdiction over their own demarcated territory. War becomes war between States, and the States prove to be States by putting an end to civil war. "Whatever does not put an end to civil war is not a State. The one excludes the other." Were reality to correspond to the etatist idea, then—as long as the "epoch of the State" lasted—there would "no longer be any enemies" within the State, and outside of its territory the State would be concerned solely with "just enemies" in the form of other States. Politics would be synonymous with foreign policy. Everything else would fall to the police.[4]

With his advocacy of the modern State, Hobbes drew the most extreme consequences from the new situation. The "thought of the sovereign *political* decision which neutralizes all theological-ecclesiastical oppositions and secularizes life," already arose in France in the sixteenth

3. *NdE*, 97–98; "Staatliche Souveränität," 79; *VA*, 383; *ECS*, 16, 71.
4. *L*, 47, 72; *NdE*, 98–99, 128–129; *BdP*, 10.

century from the confessional civil wars.[5] Yet the thought of the State "as a machine that has its 'right' and its 'truth' only in itself, that is in *performance* and *function*, was first grasped and systematically developed as a clear concept by Hobbes." If the "*historical meaning* of the modern State," as Schmitt cannot emphasize enough, consists in its putting an end to "the whole quarrel over the *justa causa*, i.e., over material law and material justice,"[6] then this meaning finds its perfect expression in the "technological character" of the Hobbesian State: "Either this State really exists as a State, and thus functions as the irresistible instrument of quietude, security, and order, and has all objective and all subjective right on its side since, as the sole and highest legislator, it itself *makes* all law; or it does not really exist and does not fulfill its function of securing peace, and then the state of nature prevails once again, and it is no longer a State at all."[7] As soon as the "technological character" of the State is discerned, however, the question arises, for what purpose the machine that has its "right" and its "truth" in itself can and should be used concretely. Saying that it has to do with an instrument for the establishment of quietude, security, and order, in no way answers the question about its purpose. Quietude of what kind? Security at what price? And order of what sort? Asked from the perspective of the Christian Epimetheus: Does the State's mechanism of command serve Christian or anti-Christian purposes? The question appears all the more obvious inasmuch as Hobbes states in the *Leviathan* that the command of the sovereign would also have to be obeyed were he to forbid the Christian religion and require the public denial of one's Christian faith.[8]

Schmitt attempts to dissolve the question historically. At the beginning of the four-hundred-year-long "epoch of the State," the State that has its "right" and its "truth" only in its performance and its function *was* the right answer; upon its end, it *is* no longer the right answer. It was the right answer because it really decided the quarrel over right, truth, and purpose by establishing "quietude, security, and order" in a historical moment, when nothing seemed more urgent than to establish "quietude, security, and order." Its historical rightness was founded precisely on its having understood how to defuse the question of what is right and to push

5. "Staatliche Souveränität," 79; "Die Formung des französischen Geistes," 12, 19, 21, 23.

6. *NdE*, 128–129 (my emphasis).

7. *L*, 71–72 (my emphasis).

8. Hobbes, *Leviathan*, XLII, ed. Oakeshott, 372. Schmitt makes no mention of this statement by the philosopher. In fact it is not very well suited to support the assertion that Hobbes *presupposed* a Christian community or that the sentence "Jesus is the Christ" forms an *axis of his conceptual system of thought*.

it into the background at a time when what on Schmitt's view is most important could still be *presupposed* and therefore defended through the sheer establishment of "quietude, security, and order." In other words, the historical truth of the State consisted in its having protected the truth of faith without raising it to its own truth. Its truth remained true as long as those presuppositions to which the State's "meaning" was bound retained validity, but which the modern State itself was incapable of guaranteeing. Due to the dominant role it played in the process of neutralization and depoliticization, however, the State did in fact contribute decisively to the erosion and destruction of the presuppositions on which its historical truth was based. At the end of the "epoch of the State," for the first time even the political seems to be threatened and in need of defense. The truth of faith sees itself confronted with an unprecedented challenge. The "vehicle of secularization" paved the way, as now becomes apparent, for the "mass faith of an antireligious this-worldly activism" that peaks in a "religion of technicity." And since it was somewhat successful in establishing "quietude, security, and order," it helped to nourish the dangerous illusion of an "age of security": The State is said to be nothing but an "apparatus" that can be employed at any time, or rather a "big business," in which exclusively practical constraints prevail; the State's highly successful police need only be extended to a Leviathan of global proportions in order to allow the promise of peace and security to become a universal reality; then it would no longer be necessary to distinguish between friend and enemy, and the question of what is right could finally be allowed to fall into oblivion, since it would have proved itself to be historically obsolete.

Hobbes devised the "*machina machinarum*" which liberalism, Bolshevism, and National Socialism used three hundred years later as a technological-neutral instrument or as a weapon for the accomplishment of their aims. Theoretically he laid the foundation for the "security State" in which the existence of the bourgeois is satisfied, of the bourgeois "who does not want to leave the sphere of the unpolitical, risk-free private," of the bourgeois "who wants to remain exempt from courage and removed from the danger of a violent death." He especially fostered the "neutralization of every truth" that sharpens the danger of the State's mechanism of command being placed in the service of anti-Christian ends. Yet Hobbes "does not mean it that way." And in the concrete moment for which Hobbes's "answer"—on Schmitt's faith—was determined, it did

9. *L*, 47, 63, 65, 69, 103; *BdP*, 62; *VA*, 384–385; "Die vollendete Reformation," 62. Cf. *Carl Schmitt and Leo Strauss: The Hidden Dialogue*, 37–38.

not serve—again on Schmitt's faith—the Antichrist.[9] But what is Schmitt's opinion based on? And granted that Hobbes acted out of "genuine piety," could he have believed with a good conscience that his theory would not serve the Antichrist? Would Hobbes have had reason to understand himself as a "restrainer"? Or would he not instead have had to fear becoming a "hastener"? Does any theoretician who wants to think and act "for his historical moment," have reason to understand himself as a "restrainer"? Regardless of the danger that the success of his "answer" will later make him a "hastener"? Can "restrainers" and "hasteners" be distinguished at all so long as history has not reached its end? But once the *cui bono?* has suppressed the *quid est bonum?* and the question *What?* has been silenced by the speculation *Who?*—by what does historical action take its bearings? Both prospectively, or in his humble-daring "post-anticipation," and retrospectively, or in his look back to "accomplished events," which strengthens his historical action, the judgment of the Christian Epimetheus seems to find support solely in the blind will to obedience or in the good intention of faith.[10]

Granted the agents had the good intention of faith, the beginning of "secularization" can be interpreted virtually as an enterprise of Christian rescue. First in the sense of a great effort to save what could be saved after the schism, which had been a "severe punishment for both sides."[11] But then also in the sense of seizing a Christian possibility, which the "specifically theological-political crisis" of the Reformation initiated in history. If one recognizes Protestantism as an original, if not "eternal" possibility of Christianity—as Schmitt did early on in one of his most pronouncedly Catholic publications,[12] or as does the Catholic theologian Jean Guitton,[13] to whom the later Schmitt refers in the present context[14]—it is only consistent that one conceive of the Protestant justification of government, which emancipated the State in every form from the authority of the Pope, likewise as a Christian possibility.[15] Later Schmitt

10. Cf. "Drei Möglichkeiten," 930–931; "Die geschichtliche Struktur," 152; *G*, 114.

11. "Die Sichtbarkeit der Kirche," 78.

12. "As soon as there is contact with God, even if mediated by many members, the revolutionary force of the faith in God can no longer be gotten rid of; even in the Church the principle holds true that one must obey God more than men, and the reservation which is thereby left to the discretion of every individual is so ineradicable and sublime that it even retains its validity vis-à-vis the infallible instance." "Die Sichtbarkeit der Kirche," 77.

13. Jean Guitton, *Le Christ écartelé: Crises et conciles dans l'église* (Paris 1963), 228, 230–231; cf. 17–18, 32, 49, 217, 219, 226, 240, 253–255.

14. "Die vollendete Reformation," 65 n. 5.

15. Schmitt's most important witness here is Rudolph Sohm, who describes in detail in the third chapter of his *Kirchenrecht* the attitude of the Reformation towards the State. See esp. vol. I, 487–488, 548–561, 565–566, 570.

goes one step further. He declares Hobbes's decision for "secularization" to be the completion of the Reformation. Hobbes's advocacy was comprehensible not merely *faute de mieux* given the difficulties of his age or defensible for a *vir probus* insofar as it could at least be brought into harmony with the Protestant view. Rather, it was the expression of a far-reaching historical—theological and political—upheaval, which was fulfilled in Hobbes's actions. Schmitt's last word on the "concrete historical identification of the controversial philosopher's locus" is that Hobbes "achieved in a conceptual-systematic way the clear State alternative to the Roman-ecclesiastical monopoly on decision-making and thereby *completed the Reformation*. That was the fruit of an epoch still determined by the notion of the medieval *jus reformandi* and was already determined by the claim to sovereignty by the epoch-bound 'State' that was just emerging."[16] With that, Hobbes seems to have been definitively historicized and Christianized. The *Leviathan*, in which Schmitt sees "the fruit of a specifically theological-political age," receives a place if not in the history of the Church, then at least in that of European Christianity. With the conception he developed in the *Leviathan*, Hobbes wanted to oppose a "State counterpart" to the "hierocratic doctrine of the *corpus* proper to Roman theology," a counterpart that was inspired and historically borne by Protestantism. Taking up a reference from his friend, the Catholic theologian and professor of canonical law Hans Barion, Schmitt is inclined in 1965 to suspect in Hobbes's employment of the biblical symbol for the strongest power on earth an answer to the "conspicuous conjuration of the image of the Leviathan" in John of Salisbury's *Policraticus*. In that case, Hobbes would have positivized and appropriated the negatively charged image in the *Policraticus* from a "monistic-hierocratic" standpoint and used it for the *corpus unum* of evil men, just as he himself would have "overturned" the hierocratic position and transferred the *plenitudo potestatis*, which John of Salisbury claimed for the Pope, to the State.[17] To Schmitt it is obvious that the addressee of the "State counterpart" devised by Hobbes was a Christian sovereign, that Hobbes had a Christian sovereign in view when he unfolded "the all-governing question" *quis iudicabit?* and that Hobbes presupposed a Christian sovereign when he secularized the "eternal correlation between protection and obedience" in order to gain from it the foundation of his edifice. In the "world-battle between Catholicism and Protestantism,"

16. *PT II*, 121; "Die vollendete Reformation," 56, 65.

17. "Die vollendete Reformation," 63, 66, 68–69; Hans Barion, *Kirche und Kirchenrecht*, 431; John of Salisbury, *Policraticus* (1159), VI, 1.

Hobbes sided with Protestantism. In foreign policy, he strengthened "the front against the world enemy of England at that time, the Roman church," with his defense of the *potestas directa*.[18] Domestically his construction corresponded in its overall design, far more to the expectations and demands of a Lutheran "who bows to every government" than it could have satisfied the "self-confident greatness of a spiritual descendant of grand inquisitors."[19] Completed in advanced years, the Christian reinterpretation of the *Leviathan* sheds light on the significance for Schmitt of a modified sentence of Barbey d'Aurevilly, a sentence he cites in one of his last essays, seemingly in passing and with the succinct comment that Hugo Ball did "not understand" it. The talk is of Barbey d'Aurevilly's remark in *Les prophètes du passé* on Hobbes's *Leviathan* and de Maistre's *Du Pape*, where he, as Schmitt says, "declared" the *Leviathan* and *Du Pape* "to be the two most important books of modernity." To the designation of his alternative, which is hidden in a footnote, Schmitt adds only the reference to "Die vollendete Reformation."[20] In fact beyond this reference there is no need of any further explanation on Schmitt's part that he sees the importance of the two books in the fundamental alternative they represent for him, an alternative based to be sure on a still more important common feature he believes to have secured through his interpretation of the *Leviathan*. For the paramount importance Schmitt ascribes the two so very unequal works cannot be based on the influence each exerted in history. Here the comparison would be far too unfavorable for *Du Pape*. Did Maistre's "answer" come too late or too early?[21]

18. *L*, 126; "Staatliche Souveränität," 79, 89, 93; "Die Formung des französischen Geistes," 22–23; "Die vollendete Reformation," 68.

19. Cf. *PT*, 51 (74) and consider Chapter III, nn. 137, 145, 146 above.

20. "Clausewitz als politischer Denker," 493 n. 7; cf. Hugo Ball, *Die Flucht aus der Zeit* (Lucerne 1946), 222. It is Schmitt, and not Barbey d'Aurevilly, who declares the *Leviathan* and *Du Pape* "to be the two most important books of modernity." The French Catholic had written: "Ainsi, au bout de toutes les philosophies, le système du Pape de Joseph de Maistre *et de toute l'Église* ou le Léviathan de Hobbes! Ou le droit absolu avec son Interprète infaillible qui juge, condamne et absout, ou des luttes sans fin, sans dernier mot, sans apaisement; le vivier de sang de la force (car l'intelligence n'est qu'une force) et le pauvre Esprit humain, secoué par ses passions comme un arbre ébranché et fendu, pour toute mesure du droit et du devoir des hommes! Voilà l'alternative. On verra comme le monde s'en tirera, mais il faudra choisir." Jules-Amédée Barbey d'Aurevilly, *Les prophètes du passé* (Paris 1851; 2d ed., 1889), 55 n. (my emphasis).

21. Four decades earlier Schmitt said of Maistre in his *Politische Theologie*: "The value of the State lies in the fact that it makes a decision; the value of the Church lies in the fact that it *is* the ultimate, unappealable decision" (50 [71]). When Schmitt claims a few lines later that Maistre declared "government as such to be good when it merely exists: tout gouvernement est bon lorsqu'il est établi," he has him, to stick to Schmitt's terminology, appear "more Lutheran" than he is, for in Maistre the passage, the source of which Schmitt does not name, reads: "Il faut partir d'ailleurs d'un principe général et incontestable: savoir que tout

Was his "anticipation of a commandment that is to be obeyed" hitherto denied its historical confirmation because Europe was not yet prepared to pay the price "that Donoso demanded for the salvation of Europe, that is, the return to the Catholic Church"?[22]

Hobbes is historicized by Schmitt; by contrast, the historical Hobbes is of lesser interest to Schmitt. True, Schmitt reminds the interpreters of Hobbes that they should learn to understand Hobbes's statements as answers to questions such as "those he himself raised," and at one point Schmitt even comes close to a formal declaration in favor of the hermeneutic maxim that "everything depends on first understanding Hobbes just as he understood himself."[23] But in fact all of Schmitt's attention is directed to those questions he believes he knows that "history" put to Hobbes,[24] and since, in the security of his faith in history, he believes he is able to know in retrospect both the historical "call" and the appropriateness or inappropriateness of Hobbes's "answer," he always already makes the tacit claim to understand Hobbes better than he understood himself. Just as Schmitt in truth hardly inquires into the philosopher's self-understanding, he likewise does not address the claim to truth that Hobbes makes and that is by no means bound to the historical moment in which Hobbes lived and thought.[25] Just as Schmitt comforts himself with his belief "that in Hobbes there was genuine piety," he also relies on the opinion that the "concrete historical identification of the locus" is able to unlock and lay bare what is most important in Hobbes's thought. Schmitt relies avowedly upon the "principle of the question-

gouvernement est bon lorsqu'il est établi *et qu'il subsiste depuis longtemps sans contestation.*" *Du Pape*, II, 8, ed. Lovie/Chetail (Geneva 1966), 181 (my emphasis).

22. *DC*, 113. A few lines prior to the sentence to which Schmitt refers in order to let those readers who follow up on his references know which "two books" *he* regards "as the most important in modernity," Barbey d'Aurevilly writes: "Et puisque j'ai cité le livre du *Pape*, qu'il me soit permis d'ajouter en passant qu'il est à lui seul, sous sa forme historique, toute une Prophétie que le temps se chargera de justifier, et plus prochainement qu'on ne croit. Les peuples chrétiens, qui ne le sont actuellement que de nom et de baptême, doivent revenier, dans un temps donné, à cette théorie du Pape, qui est la théorie de l'unité dans le pouvoir et qui a fait pousser à l'Erreur le cri qu'on pousse quand on est frappé. Lorsque nous serons las, et cette fatigue commence déjà, des pouvoirs fictifs, conventionnels, et remis en question tous les matins, nous reviendrons au pouvoir vrai, religieux, absolu, divin; à la Théocratie exécrée, mais nécessaire et bienfaisante, ou nous sommes donc destinés à rouler, pour y périr, dans les bestialités d'un matérialisme effréné" (*Les prophètes du passé*, 54–55 n.).

23. "Die vollendete Reformation," 66, 68.

24. The questions *quis iudicabit? quis interpretabitur? quis interrogabit?* are, in Schmitt's sense, "answers" to the historical challenge of the age. They are questions which Hobbes directs to others and not ones he, in a precise sense, puts to *himself*.

25. Cf. Hobbes, *Leviathan*, XXX, ed. Oakeshott, 220; *De cive*, Ep. ded. and Praef., ed. Warrender (Oxford 1983), 75 and 77 ff.

and-answer logic" he takes from R. G. Collingwood in order to "concretize" it in Christian terms.[26] The dogmatic narrowing that results from Schmitt's historicism finds expression everywhere, in the whole as well as in its parts.[27] It is expressed with the casualness with which Schmitt assumes that Hobbes "presupposed" a Christian community. It manifests itself likewise in the fact that what Schmitt calls Hobbes's "scientificity" ultimately comes into view only as an answer to the loss of another kind of evidence that guaranteed security, one that previously "was hopelessly lost in the quarrel of the theologians."[28] And since Hobbes must have "answered" to the shattered unity of the medieval *respublica Christiana* with his theory, his confrontation with ancient philosophy—which was of central importance to Hobbes "as he understood himself"—is nowhere to be found in Schmitt. However, the "concrete historical identification of the locus" at least permits Schmitt to draw parallels with his own situation, to perceive his own dependencies, and, by means of the historical classification of his "predecessor," to consider his own case and portray it by means of alienation. Something else occurs. When Schmitt reaches the conclusion that the "epochal significance of Thomas Hobbes" consists in his "having seen with conceptual clarity the purely political meaning of the religious claim to decision making,"[29] he grants Hobbes a knowledge, the truth of which was not "true only once"—and for the time being we want to disregard the fact that that truth was no less accessible to a philosopher of the fourteenth or sixteenth century, as every reader of Machiavelli's *Discorsi* or Marsilius of Padua's *Defensor pacis* can convince himself—but is still true.

Of his own case Schmitt said in the summer of 1945 that it can be called "by a name a great poet coined. It is the bad, unworthy, and yet authentic case of a *Christian Epimetheus*."[30] Bad, unworthy, and yet authentic—Schmitt's characterization refers especially to the years during which he supported the National Socialist regime, the years that occur in the middle of his life and that are the center of attention in the quarrel over his persona. For many, they are what make Schmitt into a case in the first place. But Schmitt's characterization refers not only to the role he

26. "Die vollendete Reformation," 66–67. Consider "Die geschichtliche Struktur," 151–152.

27. Thus, e.g., Schmitt says of Hobbes: "In the concrete situation of his age he reaches the conclusion that the dangers, from the Church and the prophets, that threaten an individualistic freedom are worse than everything to be feared from a State-secular government" ("Die vollendete Reformation," 61). Cf. Chapter III, 109 f. and 116.

28. "Die vollendete Reformation," 59.

29. "Die vollendete Reformation," 64.

30. *ECS*, 12; cf. 31 and 53; *G*, 23, 24, 66, 101, 159, 238.

played during those twelve years, just as his case is not confined to his actions in the Third Reich. Schmitt's self-characterization—which comes closer to a public confession of Christian repentance than any other remark published during his lifetime, in order thereby to pave the way at the same time for his Christian justification—considers his National Socialist past without stopping there.

The attributes *bad, unworthy, and yet authentic* may serve as a starting point for contemplation of the case of Carl Schmitt, contemplation to which the intention to prosecute is just as foreign as are apologetic motives. We assume that Schmitt hit upon what is essential when as a Christian Epimetheus he called his case *bad* and *unworthy*, and we leave it to future biographers to instruct us whether in truth he is to be judged as worse or not as bad, as unworthier or not as unworthy. If we take Schmitt's opinion as our starting point, of course not merely because a biography that deserves this name is unavailable, but because for us the chief interest of Schmitt's judgment lies in the attributive *and yet authentic*. Of interest to us is how the Christian Epimetheus, who wants to have his actions—in view of the unfathomability of the providential will that he believes rules history—understood only in the sense of an "anticipation of a commandment that is to be obeyed," how this Christian Epimetheus classifies his activities *post festum*. Of interest to us are the consequences the political theologian draws for his theory, or whether the concrete historical experience of his own case remains without consequences for his theory. For that reason we are chiefly interested in the fact that Schmitt claims for his case that he is, although bad and unworthy, the *authentic* case of a *Christian Epimetheus*. Accordingly, regarding Schmitt's decision in 1933 to join the NSDAP [National Socialist German Workers' Party] and to be actively involved in the construction of the Third Reich, the central question is how Schmitt could believe—in the "historical moment" of 1933 and in retrospect in 1945—that his decision is compatible with his political theology. In comparison with this question, a whole series of questions that preoccupy historians, and in particular move apologists and prosecutors, fade in importance. For example, the considerations of Schmitt's personal motives or conjectures about the influence friends and acquaintances, even well-known public figures with whom he was not on close terms, might have exerted on his decision.[31] We shall not investigate whether Schmitt's fear or vanity

31. Among the legends that have grown up around Schmitt's biography counts the rumor spread by various historians and journalists that Heidegger asked Schmitt to join the NSDAP or "not to shut himself off" from the Movement. As evidence a letter from Heidegger dated April 22, 1933 is cited. In fact this letter does not exist. No more than there is any

played a greater role—to mention only the Hobbesian alternative with which Schmitt was well acquainted—and we shall certainly not get involved in the intricate casuistry as to which of the motives in question, considering all of the circumstances, is to be regarded possibly as more incriminating or more exonerating. Of incomparably greater importance for us is that after the Second World War Schmitt was of the opinion that the readiness with which he served the tyranny in Germany for years and the anti-Semitic outbursts he allowed himself from 1933 on can be brought into harmony with the case of a Christian Epimetheus and do not speak against its authenticity. No future historical instruction will ever equal what Schmitt's own judgment, which has been accessible to everyone for decades, can teach us about his faith and about the political theology grounded in his faith.[32]

To what extent does Schmitt's teaching promote despotism? Does it perceive the latter at all? Or is it constitutionally blind to despotism?[33] In one case his teaching seems to be virtually overwhelmed by the danger of it. The thought of the impending despotism of the Antichrist captivates Schmitt so forcefully that his attention to all other sources and forms of despotism in political reality wanes (not to mention those expressions that Hobbes summarized under the title "Kingdom of Darkness"). Schmitt's fixation on the danger of the Antichrist, on the one case that matters, leads us straight to the center of his own case, which cannot be properly understood without considering that fixation. For it marks out the horizon in which Schmitt moves with his political advocacy. The eschatological anticipation, the tense expectation of the threat that overshadows every other threat, has an ambivalent character from the beginning. It makes one acutely aware of the seriousness of the decision, shakes the security of the status quo, cancels the comfort and ease of self-satisfaction. At the same time, however, in the usual course of events it makes it easier for one to comfort oneself with trite subterfuges along the

---

other indication that Schmitt, who followed the political events of 1932–33 in Berlin at close range, let himself be advised by the Freiburg philosopher with whom he had a definite nonrelationship. The sole letter from Heidegger to Schmitt available to us is dated August 22, 1933. In it Heidegger conveys his thanks in general terms for the third edition of *Der Begriff des Politischen*, which the Prussian State Councilor had sent to the Rector of the University of Freiburg. Beyond that there is no indication that Schmitt, who sent books and offprints to innumerable scholars throughout the world, actually exchanged publications or corresponded with Heidegger.

32. Cf. Johann Wolfgang von Goethe, *Noten und Abhandlungen. Israel in der Wüste*, ed. Trunz, vol. II, 223–224.

33. Cf. Chancellor Friedrich von Müller, *Unterhaltungen mit Goethe*, ed. Grumach (Weimar 1959), 99 (entry from October 19, 1823); *PT II*, 123; furthermore, Chapter I, 18 f. and 20 above.

lines of the supposedly "lesser evil" or of the "necessary antidotes" and "unavoidable risks," subterfuges that can be justified in view of the uniqueness of the peril and of what is at stake in *it*. The eschatological anticipation increases, in a word, the danger of self-deception.[34]

To counteract the dominion of the Antichrist, Schmitt backs the defense of the political, and the battle "for" or "against" enmity becomes for him, as we have seen, the most important political-theological criterion, since he sees in the negation of enmity the surest sign of the threat posed by the Old Enemy.[35] The apocalyptic horror of the Antichrist thus stands in a very precise sense before and behind Schmitt's action as a political theologian. It is voiced for the first time in a book published in the middle of the First World War, a book about "the Elements, the Spirit, and the Actuality" of the epos *Nordlicht* by his friend Theodor Däubler. It is the only one among his numerous writings for which he takes a saying of Christ as his motto. The conjuration of the Antichrist, which represents the apex of the most vivid description and critique Schmitt bestows upon the "moral significance of the age," proves to be the central point for everything that follows.[36] In its light what links Schmitt's subsequent decisions about and determinations of his own position to one another—decisions and determinations that appeared to many of his contemporaries to be the expression of mere "occasionalism" or sheer opportunism—and what persists in them becomes visible. For the defense of the political is not confined to Schmitt's efforts—in *Der Begriff des Politischen* and *Politische Theologie*—to provide it with a theoretical foundation or to prove its "inescapability." It is also the leitmotif of those studies on which Schmitt built his reputation as a jurist. From the in-depth treatment of the problem of the realization of law or the insistence on the personal as-

34. On the evening before his fiftieth birthday, in an after-dinner speech to a circle of his closest friends, Schmitt states: "Each of you knows my great weaknesses, my curiosity, my capacity for enthusiasm, my capacity for letting myself be deceived." (Ms. Hauptstaatsarchiv Düsseldorf.) Cf. *G*, 95, 174, 227, 238. (Among the four birthday guests were the Prussian Minister of Finance, Johannes Popitz, and the Protestant Regional Bishop, Heinrich Oberheid, of whom Schmitt says that "for me, who comes from the Catholic part of Westphalia," he has become "a true initiator into the world, without the inner conquest of which one cannot be a German—into the world of Lutheran Christianity, of the Lutheran faith in God and grace.")

35. In 1947 Schmitt notes that people were "appalled by the observation"—by *his* observation—"that there is a distinction between friend and enemy and that there is still something like enmity among men. That struck a nerve. The Devil jumped up when his bush was beaten that way, and he taught the bush-beater mores" (*G*, 12). See Chapter I, 24 f. and Chapter II, 56 ff. and 65 above.

36. *Theodor Däublers "Nordlicht,"* 59–72. The saying of Christ (Luke 12:56), which Schmitt takes as his motto, reads: "Ye hypocrites, ye can discern the face of the sky and of the earth; but how is it that ye do not discern this time?"

pect involved in applying the law—in *Die Diktatur* and, prior to that, already in the early writings *Gesetz und Urteil* [*Law and Judgment*] and *Der Wert des Staates und die Bedeutung des Einzelnen*—via his emphatic insistence on the political decision which precedes every constitution and on which the entire legal system is based—in *Verfassungslehre*, in *Hüter der Verfassung*, and in *Legalität und Legitimität*—down to the centerpiece of Schmitt's works on public law, down to the legal implementation and historical actualization of the "teaching of sovereignty."

Appropriately enough Schmitt's leitmotif emerges particularly clearly in the pros and cons of his immediately polemical statements and concepts. For example, in his critique of political Romanticism, which he maintains sought to evade the Either-Or of the moral and political decision by taking flight into an eternal conversation; in his battle against anarchism, which is said to paralyze the "demanding moral decision," the "core of the political idea," in a "paradisiacal, this-worldliness of immediate, natural life and unproblematical carnality"; or in his revolt against "the economic-technological kind of thinking prevailing today," which is "no longer even capable of perceiving a political idea." Against these and other enemies of "the political," Schmitt advances in 1922 the "political idea of Catholicism." In 1939 he proclaims the Reich to be the bearer of a political idea that "extends into a certain *Großraum*" and to be the center of a new, polycentric, political order of the earth. In 1963 he offers the guerrilla as the last example of the power of resistance which a political idea or the "most extreme intensity of political engagement" is in a position to mobilize against the "system of infallible objectivity."[37] This does not exhaust the risky ventures and misjudgments that follow the same pattern. In 1933, after "Hegel had died" and the "bureaucratic State of the nineteenth century had been replaced by another conception of the State" on January 30, Schmitt attempts to steer National Socialism towards a "tripartite structure of political unity," one divided into State, Movement, and People, and to bring it into place against the "bipartite" construction of "liberal democracy," behind which "an anarchic pluralism of social forces grew rampantly": the "total Führer-State" as the guarantor of the primacy of the political and as the way out of "a chaotic mixture of the civil and the non-civil, the public and the private, the po-

37. *PR*, 162; *PT*, 55–56 (82–83); *RK*, 56–57 (37–38); *Völkerrechtliche Großraumordnung mit Interventionsverbot für raumfremde Mächte. Ein Beitrag zum Reichsbegriff im Völkerrecht* [*The Order of International Law based on* Großraum, *with a Prohibition of Intervention by Foreign Powers: A Contribution to the Concept of the Reich in International Law*] (Berlin/Vienna 1939), 69, 72; *TdP*, 92.

litical and the fictively unpolitical."[38] This attempt was preceded at the outset of the thirties by Schmitt's last effort to hand the political over to the State's monopoly on decision-making in the classical sense, and in fact by offering the conception of a "total State" that "no longer knows anything that is absolutely unpolitical" and that decides sovereignly what is political and what it will accept as unpolitical, thus by offering a conception of a total State that "consists of power and strength" or "in the sense of quality and energy" to a regime that is authoritarian in character, one that would be in a position to provide the interests of the whole with validity over the particular interests of society and the parties effective within it.[39] For the same reason Schmitt places great hopes in Mussolini's *stato totalitario* already in the twenties.

The "superiority of fascism over economic interests, whether those of the employers or of the employees, and, one can say, the heroic attempt to hold [onto] and assert the dignity of the State and national unity over the pluralism of economic interests," gain Schmitt's unlimited support. In the guise of a book review in 1929 he publishes a panegyric to the "Wesen und Werden des fascistischen Staates" [Essence and Development of the Fascist State], which reveals in a few pages his own political preferences just prior to the Third Reich: "The fascist State does not decide as a neutral but as a higher third. Therein lies its supremacy. Whence this energy and this new strength? From national enthusiasm, from Mussolini's individual energy, from the war veterans movement, perhaps even from other sources."[40] What in Germany remained "a magnificent philosophical theory," the State as the *higher* third, Schmitt sees become reality in Italy because, he contends, fascism has understood that the "supremacy of the State over the economy can only be implemented with the aid of a closed, order-like organization." "Both fascism and communist Bolshevism require such an 'apparatus' for this superiority over the economy." For how "could the State be the higher and more powerful third if it does not have a strong, solidly formed, self-contained organization at its disposal, and

38. *SBV*, 17, 23, 27, 31–32, 42, 44, 46.

39. *Der Hüter der Verfassung* [*The Guardian of the Constitution*] (Tübingen 1931), 73, 78–82; "Die Wendung zum totalen Staat" (1931), in *PuB*, 146, 151–154, 157; *BdP*, 24, 26; *Legalität und Legitimität* [*Legality and Legitimacy*] (Munich/Leipzig 1932), 95–97; "Gesunde Wirtschaft im starken Staat" [A Healthy Economy in a Strong State] (address from November 23, 1932), in *Langnamverein*, no. 1 (1932): 13–32, esp. 16–18, 21–23, 31–32; "Weiterentwicklung des totalen Staates in Deutschland" (1933), in *VA*, 361–362, 364–365.

40. "Wesen und Werden des fascistischen Staates," in *Schmollers Jahrbuch für Gesetzgebung, Verwaltung und Volkswirtschaft im Deutschen Reiche* 53, no. 1 (1929): 108, 111 (*PuB*, 110, 113; I am quoting the wording of the original publication).

thus not one like the Party, which is hierarchical and based on free recruitment? Only such a new organization is up to such an enormous, new task."[41] Since Schmitt had already become involved in the "sociological reality," he also raises the further question about whom the "apparatus constructed by Mussolini," which according to its claim is obliged solely to the whole, "has to serve in the long run by virtue of its essence, the capitalist interests of the employers or the socialist interests of the employees?" Schmitt's prognosis is "that it, and precisely as far as it is a *genuine State*, in the long run is beneficial to the employees, and precisely because *today* they are the people and the State is after all the political unity of the people. Only a weak State is the capitalist servant of private property. Every strong State—if it is really a higher third and not simply identical with those who are strong economically—demonstrates its proper strength not vis-à-vis the weak, but rather vis-à-vis the socially and economically strong. Caesar's enemies were the optimates, not the people; the State of the absolute prince had to assert itself against the upper classes, not against the farmers, etc. For that reason the employers and especially the industrialists can never trust a fascist State completely, and they have to suspect that as a result it will one day develop into a worker State with a planned economy." Were this prognosis to prove well founded, "a nice example" would be yielded "for the cunning of the world-historical idea" inasmuch as "Mussolini would have created a socialist instrument in the bitter fight against the official guardians of socialism." By contrast, the success of fascism in the confrontation with the main enemy, liberalism, does not lie in an uncertain future. True, Schmitt does not want to rule out "that a few liberal setbacks could possibly occur at some point if Mussolini's leadership were to end," yet for Schmitt Italian fascism has now already "broken through the atmosphere of deception" surrounding liberalism and allowed the position of the political, which Schmitt believes to be most seriously endangered by liberalism, to take historical shape. What fills Schmitt with admiration regarding Mussolini's fascism is the decided antithesis to liberalism which Schmitt sees

41. "Wesen und Werden," 111 (*PuB*, 112). "It is part of Germany's fate that it produced a magnificent philosophical theory of State as the higher third already a hundred years ago, a theory that extends from Hegel via Lorenz von Stein to the great economists (such as Schmoller and Knapp), which then fell victim to a rather blatant trivialization. It was then easy for it to become notorious as a doctrine of the governmental State because no new organization, created with a sociologically-informed awareness of the new situation, corresponded to it, but rather was only a well-disciplined and technologized civil service in connection with a traditionalistically hardened, nationally confusing plurality of dynasties, whose ideal foundation was the politically paralyzing concept of legitimacy. By contrast, fascism places value on being revolutionary, and with good reason" (111; *PuB*, 112–113).

in it or projects into it, the antithesis to the dominion of money, of the invisible, of indirect powers: "With ancient honesty the fascist State wants to be a State again, with visible bearers of power and representatives, but not the facade and antechamber of invisible and irresponsible rulers and financial backers." Matters are completely different regarding liberalism, which is "an elaborate system of methods for weakening the State" and which dissolves "everything that is specifically political and specifically State," including democracy, for democracy "is a concept that belongs just as specifically to the sphere of the political." Schmitt expressly defends fascism therefore against the reproach that it stands in "absolute opposition to democracy."[42] Fascism does not take a stand against democracy but rather against "the liberal dissolution of genuine democracy." And in view of what is fundamental, Schmitt observes: "As things stand today, the battle for the State and the political is in no country a battle against a genuine democracy, but it is just as necessarily a battle against the methods by which the liberal bourgeoisie of the nineteenth century weakened and toppled its monarchic State, which today has long since been disposed of."[43]

When the concern is the defense of the political, Schmitt is resolved to consider revolutionary forces also as possible "restrainers," and to the extent that it is aimed at liberalism, he is, as things stand *today*, that is, after the caesura of the First World War, even prepared to get involved to a point with democracy. For despite the burden of its Spinozist-Rousseauian provenance, Schmitt is at least able to see a "formative political principle" in modern democracy, which "in the battle for the State and the political" can be played off against the dominant "antipolitical" liberalism of the present. Thus he devotes several publications from the twenties and early thirties—first and foremost, *Die geistesgeschichtliche Lage des heutigen Parlamentarismus* and *Verfassungslehre*—to dissecting "liberal democracy" into its heterogeneous component parts and to demonstrating the hostile conflict of its fundamental principles: the political principle, on the one hand, which characterizes democracy as a form of dominion, and on the other the un- or antipolitical principles,

42. "Wesen und Werden," 112–113 (my emphasis); 108 (*PuB*, 113, 114; 110). "That fascism does without elections and hates and despises the whole '*elezionismo*' is not undemocratic but rather antiliberal and springs from the right knowledge that the contemporary methods of a secret individual ballot endanger everything political and of the State through total privatization, that they drive the people as a unity completely out of the public [sphere] (the sovereign disappears in the voting booth), and that they degrade the State development of informed opinion to a summation of secret and private individual wills, i.e., in truth of uncontrollable mass wishes and resentments" (109; *PuB*, 110–111).

43. "Wesen und Werden," 108, 110 (*PuB*, 110, 111).

which determine the bourgeois legal State.[44] Under the title "Der bürgerliche Rechtsstaat" [The Bourgeois Legal State] Schmitt publishes in 1928 a critique focused on the political quintessence, a critique that forms in almost every respect the complementary counterpart of the panegyric he will dedicate to the fascist State a year later. Schmitt identifies "the uncontrollability of the individual" as the "fundamental principle" of the legal State. From this principle derive the demands that are essential to legal liberalism, namely, that basic rights be secured and that powers be separated. "As a result the freedom of the individual becomes in principle unlimited, the State and its authority are posited as limited. What the State is allowed to do is precisely apportioned. Monitoring bodies are installed everywhere and secured legally." In the strict sense, the bourgeois legal State does not decide on any form of State, nor for democracy. Rather, it reduces democracy to a mere organizational form, such as legislation, which is to counterbalance the other organizational forms, the monarchic form, for example, as the executive. Thus a *status mixtus* arises "which intentionally balances opposing principles, one with the other, though not in the interest of political unity, but of individual freedom."[45] In accordance with its essence and development, the bourgeois legal State is in Schmitt's eyes the expression of the *decision for the unpolitical*.[46] Schmitt sees its "typical manifestation" in the parliamentary

44. *GLP*, 14, 16, 18, 21–23, 45–46, 58; *VL*, 41, 213, 216–217, 255–256, 305. The two central sections of the *Verfassungslehre* are entitled "Der rechtstaatliche Bestandteil der modernen Verfassung" [The Legal-State Component of the Modern Constitution] and "Der politische Bestandteil der modernen Verfassung" [The Political Component of the Modern Constitution]. In the Preface Schmitt says of his work: "In the main the constitutional theory of the bourgeois legal State is presented. In that respect, no one will be able to raise *any objection* to the book, for this kind of State is *in general still predominant today* and the Weimar constitution corresponds completely to its type" (ix; my emphasis).

45. "Der bürgerliche Rechtsstaat," in *Die Schildgenossen. Zweimonatsschrift aus der katholischen Lebensbewegung* 8, no. 2 (March-April 1928): 128, 129. The editors added this reference to the text: "The following exposition is Dr. Werner Becker's transcript of a talk given by Prof. Dr. Carl Schmitt. The manuscript has been checked by Carl Schmitt and is published in the *Schildgenossen* with his permission" (127). Schmitt published it shortly thereafter also in the journal *Abendland*, no. 3 (1928): 201–203.

46. "The two principles of the bourgeois legal State, freedom of the individual and the separation of powers, are both unpolitical. They do not contain any form of the State but rather methods of organization for the *inhibition* of the State. Here the immediate influence of liberal thought hostile to all formal elements manifests itself. 'Freedom constitutes nothing' (Mazzini). It must be especially emphasized that the bourgeois legal State is not a form of State and, taken on its own, not a constitution, but only a system for the control of the State" (129). "The bourgeoisie found the definitive scheme of the bourgeois legal State, the meaning of which consists precisely in its avoidance of a political form, in the French constitution of 1875, which is still in force today. It culminates in the parliamentary system. The parliament, which is independent of the people, constitutes the peak of the bourgeois legal State" (129–130).

system. "It contains aristocratic and monarchic elements and is all in all a mixture of forms that arose from the liberal interest in inhibiting the properly political wherever it appears. It is the form the bourgeoisie created to protect itself from the State, thus it is an antipolitical form, just as the liberal bourgeoisie itself is something unpolitical." The principial attack is followed by the historical disposal. In the past the bourgeois legal State had "a specific task" to fulfill "with its parliamentarianism." It served "to integrate the bourgeoisie, i.e., a segment of the population characterized by the two features of possessions and education, into the then existent monarchic State." It fulfilled that task. It is all the more important now, Schmitt argues, translating his historicism into practical politics, that one become clear on the "relativity of that attempt." Especially as the earlier opponent of parliamentarianism, the monarchy, no longer exists, an opponent "that drew its strength from another age. Already for that reason the entire system has to run dry." *Today* a completely new task has been set. "Today the aim is to integrate the proletariat, a non-possessing and uneducated mass, into a political unity." In view of this "central task," which must be "mastered politically" and which "reveals the inadequacy of the methods of the bourgeois legal State," Schmitt pleads for the activation of the "political component" of the constitution, for the mobilization of the "democratic"—which is, after all, "emphasized strongly enough" in the Weimar constitution—"so that the people has the possibility at any time, despite all obstacles and outlets and behind the wall built by the ideas of the bourgeois legal State, of finding its political form." "[F]or the constitutional development of the near future," Schmitt adds to this the demand that "democracy be saved from its veiling by liberal moments."[47] But what is to be saved? Which figure will come to light once the liberal veil has been shed, once the constitutional obstacles have been overcome? Is the turn to democracy more than a euphemism for somehow taking the bull by the horns? Does it indicate anything more concrete than the turn away from liberalism or the wish for such a turn?

It is certain that Schmitt makes a case for a rapid hastening that has an uncertain outcome. In a historical moment in which "drawing the consequences of the democratic is avoided everywhere in German democracy," Schmitt acts as the advocate of a democracy in which one has to take seriously just these consequences. "The democratic principle requires that the people decides and rules responsibly in its totality." In "today's democracy" the democratic principle has not been fulfilled since today's

47. "Der bürgerliche Rechtsstaat," 129, 130–131.

democracy uses liberal, instead of democratic, methods to establish the sovereignty of the people. That is, the sovereign's decision comes about "by means of a secret individual ballot. That means: the individuals are isolated in the sole moment in which they bear public responsibility." They decide as individuals and in secret, not as a people and in public. For that reason liberal democracy remains a "democracy without a *demos*, without a people." In his fight against liberalism Schmitt makes himself the advocate of the people. In this connection the people is for him "only an assembled people," visible and really existing. To be able to be "the bearer of political responsibility," it also has to be—unlike "today's people of the State," which is "divided culturally, socially, into classes, racially, religiously"—politically unified and homogeneous. The democracy proclaimed by Schmitt thus proves to be a democracy founded on publicity, acclamation, and homogeneity: Publicity, because without publicity "there is no people"; acclamation, because the assenting or rejecting of the assembled multitude or the public opinion in the major modern States is the form of the people's expression of its will, which seems to be least accessible to channeling, domestication, or falsification by "liberal methods"; homogeneity, because democracy as an identity of the ruling and the ruled presupposes a sameness of kind, however it may be determined.[48] It is obvious that Schmitt leaves nearly every concrete question unanswered and keeps almost every political option open with his conception of democracy, which he opposes polemically to the bourgeois legal State, and he himself was certainly not unaware of this.[49] An author who repeated the Hobbesian sentences *quis iudicabit? quis interpretabitur? quis interrogabit?* innumerable times during his lifetime, must have known what he was doing when he defined democracy as a majority decision and then added in the next sentence: "It means that political questions are settled in keeping with the politically responsible conviction of the majority of the people."[50]

Genuine nationalism calls for democracy. It is grounded on the sovereignty of the people, or it is not grounded at all. Schmitt explains in his essay on Italian fascism that "genuine nationalism, compulsory military service, and democracy are after all 'triune, [and] not to be sepa-

48. "Der bürgerliche Rechtsstaat," 131, 132, 133. See *VL*, 205, 214–215, 231, 234–237 (on homogeneity); 208, 244–246, 280–282 (on publicity); 83–84, 243, 246–247 (on acclamation). Concerning the significance Schmitt ascribes to acclamation, cf. Peterson, Εἷς Θεός. *Epigraphische, formgeschichtliche und religionsgeschichtliche Untersuchungen* (Göttingen 1926), Parts III and IV, esp. 141, 145, 146–152, 213, 215.

49. Cf. *VL*, 84.

50. "Der bürgerliche Rechtsstaat," 132.

rated.'"[51] Was Schmitt a supporter of this trinity? Might he have become involved, in his own way, in democracy in order to promote nationalism? Was Schmitt thus a nationalist? Or is he a theoretician of nationalism? In 1929 Schmitt confirms that fascism has achieved a "great increase in the civil and national self-confidence among the mass of Italians, especially among the farmers,"[52] and in view of his prognosis regarding the fascist State as a promising realization of the theory of the "higher third," it is safe to assume that he also thought it the one most likely capable of managing that "central task," of which he had said a year earlier "had still hardly been considered" in Germany: the political integration of the proletariat, or more precisely, the "integration" of the people in its totality, "into a political unity from within."[53] To be sure, Schmitt's hopes were based not on actual successes or on the practices of fascism so much as on its statements or on fascist rhetoric. The fascist reference to the myth of the nation serves him, just a few months after il Duce's seizure of power, as evidence of the "superiority of the national" over international socialism and its myth of the class struggle. In 1923 he enlists the orator Mussolini as the principal witness to the strongest political force he believes he sees in the present. "In his famous speech of October 1922 in Naples, before the march on Rome, Mussolini said: 'We have created a myth, the myth is a faith, a noble enthusiasm, it need not be a reality, it is a drive and a hope, faith and courage. Our myth is the nation, the great nation we want to make a concrete reality.' In the same speech he calls socialism an inferior mythology." Commenting on this, Schmitt continues: "Just as back in the sixteenth century, once again an Italian expressed the principle of political reality."[54] What counts in the political reality are drive, hope, faith, and courage; what matters today is to discern the mythology that is capable of awakening and developing these forces and virtues with the greatest intensity; and here Schmitt thinks, as far as the "more recent age" is concerned, he observes "the superiority of the national" or, as he corrects himself three years later, he can rely on the fact "that the stronger

51. "Wesen und Werden," 109 (*PuB*, 110); *VL*, 231; see also Heinz O. Ziegler, *Die moderne Nation. Ein Beitrag zur politischen Soziologie* (Tübingen 1931), esp. 233, 243, and by the same author *Autoritärer oder totaler Staat* (Tübingen 1932), 7, 9–11, 16, 18; cf. *LuL*, 93 and "Völkerrechtliche Neutralität und völkische Totalität" [Neutrality in International Law and National Totality] (1938), in *PuB*, 255.

52. "Wesen und Werden," 109 (*PuB*, 110).

53. "Der bürgerliche Rechtsstaat," 130, 133.

54. *GLP*, 1st ed. 1923, 64, 65 (2d ed. 1926, 88, 89). Compare the changes made in the text of 1926 with the first edition. The commenting remark is to be found in both versions of the book, but not in the original publication in the *Bonner Festgabe für Ernst Zitelmann* (Munich/Leipzig 1923), 472, nor in the reprint in *PuB*, 17.

myth lies in the national." But this means neither that Schmitt shares the faith "of the national myth" nor that he refers to it for the sake of the nation, considers it in view of the nation, or supports it in the interest of the nation. Schmitt is not a theoretician of nationalism, but rather a political theologian. In the decisive respect, nationalism has a status for him no different from that of the "inferior mythology" of socialism. And Schmitt by no means leaves his readers, as long as they do not deliberately close their eyes to what is most important, in the dark about his fundamental distance from the national myth: "For political theology it is polytheism, just as every myth is polytheistic." Thus a deviation from the true theology, a fall from the right faith. "But," the historical agent concedes, "one cannot ignore it as a strong tendency in the present."[55] In the same sense Schmitt notes that between 1815 and 1918 a "development from dynastic to democratic legitimation" took place and "that the kind of legitimacy prevailing today is indeed democratic,"[56] without, however, forgetting for a moment that for political theology, according to that "immeasurably fruitful parallel between metaphysics and the theory of State," democracy has its "equivalent" in pantheism, in "immanence pantheism," or in "immanence philosophy."[57] Judging in light of this, pantheism, immanence philosophy, and polytheism seem to have no serious difficulties in being compatible with one another. Be that as it may. No theoretician who intended to support the sovereignty of the people would think of presenting the teaching of sovereignty that Schmitt presents, and it would not have occurred to anyone whose political thought revolves around the nation to develop the conception of the political that Schmitt develops.[58] If we turn to the political agent in the usual sense, no other image emerges. Just as the insight that democratic or plebiscite legitimacy is indispensable today as "State justification" and "sanction," "because today there is simply no other sanction,"[59] just as the insight into the political possibilities of the reference to democracy—

55. *GLP*, 65 (89); cf. *VL*, 238. Peterson writes in "Politik und Theologie": "It is just part of the peoples, the *gentes*, that they belong to metaphysical pluralism, polytheism, paganism" (Nichtweiß's transcription, 4).

56. *GLP*, 18 (39).

57. *PT*, 44–46, 52 (62–65, 76); cf. *D*, 142; *GLP*, 20 (41); *VL*, 79–80, 237–238; "Die legale Weltrevolution" [The Legal World Revolution], in *Der Staat* 21, no. 3 (1978): 397. See further Donoso's speech from January 30, 1850 (ed. Veuillot, *Œuvres de Donoso Cortés* [Lyon 1877], I, 394–395) and his letter to Cardinal Fornari from June 19, 1852 (ed. Maschke, *Essay über den Katholizismus, den Liberalismus und den Sozialismus* [Weinheim 1989], 309–312).

58. See Chapter II, 32–35, 61, and Chapter III, 67–71 above.

59. *LuL*, 93, 94.

which increases appreciably in his work from 1923 on[60]—hardly makes Schmitt a democrat, likewise the conviction that the stronger myth presently lies in "the national" does not make Schmitt a nationalist. For a nationalist, the identification with the nation forms the center of his own existence. For Schmitt this never held true: his center was occupied differently.[61] For that reason even his oft discussed "battle with Geneva and Versailles" is insufficient to prove that Schmitt was a nationalist. Taking a stand for the interests of one's nation or, to formulate it more in accordance with our case, for the interests of the State in which one lives is no proof of nationalism, but rather—under normal circumstances—a matter-of-course. Insofar as Schmitt's "battle with Geneva" went beyond this, it was more a battle against an institution, in which Schmitt saw a liberal instrument for the domestication of the political, than a battle for the nation; and insofar as his "battle with Versailles" stood out from the

60. Whereas in 1929 Schmitt thinks it necessary to protect fascism against the claim that it stands in opposition to democracy, he still writes in 1923: "Only Italian fascism broke theoretically and practically through this dominion <of democratic principles>. Apart from it, one will have to say that until now the democratic principle has been indisputably recognized" (*GLP*, 18). In 1926 this changes to: "Only Italian fascism apparently places no value on being 'democratic.' Apart from it, one will have to say that until now the democratic principle has been indisputably recognized universally" (2d ed., 39). In the penultimate paragraph of the book, it reads: "To this point there has been only one example for democracy's and parliamentarianism's being contemptuously pushed to the side with conscious reference to the myth, and that was an example of the irrational force of the myth" (64). In 1926 Schmitt replaces the 'democracy' which was contemptuously pushed to the side by Mussolini, with the 'democracy of mankind' (*Menschheitsdemokratie*; 2d ed., 89).

61. Cf. *G*, 283. In the "Entwurf eines Berichtes an [Draft of a Report to] P. Erich Przywara," which he wrote in "winter 1945–46" in the internment camp in Lichterfelde, Schmitt introduces himself to the Jesuit priest as follows: "I come to you, Honorable Father, with the request that you accept this report as a *depositum* that you will either keep with you or send somewhere else as seems fit to you given the abnormality of our situation today. The *depositum* concerns discoveries and insights that could arise only from long research and experiences and only from out of the innermost core of German events and could only be made by a *German Catholic*, i.e., by a German who had a legitimate share, who had complete *participatio, without identifying himself* [with Germany]" (Typescript Hauptstaatsarchiv Düsseldorf; my emphasis). Schmitt concludes the "report" with the request that Przywara "accept this letter in our fantastic age as if a wave had carried the map of a treasure island to you in a sealed bottle which some pirate had thrown into the sea, a wretched pirate whom you, however, nevertheless do not need to deny your priestly blessing, which he requests in his kind of piety and humility for the sake of our crucified God and his purest and most Holy Mother Mary." (Thus far the "report" could not be found in Przywara's literary estate. On the other hand, a letter of Schmitt's from October 10, 1959 has been retained, in which he says: "Fourteen years ago in the forsakenness of the camp your image appeared to me as that of a comforting angel." Concerning his contribution "Nomos-Nahme-Name" to the *Festschrift für Erich Przywara*, which he encloses with his letter to the theologian on the occasion of the latter's seventieth birthday, he writes: "After the letter from the camp from February 1946, this is, so to speak, the attempt at a second message to you, Honorable Reverend Father Przywara.")

consensus of that time in Germany which extended from the Left to the Right, it was in turn first and foremost a battle against the "system of Western liberal democracy." If one were to want to determine just how deep Schmitt's reference to "the national" actually went, it seems that greater importance must be attached to two further considerations: Once "history" had decided against the German nation and the country lay in ruins and division after 1945, Schmitt would not write anything, in the four decades in the seclusion of his "San Casciano," which would even remotely recall an "*Exhortatio ad capessendam Germaniam in libertatemque a barbaris vindicandam.*" But especially: could a nationalist get mixed up with Hitlerism in 1933, could he have been willing to serve the "total Führer-State" for years hence, could he subjugate the freedom, integrity, and honor of the nation to the arbitrariness of an individual and his acclaiming followers?

Let us return to the central question. The decision Schmitt made in the spring of 1933 was not the decision of a nationalist, but rather that of a political theologian. How was he able to reconcile it with his political theology? Ten years earlier he had made another decision the object of a public meditation. It concerned the Catholic Church immediately and expressly. He would therefore have been able to leave that decision to the discretion of the proper authorities and to take his bearings by their policy. Yet, as on so many occasions before and after, Schmitt instead behaved more "like a Protestant," neither respectful of the intermediate instances nor relying on representation, referring solely to his own faith or to the sovereign authority, emulating more the "Protestant theologian" from Denmark in seeking the Either-Or of the historical moment than satisfying the traditional rules of the Institution of Rome with which he identified himself. In 1923 Schmitt is haunted by the opposition between Western European education, morality, and civilization and Russian barbarism, an opposition that after the October Revolution seems to have its politically concrete intensification in the alternative: liberalism or Bolshevism. Schmitt knows that at issue is not the final, not that "great alternative" "which no longer allows any mediation." The situation is too confused, and the choice apparently still lacks the eschatological sharpening too much for Cardinal Newman's guiding principle to be directly applicable: *No medium between catholicity and atheism*.[62] What is to be done when atheism appears in very different forms? How is a decision to be made when the enemy can be discerned on several fronts? Schmitt does not underestimate the exceptional position of the Church: "*Sub*

62. *PT*, 49 (69).

specie of its duration that outlives everything else, here too the Catholic Church does not need to decide; here too it will be the *complexio* of all that survives. The Church is the heir. But," he continues following the reaffirmation of his confession, "there is nevertheless an unavoidable decision for the present day, for the current constellation, and for the present generation. Here the Church, even if it cannot declare itself in favor of any of the battling parties, really must take sides, just as, for example, in the first half of the nineteenth century it took the side of the counterrevolutionaries," that is the side of the political theologians Bonald, Maistre, Donoso Cortés.[63] To indicate with the necessary caution how the "unavoidable decision for the present day" has to turn out, Schmitt conjectures about the "decision" for a day long since past. He leaves the present and goes back half a century in history, back to the "symbolic outlying skirmish" that Bakunin fought against the *théologie politique de Mazzini*. "And here *I believe*," reads Schmitt's tangled answer, "that in that outlying battle of Bakunin's, the Catholic Church and the Catholic concept of humanity were on the side of the idea and Western European civilization, close to Mazzini and not close to the atheistic socialism of the anarchic Russian."[64]

It becomes even clearer just how tangled Schmitt's answer is when we recall that Mazzini's name can stand for liberalism or for the freemasonry which in the eighteenth century, as Schmitt remarks, was Catholicism's "last European adversary," but it also can stand—in the same breath with "idea," "morality," and "civilization"—for the "faith in God," for "religion" in the broader sense, and even for "national enthusiasm."[65] Only the decision against the barbarians of the "Russian republic of soviets," with its atheistic socialism, takes on comparably clear contours. To be sure, in the same passage Schmitt makes the statement: "I know that more Christianity can lie in the Russian hatred of Western European education than in liberalism or German Marxism, that great Catholics regarded liberalism as a more terrible enemy than open, socialist atheism, and that ultimately, perhaps, the strength for a new form that would shape even the economic-technological age could potentially lie in formlessness."[66] Hardly anything seems impossible, almost everything may prove right—or wrong—in the future. With these considerations,

63. *RK*, 79–80 (52).

64. *RK*, 80 (my emphasis). In the second edition of 1925 the last sentence of the text is formulated more cautiously: ". . . closer to Mazzini than to the atheistic socialism of the anarchic Russian" (53).

65. *RK*, 73, 75 (48, 49).

66. *RK*, 79 (52).

Schmitt has prepared the most important reasons that he can fall back on ten years later, in order to convince himself that going along with National Socialism after its victory in March 1933 can be justified by political theology.

Other factors are added over the turbulent decade. A few months after Schmitt had put his late option in favor of "Mazzini" to paper, he became witness to how the break of "national enthusiasm" away from the "ideology of Anglo-Saxon liberalism" occurred "on Italian soil."[67] Mussolini was neither liberal nor was he a Freemason. With Italian fascism a new political formation entered the European arena, a formation agreeable to Schmitt already because it behaved in a decidedly antiuniversalistic way and emphatically took up the cause of "defending one's own." In 1933 something analogous holds for National Socialism in Germany: The instrumentalization of the "national myth" as a promising strategy to counteract the realization of the terrifying apocalyptic vision of the "world-State," which seizes and devours everything. In addition, during the decade from 1923 to 1933 in which Schmitt, filled with admiration, followed Mussolini's career, his conviction grew that liberalism and Marxism agreed in essence or with regard to their "metaphysics"; for Marxism its liberal inheritance is said to have remained decisive, it was "only a case of the application of the liberal way of thinking proper to the nineteenth century." The synopsis of liberalism and Marxism as the "new faith" of the present—which arose out of a "century filled with illusion and fraud," had a stock of shared dogmas at its disposal and pursued a shared, antipolitical final purpose—had to let fascism and National Socialism appear to be the most resolved and, where the hopes for an "authoritarian solution" had actually failed, to be the sole political antipodes of any real significance.[68] A third element may have made Schmitt's justification to himself easier. Like no other political force, National Socialism referred to "historicity" and to "fate." What mass movement would have come closer to the "arcanum" that all historical truth is only true once? Was there not a considerable resonance here with Schmitt's own "historical thought," with his Christian faith in history? And might not at least an antidote to the overpowering "religion of technicity" have lain in the new faith in destiny, however diffuse, vulgar, and unchristian it may have looked? It is certain that National Socialism reaped approval and sympathy among Christian theologians—among Protestant and Catholic, more and less important theologians alike—precisely with its refer-

67. *GLP*, 65 (89).

68. Cf. "Wesen und Werden," 113 (*PuB*, 114); *BdP* III, 55–56.

ence to historicity and the primacy of historical action.[69] It built a bridge across the whole lot of them for the support of the "national movement." The "defense of one's own" and the hostile stance towards the "activistic metaphysics" of liberalism, as well as of Marxist socialism, contributed in turn to the "unavoidable decision for the present day" having the same outcome in 1933 for the political theologians Emanuel Hirsch and Friedrich Gogarten, for Schmitt's theological friends Karl Eschweiler and Hans Barion, for a Paul Althaus or Gerhard Kittel.

Five years later Schmitt had changed his mind in a number of ways. The treatise on the Leviathan, which he publishes on the occasion of July 11, 1938, is also a critique of the reigning regime. Little remains of the illusion of being able "to lead the leader" [*den Führer führen*], save the sad results that illusion had led to earlier. Schmitt no longer holds Party offices at the end of 1936 after *Das Schwarze Korps*[TN10] publicly "exposed" his Catholic background to the National Socialist authorities. If Schmitt says of Hobbes at the end of his treatise that he is "for us the genuine teacher of a great political experience" and defines "for us today the recognizably and constantly fruitful achievement" of the Englishman a few lines earlier to be "that of the great teacher in the battle against all kinds of indirect power," then Schmitt's experiences may have played a part in this singularly unambiguous and unqualified praise he bestows on Hobbes within the book, that is, the experiences he had gained in the first years of the Third Reich with the most diverse party subdivisions and National Socialist organizations, from the *Amt Rosenberg*[TN11] to the SS.

69. The only thing that Rudolf Bultmann, who did not support National Socialism, grants the latter in his lecture course *Theologische Enzyklopädie* in 1933 is, typically enough, the "concealed knowledge of the historicity of existence," which is inherent in the "Movement" and which places it in the tradition of the struggle for "historical consciousness" extending from Kierkegaard to dialectical theology: "The true positive strength of the Movement becomes a consciousness of its own in an ideology that threatens to cover it up and thereby ruin it. Its strength springs from a concealed knowledge of the historicity of existence, thus from the knowledge that the concrete historical conditions with their claim and the concrete historical decisions constitute the reality of life. That is why it turns away from idealism, rationalism, from liberalism and democracy, insofar as in them timeless ideas want to give life its challenge and reality and the particular is to be measured by the universal. [. . .] In the reaction against idealism and rationalism, however, the danger of falling into Romanticism and a materialistic biology is great. The concrete conditions of life that constitute our reality can do so only as *historical conditions*." *Theologische Enzyklopädie*, 64. Compare Gogarten, *Ich glaube an den dreieinigen Gott. Eine Untersuchung über Glauben und Geschichte* (Jena 1926), 43, 44–45, 78, 81, 100–102, 123, 180. Emanuel Hirsch, *Die gegenwärtige geistige Lage im Spiegel philosophischer und theologischer Besinnung. Akademische Vorlesungen zum Verständnis des deutschen Jahres 1933* (Göttingen 1934), 32–33, 35–36. *Christliche Freiheit und politische Bindung* (Hamburg 1935), 19. Konrad Weiss, "Die politische Spannung von Inbegriff und Geschichte," in *Die Schildgenossen* 13, no. 1 (1933): 39, 40, 42–43, 44.

The current reference of the attack on the *potestas indirecta*, regardless of the form in which it appears and makes its claim, in any case could hardly have escaped the notice of those contemporaries who were politically alert.[70] The same holds for the pointed "rendition" of relevant Hobbesian positions. For example, the statement that "the full assumption of political risk and in this sense the responsibility for the protection and security of the State's subjects always belongs especially to a rational State power. If the protection ceases, then the State also ceases and all duty to obey it ceases to be binding. Then the individual regains its 'natural' freedom."[71] Matters are more complicated where the talk is of Hobbes as a "spiritual forefather of the bourgeois legal and constitutional State."[72] There are at least new overtones here. In the assertion that Hobbes has "in the meantime" come to be "*recognized* as a theoretician of the 'positive legal State'"—an assertion Schmitt makes in reference to a remark by a National Socialist jurist from 1930, from the period before the jurist's conversion to National Socialism—resonates a belated note of respect for the "bourgeois legal State," which Schmitt had severely attacked a decade earlier and in whose destruction he actively participated from 1933 to 1936.[73] After five years of the "total Führer-State," the much-maligned "bourgeois legal State" appears in a less severe light, and the meaning of a formula such as *nulla poena, nullum crimen sine lege* re-

70. *L*, 131–132; cf. esp. 116–117.

71. *L*, 113.

72. *L*, 103, 114; cf. 100–102, 110–111, and esp. 70–72; consider Chapter III, 105, 108, 114 f. above.

73. "In the historical situation of the German nineteenth century, 'legal State' [*Rechtsstaat*] is the counterconcept of two kinds of State: the Christian State, thus one defined by *religion*, and the State understood as a realm of *morality* [Sittlichkeit], that is, the Prussian civil servant State of Hegel's philosophy of State. In the battle against these two opponents, the legal State goes out into the world. That is its provenance, its *principium*, or if I may say so: its race [*Rasse*]." "A Christian State was able to gain its totality and entirety from the religious faith of a then still thoroughly Christian people; the State as the realm of morality and of objective reason was likewise still capable of a totality and in any case superior to bourgeois society; the legal State of the nineteenth century is, by contrast, nothing but the neutral State which has become the means and tool of individualistic bourgeois society." "Was bedeutet der Streit um den 'Rechtsstaat'?", 191 and 192. Cf. 198, 199, 201; further *Fünf Leitsätze für die Rechtspraxis* [*Five Guiding Principles for Legal Practice*] (Berlin 1933), esp. guiding principles 4 and 5; "Nationalsozialistisches Rechtsdenken" [National Socialist Legal Thought], in *Deutsches Recht* 4, no. 10 (May 25, 1934): 229; "Der Führer schützt das Recht" [The Führer Protects the Law], in *Deutsche Juristen-Zeitung* 39, no. 15 (August 1, 1934): col. 946, 947, 948, 949 (*PuB*, 200, 201, 203); *DA*, 35, 58–59; "Die Verfassung der Freiheit" [The Constitution of Freedom], in *Deutsche Juristen-Zeitung* 40, no. 19 (October 1, 1935): col. 1133 and 1135; the Epilogue to *Disputation über den Rechtsstaat*, 86, 88.

quires neither an extended jurisprudential discussion, nor an explicit defense against the postulate *nullum crimen sine poena*.[74]

Of incomparably greater significance is the fundamental confrontation with the "security State" of the Leviathan which Schmitt undertakes in 1938. The politically explosive quality particularly of the argument Schmitt develops, as we have seen, *e contrario*—where he argues that *post Christum* the "unity of religion and politics" can no longer be established by "politics," based on the mere "work of men"—requires no commentary. Thus what is perhaps the most important sentence in the book aimed at the regime reads: *Nothing divine can be forced externally*. In the two lines that immediately follow, Schmitt evokes the "political situation of a Seneca" under Nero. He begins the paragraph where that evocation is found in a hardly less provocative way: "But if the public power really wants to be only public, if State and denomination push aside the inward faith into the private [sphere]," or—as every reader can add for himself—if they no longer reach that faith, "then the soul of a people sets out on the 'mysterious path' that leads inward. Then the counterforce of silence and stillness grows."[75] What could we add to the political-theological thrust of a book that recalls clearly enough the "ultimate superiority of the inward over the outward" and of the "other world over the secular world" and that emblematically strengthened gives expression to the belief that the Leviathan hangs from God's fishhook?

The changes of the Christian Epimetheus do not extend to his anti-Semitism. Despite its turn against the faith or errant faith of National Socialism, *Der Leviathan in der Staatslehre des Thomas Hobbes* is an anti-Semitic book. Its anti-Semitic attacks are not merely lipservice so as to disguise the critique of the regime. Schmitt uses various rhetorical devices in order to link positions he opposes to Judaism, beginning with the split of Hobbes's own position into that of a well-meaning Englishman who wants "to stay within the faith of his people" and that of a "Jewish philosopher" named Spinoza who wants to promote the *libertas philosophandi*. In the dramatic narrative of the erosion and ultimate destruction

74. *L*, 111, 113–114, 115. In 1940 Schmitt does not include the essay "Der bürgerliche Rechtsstaat" from 1928 in the collection *Positionen und Begriffe*. For Schmitt's earlier critique of the sentence *nulla poena sine lege*, see "Nationalsozialistisches Rechtsdenken," 228 and "Der Weg des deutschen Juristen" [The Path of the German Jurist], in *Deutsche Juristen-Zeitung* 39, no. 11 (June 1, 1934): col. 692–693.

75. *L*, 94–95. In *ECS*, 21 Schmitt cites these two sentences in a distorted form, which does not change the fact that the intention Schmitt ascribes the passage in 1945–46 coincides with his intention in 1938. A careful reader of the entire book and of pp. 94–95 in particular could have discerned that intention during the Third Reich. See Chapter III, 113 ff. above with nn. 138 and 139.

of the "unity of religion and politics," in which Schmitt dresses his argumentation for the "failure" of Hobbes's enterprise, the main roles of the three most spectacular wrongdoers are given to Spinoza, Mendelssohn, and Stahl.[76] A drama of villainy with such a cast may have been a timely and an effective cloaking for a quite untimely endeavor. But it was not just rhetorical cloaking. The moral indignation with which Schmitt encounters the philosopher Spinoza reaches into the innermost core of his being,[77] and the bitter hatred with which he pursues the political theologian "Stahl-Jolson" likewise goes far beyond mere rhetoric.[78] It is

76. *L*, 16–18, 86–89, 92–94, 106–110, 118, 124.

77. Schmitt's moral indignation finds expression in an entry on the first page of Leo Strauss's book on Spinoza where Schmitt records six passages which were particularly important to him. The last one concerns a lengthy note (228), which he recalls once again elsewhere in a context of central importance (see Chapter III, n. 148). In it Strauss explains the "joy of the *spectator* Spinoza" with the help of a biographical account of the pleasure Spinoza took in observing the battle between spiders and flies. To the reference at the beginning of the book Schmitt adds the exclamation: *atrocious.* Three pages prior to the example of Spinoza's "atrocious" attitude, Schmitt notes in the text (in a passage where Strauss discusses Spinoza's conception of natural right) Spinoza's phrase, of which he says in the *Glossarium* that it is the "the most audacious insult ever to be inflicted upon God and man." See Chapter I, 15 f. above.

78. From 1933 to 1938 Stahl is the enemy whom Schmitt most frequently attacks by name and reviles personally. The attacks begin in the third edition of *Der Begriff des Politischen*: "This conservative man changed his faith and his people, changed his name and then taught the Germans about piety, continuity, and tradition. He found the German Hegel 'empty and untrue,' 'tasteless,' and 'hopeless'" (44; cf. Chapter III, n. 99 above). In the Conclusion to *Die deutsche Rechtswissenschaft im Kampf gegen den jüdischen Geist* (*Das Judentum in der Rechtswissenschaft*, no. 1 [Berlin 1936]), Schmitt says of the "Jew Stahl-Jolson," among other things: "It is completely wrong to make him out to be an exemplary, conservative Jew compared with other, later Jews, who unfortunately were no longer so. Therein lies a dangerous failure to appreciate the essential insight that with every change of the general situation, with every new period of history, a change of the general behavior of the Jews, a *change of masks* possessing demonic enigmaticness also occurs so quickly that we grasp it only with the most careful attention; by comparison, the question about the subjective credulity of a particular participating Jewish individual is altogether uninteresting" (33; also *Deutsche Juristen-Zeitung* 41, no. 20 [October 15, 1936]: col. 1198). See further *SBV*, 30; "Was bedeutet der Streit um den 'Rechtsstaat'?" 192–193; the Epilogue to *Disputation über den Rechtsstaat*, 86; *PuB*, 275, 293. In 1938 Schmitt believed it necessary to defend himself against critics of his campaign: "They slung mud at me because of my remark that 'I cannot look into the soul of this Stahl-Jolson' (cf. *Deutsche Juristen-Zeitung* [1936]: col. 1197), but they never asked how I came to make such a remark" (*L*, 109 n.). The remark Schmitt cites—as so often—with a seemingly small, but in fact significant change, clearly did not give occasion to ask what Schmitt called for: "The Jews notice quickly where German substance is, which attracts them. We need not consider this characteristic to be to their credit for us to exercise restraint here. It is simply the general situation of the Jew, based in his parasitic, tactical, and merchant relation to German intellectual treasures. Even such a gruesome, uncanny change of masks as that on which Stahl-Jolson's entire existence is based, can then no longer disconcert anyone. When it is stressed again and again that this man was 'subjectively honest,' that may be, yet I must add that I cannot

possible that Schmitt judged the individual activities of the three representatives he selected as examples of the "tireless spirit of the Jew" and his work of determined "undermining" differently than he staged them for his purposes. But there is no question that he ascribes to "the Jews"—next to the philosophers—a far-reaching influence on the modern process of dechristianization. With this process Schmitt considers the nearly two millennia long battle between Christianity and Judaism to have entered into a new phase, a battle that takes on an exceptional position among the battles of faith in world history. For Judaism is, according to a famous phrase by Bruno Bauer, whom Schmitt esteemed not least because of his writings on the Jews,[79] "the incorporated doubt of the heavenly origin of Christianity, the religious enemy of the religion which announced itself as the completed, solely legitimate religion, and could not even overcome the small flock from whose middle it emerged."[80] Judaism has denied from the beginning and without fail that "Jesus is the Christ." Regarding its deepest roots, Schmitt's enmity towards the Jews grows out of his faith in revelation. It stands in the terror-filled tradition of Christian anti-Judaism, which by no means induces him to keep his distance from the National Socialists' enmity towards the Jews, an enmity that gains its sustenance from a quite different source. Considered more closely, one has to say on the contrary that enmity towards "the Jews" is what binds Schmitt to National Socialism the longest. A few days

---

look into the soul of this *Jew and that we do not have any access whatsoever to the innermost essence of the Jews*" (col. 1197; my emphasis).

79. In addition to the *Judenfrage* of 1843, which became known through Marx's response to it, *Das Judentum in der Fremde* (Berlin 1863) already contains the entire arsenal of the anti-Semitic polemic of the first half of the twentieth century. In his "*depositum*" to Erich Przywara from the winter of 1945–46, which names Bruno Bauer "in the first place," Schmitt mentions both treatises and then confides to the priest: "In a book by the emigrant Karl Löwith, *Von Hegel bis Nietzsche*, the spiritual-historical spoor signified by Bruno Bauer, is well noted. But Löwith suppresses Bruno Bauer's writings on the Jews, and thereby a specifically German-Protestant concern, so that the book *Von Hegel bis Nietzsche* wears the blindfold worn by medieval statues representing the synagogue." In public Schmitt exercises caution: "Nor have diligent scholars, such as Ernst Barnikol, and *spiritual-historical initiates*, such as Karl Löwith, succeeded in laying bare the core of his <Bruno Bauer's> spiritual existence . . . . Löwith completely disregards *essential questions* in Bruno Bauer" (*DC*, 99 and 99 n. 1; my emphasis).

80. Bruno Bauer, *Die Judenfrage* (Brunswick 1843), 114. "The hostility of the Christian world towards Judaism is thus perfectly understandable and based on their mutual, essential relationship. Neither of the two can retain and recognize the other; if the one exists, then the other does not exist; each of the two believes that it is the absolute truth, and thus if it recognizes the other and disowns itself, it denies that it is the truth" (16). Need we add that Schmitt does not share Bauer's belief in the historical sublation of the conflict in a higher truth? Cf. Yosef Hayim Yerushalmi, *Freud's Moses: Judaism Terminable and Interminable* (New Haven 1991), 91–92, 94.

after joining the NSDAP on May 1, 1933, Schmitt audibly joins in the chorus of anti-Semitic polemic for the first time.[81] And he remains true to anti-Semitism above and beyond the collapse of the Third Reich, to an anti-Semitism which knows how to track down "the Jew" behind every "mask" and does not accept any difference of denomination, spirit, or political decision. At the peak of his public effectiveness in the "battle against the Jewish spirit," at the conference "Das Judentum in der Rechtswissenschaft" [Judaism in Jurisprudence], which he organized and which took place on October 3–4, 1936, Schmitt reveals in the midst of the ugliest tirades he would ever publish, what he, Schmitt, wants to read into the battle of the National Socialists against "Judaism and Bolshevism": "But the most profound and ultimate meaning of this battle," he states at the outset of his inaugural address, "and thus also of our work today, lies expressed in the Führer's sentence: 'In fending off the Jew, I fight for the work of the Lord.'"[82] The sentence in which the most profound and ultimate meaning of the battle against Judaism is said to *lie expressed*, without him who "expressed" the meaning ever having to have *understood* it, the sole sentence from *Mein Kampf* that Schmitt quotes literally and italicizes, is so important to him that he cites it yet a second time and concludes his closing remarks to the conference with it.[83] This

81. "Das gute Recht der deutschen Revolution" [The Legitimacy of the German Revolution], lead article from May 12, 1933 in *Westdeutscher Beobachter*, and "Die deutschen Intellektuellen," lead article from May 31, 1933 in the same newspaper. Cf. "Was bedeutet der Streit um den 'Rechtsstaat'?", 191–193; "Die Verfassung der Freiheit," col. 1133–1135; the Epilogue to *Disputation über den Rechtsstaat*, 86; *VGO*, 64; "Das 'allgemeine deutsche Staatsrecht' als Beispiel rechtswissenschaftlicher Systembildung" ["General German State Law" as an Example of the Formation of a Jurisprudential System], in *Zeitschrift für die gesamte Staatswissenschaft* 100, no. 1–2 (1940): 13–14, 22. See n. 78 and Chapter II, n. 101 above.

82. *Die deutsche Rechtswissenschaft im Kampf gegen den jüdischen Geist*, "Eröffnung der wissenschaftlichen Vorträge durch den Reichsgruppenwalter Prof. Dr. Carl Schmitt," 14. In his Conclusion, Schmitt says: "If for objective reasons it is necessary to cite Jewish authors, then only with the addition 'Jewish'. The *healing exorcism* will set in already with the mere mention of this word 'Jewish'" (30; my emphasis). Prior to this he had explained: "The addition of the word and the designation 'Jewish' is no formality, but rather something essential because, after all, we cannot prevent the Jewish author from using the German language. Otherwise the purification of our law literature will not be possible. Whoever writes 'Stahl-Jolson' today has brought about more thereby in a genuinely scholarly and clear way than through lengthy expositions against the Jews which move in abstract general phrases and by which not a single Jew feels affected *in concreto*" (30; *Deutsche Juristen-Zeitung*, col. 1195–1196).

83. *Die deutsche Rechtswissenschaft*, Conclusion, 34 (*Deutsche Juristen-Zeitung*, col. 1199). The quotation may be found in *Mein Kampf*, 70. From the essay by Thomas Heerich and Manfred Lauermann, "Der Gegensatz Hobbes-Spinoza bei Carl Schmitt (1938)," in *Studia Spinozana* 7 (1991; *recte* 1993): 112 n. 23, I gather that the "saying of the Führer" from *Mein Kampf* was also used by Church dignitaries at public events, thus, e.g., as the

attribution of meaning, too, belongs to the "bad, unworthy, and yet authentic case of a Christian Epimetheus." For it, too, Schmitt will claim to have taken the risk of an "anticipation of a commandment that is to be obeyed" and to have attempted to answer the "call of history." Can an action that wants to listen to "history" rule out that anything or anyone serves the "work of the Lord"?

The decisive features of Schmitt's enmity towards "the Jews" go unchanged after 1945. To be sure, he exercises public restraint. One part of his previous "battle against the Jewish spirit" is continued in his "campaign against the law" and is expressed under the *signum* of the thought of the "*nomos*";[84] another part finds its expression in his efforts to articulate a "Christian view of history" that accounts for the political-theological situation. Even after he determined his case to be that of a Christian Epimetheus—thus of a Christian who knows himself to be caught up in historical errors and who, one can assume, was able to discern at least some of them after the fact—Schmitt believes he has to fend off "the Jews." From the posthumously published "notes from the years 1947–1951" we learn that he sees himself, in addition to everything else, now persecuted by "Christ's murderers."[85] The "undermining" of the Christian State, Church, and peoples, of which he accused the Jews in the thirties is not judged any differently than before, although the talk is no longer of the "virtuosity of mimicry," the "adaptability of the Jew" which takes on "enormous dimensions," or a "change of masks of demonic enigmaticness" which is proper to the "general behavior of the Jew." Induced by a remark he feels to be a "nasty dig," Schmitt notes concerning the "'Stahl' case" that it "harmed [him] greatly."[86] But of the former attacks on the "boldest man" of the nineteenth century "Jewish front," on which "each [occupied] his field of operations in the economy, journalism, art, and science," of the alleged demasking of the "Jewish philosopher," whom "the Christian sacrament of baptism [served] not only as it

---

motto of the "Closing Festivities of the Catholic Youth Gathering" in the Berlin-Neukölln stadium on August 20, 1933.

84. *G*, 64; cf. 57, 85, 154, 209, 287. "Nationalsozialistisches Rechtsdenken," 226–227; *DA*, 9, 15, 31, 35; *Die deutsche Rechtswissenschaft*, Conclusion, 28 (*Deutsche Juristen-Zeitung*, col. 1193); *VGO*, 12; "Das 'allgemeine deutsche Staatsrecht,'" 19, 22, 24; "Die Formung des französischen Geistes," 7–8; *Die Lage der europäischen Rechtswissenschaft*, 23, 30 (*VA*, 411, 422–423); *NdE*, 38–42, 44–45; *VA*, 449 and 502; "Nomos-Nahme-Name," 96–97, 98–100, 104.

85. *G*, 232; cf. 18, 61, 91, 169, 241, 255, 319.

86. *G*, 150. Schmitt does not use the name *Stahl* (the "Stahl" case) again after 1945. As a result he need not publicly dissociate himself from his practice of insisting on *Stahl-Jolson* (see n. 82 above).

did the young Heine as an '*entrée billet*' to 'society,' but as a pass for admission into the sainthood of a still very solid German State" and who "from high offices" was even able "to confuse the innermost core of this State, kingdom, nobility, and Protestant Church ideologically and to paralyze them spiritually"—Schmitt apparently has nothing to take back regarding any of these accusations.[87] That Schmitt is no less convinced in 1950 than in 1938 that Stahl worked "along the general lines of his people" and continued "purposively and instinctively" what Spinoza is said to have begun, is suggested by the following note, which under the given circumstances could hardly be clearer: "*Salus ex Judaeis? Perditio ex Judaeis?* First of all, enough of these pushy *Judaeis*! When we [Christians] were divided among ourselves, the Jews sub-introduced themselves. So long as that has not been grasped, there can be no salvation. Spinoza was the first to sub-introduce himself."[88]

Thus nothing less than salvation depends on whether one grasps just what influence "the Jews" have on the Christian peoples, in what way "the Jews" meddle in Christian affairs, how "the Jews" have wormed their way into Christian history. To be able to discern the hidden agenda and the ultimate goal of their "sub-introduction," of their "neutralizations," and their other machinations, one must know how "the Jews" interpret world history. Schmitt tells of this in *Land und Meer*: "According to the medieval interpretations of Jewish secret teachings, according to the so-called cabalists, world history is a battle between the mighty whale, the Leviathan, and the land animal, the Behemoth, which is just as strong and which was imagined as a bull or an elephant." On Schmitt's account, the cabalists think that both fighting powers kill each other. "But the Jews, they say further, stand on the sidelines and watch the battle. They eat the flesh of the animals that kill each other, skin them, build beautiful tents out of the fur, and celebrate a festive, millennial banquet. That is how the Jews interpret world history. The cabalist most frequently quoted for this interpretation of history [in terms of] the banquet of the Leviathan is Isaac Abravanel."[89] This exposure of "the Jews'" secret

87. *L*, 108–109.

88. *G*, 290.

89. *Land und Meer. Eine weltgeschichtliche Betrachtung* [*Land and Sea: A World-Historical Reflection*] (Leipzig 1942), 9–10 (2d, rev. ed. [Stuttgart 1954], 8). Thereafter Schmitt tells the reader about Abravanel: "He lived from 1437 to 1508, in the age of great discoveries, was the treasurer first of the King of Portugal, then of the King of Castille, and died in 1508 a great man in Venice. He thus knew the world and its riches, and knew what he said." Schmitt does not mention that Abravanel was forced to emigrate three times during his life and died separated from his family. For Abravanel's biography, in which the persecution of the Jews in the course of the Catholic Inquisition plays a decisive role, cf. J. B.

agenda puts every reader of Schmitt's "world-historical reflection" in a position to "grasp" their activities in the desired sense, whether Spinoza or Stahl or Disraeli is of concern, the latter of whom it is said in the same book that he was "an Abravanel of the nineteenth century, an initiate, a wise man from Zion."[90] In comparison with Stahl, Benjamin Disraeli not only ascended to a considerably higher and more influential "office" but also gave rise to an even more sustained and more dangerous "ideological confusion": "Many purposive suggestions and formulations came from him that were greedily swallowed up by non-Jews."[91] The one that filled Schmitt with indignation into the last years of his life more than any other is located in Disraeli's novel *Tancred: or, The New Crusade* and reads: *Christianity is Judaism for the multitude, but still it is Judaism.*[92] Schmitt sees himself challenged not only by this claim to the superiority of Judaism,[93] but even more so and above all by the fact that Disraeli's "purposive suggestion and formulation" makes Christianity appear to be a tool of Judaism and declares Christian history to be a part of Jewish history or its continuation by other means.[94] In view of such an interpretation of the relationship between Judaism and Christianity, an interpretation that also "was enthusiastically propagated by non-Jews and

---

Trend and H. M. Loewe, eds., *Isaac Abravanel: Six Lectures* (Cambridge 1937), xx–xxvii. Concerning his political theology, for which Christian-hierocratic influences were determinative, see ibid., 105, 107, 109–110, 117, 122–129. "His soul was the soul of a priest" (Leo Strauss).

90. *LuM*, 67 (cf. 2d ed., 56).

91. *LuM*, 67, in the second edition, this is replaced with: "Much of what he said about race as a key to world history and about Judaism and Christianity was enthusiastically propagated by non-Jews and non-Christians" (56).

92. Benjamin Disraeli, *Tancred: or, The New Crusade* (London 1847), VI, 4; ed. Langdon-Davies (London/Edinburgh 1904), 505. Schmitt calls Disraeli's sentence an *infandum scelus* (*G*, 268). Jacob Taubes seeks not only to harden the superiority of his own political theology, but also to strike a blow to Schmitt in the most sensitive spot when in his obituary for the "Apocalyptist of the Counterrevolution" he claims: "For Schmitt Christianity was 'Judaism for the peoples,' against whose power he always desired to rise up. But Schmitt saw ever more profoundly how impotent such a 'protest' against God and history is." *Ad Carl Schmitt. Gegenstrebige Fügung* (Berlin 1987), 25; cf. 51–52, 60, 61, 75 and *Die Politische Theologie des Paulus* (Munich 1993), 96, 105.

93. At another point Disraeli has the Jewess Eva say to Tancred: "We agree that half Christendom worships a Jewess, and the other half a Jew. Now let me ask you one more question. Which should you think should be the superior race; the worshipped or the worshippers?" *Tancred*, III, 4, 232.

94. "Sons of Israel, when you recollect that you created Christendom, you may pardon the Christians even their Autos da Fè!" *Tancred*, VI, 4, 510; cf. III, 4, 231; see also Bruno Bauer, *Disraelis romantischer und Bismarcks sozialistischer Imperialismus* (Chemnitz 1882), 52–56.

non-Christians,"[95] the reflection on the "knowledge of the meaning of Christian history" takes on the greatest importance for Schmitt. It comprises the recollection of "what it meant politically-historically that the Jews cried out before the crucifixion of the Savior: 'We have no king but Caesar' (John 19:15)." Schmitt does not express, he does not explain, what "every theologian of the Christian Middle Ages knew."[96] But the meaning of his purposive suggestion and considered formulation is not difficult to discern.

The political-theological battle that Schmitt wages in the forties and fifties is essentially a battle for the interpretation of history. At first this holds true of the battle with Judaism, which leads to a confrontation over the legitimacy of Christian succession and finally concerns the place "the Jews" are to occupy in Christian history. In question in this connection is on the one hand the interpretive sovereignty over the meaning and course of world history, on the other hand the active "participation in it," the orientation and effectiveness of historical action itself. It is certainly no coincidence that Schmitt calls the central figure of thought [*Denkfigur*] of his late speculations on the theology of history, that is, the notion of "restrainer" or "*katechon*," for the first time by name in the book in which he "reveals" the cabalist "secret teaching" of the millennial banquet of the Leviathan and the hope bound up with it that world history can be hastened.[97] Nor is it presumably a mere coincidence that Schmitt uses the publication of the work *Meaning in History* by Karl Löwith, whom he had recently included among the "initiates,"[98] as an opportunity to expound the "possibilities of a Christian view of history" in the most concentrated form and to defend it with the greatest determination. But Schmitt's battle for the interpretation of history is not limited to the bat-

95. In his *Notes* Schmitt speaks occasionally of "Disraelites" (*G*, 142). On December 12, 1941 he presents Ernst Jünger with a copy of Alfred Schuler's *Fragmente und Vorträge aus dem Nachlaß* (Leipzig 1940), edited and with a lengthy introduction by Ludwig Klages. In his dedication to Jünger, Schmitt characterizes Klages's introduction as "the threefold effort of an envious German, of a redeemer swollen with poison, and of a Disraeli-devout enemy of the Jews" (Ernst Jünger, "Autor und Autorschaft–Nachträge," in *Scheidewege* 17 [1987–88]: 192). Klages, the "Disraeli-devout enemy of the Jews," claims "that regardless of the concealing of the state of affairs, which is practiced intentionally by the Jews and unintentionally by the majority of Christians, so-called Christianity was and is in every form just one of the *tools* of Judah" (*Fragmente und Vorträge*, 44). In his battle against the "Judaism in Christianity" Klages refers explicitly to Disraeli's remark that Christianity is "Judaism for the multitude" (44–45). "But whoever has not seen the Judaism in Christianity, he has not seen it at all" (49).

96. *NdE*, 33; cf. Erich Przywara, *Humanitas. Der Mensch gestern und morgen* (Nuremberg 1952), 723–724, and Bultmann, *Das Evangelium des Johannes*, 515.

97. *LuM*, 11–12, 56 (10, 47).

98. *DC*, 99; see n. 79 above.

tle with Judaism and against "the Jews." It is directed at the conceptions of progress propounded by the Enlightenment, liberalism, and Marxism. It is aimed at the "unhistorical" thought in paganism and neopaganism. It opposes the eternal return of ancient, as well as Nietzschean, provenance. In Schmitt's essay on Löwith's book, the entire range of oppositions is marked out in the most confined space. And nowhere else does the shared core out of which they grow emerge more sharply.

The decisive challenge that Schmitt perceives in *Meaning in History* is represented by Löwith's thesis: "the message of the New Testament is not an appeal to historical action, but to repentance."[99] Schmitt opposes "Löwith's sentence with another, which should keep every philosophical, ethical, and other *neutralization* at a distance." It reads: "In its *essential core* Christendom is not a morality and not a doctrine, not a sermon calling to repentance and not a religion in the sense of comparative religious studies, but rather *a historical event of infinite, unpossessable, unoccupiable uniqueness.*" In order neither to allow any doubt to arise about the political character of the statement nor to allow there to be any lack of clarity about the fact that he is speaking of a *miracle*, Schmitt adds three more sentences: "It is *the incarnation in the Virgin*. The Christian creed speaks of historical events. Pontius Pilate is there *essentially* in the right place and not merely an unlucky soul who in some strange way strayed there."[100] Schmitt need not expressly recall the questions raised by the representative of the Roman government according to John 18 and 19, nor the answers he received. The oppositions that separate Schmitt from Judaism, paganism, and philosophy are all contained in his answer to Löwith.[101] Likewise his opposition to the "progressivist" reflection on history and even his later rejection of a historicism that wants to be nothing but historicism, that is, a historical "theory" of the historical. Beyond that and against the backdrop of the unchangeable determination of his own faith in revelation, Schmitt can only applaud Löwith's investigation of the "theological implications of the philosophy of history" and greet several of its conclusions heartily. Thus he is "convinced, with Karl

99. *Meaning in History: The Theological Implications of the Philosophy of History* (Chicago 1949), 196. This is the sole passage in Löwith's book to which Schmitt refers with a page number. In the subsequent paragraph Löwith writes: "If we understand, as we must, Christianity in the sense of the New Testament and history in our modern sense, i.e., as a continuous process of human action and secular developments, a 'Christian history' is nonsense. The only, though weighty, excuse for this inconsistent compound of a Christian history is to be found in the fact that the history of the world has continued its course of sin and death in spite of the eschatological event, message, and consciousness" (197).

100. "Drei Möglichkeiten," 930 (my emphasis).

101. See Chapter III, 119 above.

Löwith, that paganism is not capable of historical thought because it thinks cyclically,"[102] and he especially agrees with him "that the Enlightenment and positivist faith in progress was only secularized Judaism and Christianity and derived its '*eschata*' from them." Another of Löwith's statements gives Schmitt occasion to emphasize the unassimilability of divine Providence and human planning.[103] Schmitt sees the specific actuality of Löwith's critique of the philosophy of history, however, in the Promethians' making of great plans which fall back on clichés taken from the philosophy of history, in order to "give meaning, or better: posit meaning," so that they then can prove that they have the future on their side.[104] The positings of meaning underlying the great plans for the recreation of all things past appears to Schmitt to be all the more threatening inasmuch as they are common to both the East and the West, just as West and East meet in the common aim, each in its own way, to bring about the unity of the world in which history comes to its end.

That we have yet to reach the end of history we owe, on Schmitt's faith, to the effectiveness of the *katechon*, which is spoken of for the first time in the "mysterious passage of Paul in the Second Letter to the Thessalonians."[105] Schmitt relies on the "notion of a force that restrains the end and suppresses the Evil One." Put more precisely: he believes in the uninter-

102. "Drei Möglichkeiten," 928; concerning the concrete addressee of Schmitt's critique, see Helmut Quaritsch, ed., *Complexio Oppositorum. Über Carl Schmitt* (Berlin 1988), 154–156. With his praise Schmitt had stressed the following about the Christian Romantic J. A. Kanne already in 1918: "The spiritual actuality of this man lies in his having resolutely made the leap from the eternal circles of the lawfulness [focused on by] the philosophy of nature and from the infinite recurrences and developments of history to the paradox of Christianity and thereby found his way out of the prison of his reckless egoism" (Epilogue to Kanne, *Aus meinem Leben*, 68). Cf. "Die geschichtliche Struktur," 146–148; *G*, 160, 199, 272, 286.

103. "Thus we understand Löwith's infinitely significant sentence: The further we go back from today into the history of human reflection on history, the more the notion of planning ceases. A divine Providence which man can check or even calculate is after all only a feature of human planning" (928).

104. "Drei Möglichkeiten," 927, 928. "The planning and steering elite construe themselves, and the masses steered by them, with the help of meanings given by the philosophy of history. All mass propaganda seeks its evidence in the proof that it is on the side of things to come. All mass faith is only faith in being on the right path, whereas the opponent is not because time and future and development work against him. And even despair finds its *dernier cri* only in the threat that world history has lost its meaning" (927). It is easy to understand why Schmitt was outraged at the title "Drei Stufen historischer Sinngebung" chosen by the editors (cf. Chapter I, n. 56 above).

105. "Drei Möglichkeiten," 929. Schmitt refers to the *katechon* [neuter], *quid detineat*, in 2 Th 2:6, or to the *katechon* [masculine], *qui tenet*, in 2 Th 2:7. On the history of the exegesis of this passage in Paul, cf. Ernst von Dobschütz, *Die Thessalonicher-Briefe* (Göttingen 1909), 278 ff.

rupted succession of the historical bearers of this force. "One must," he notes in December 1947, "be able to name the κατέχων for every epoch of the past 1948 years. The position has never gone unoccupied, otherwise we would no longer exist." The necessity of the restrainer, to whom Schmitt returns again and again from 1942 on,[106] arises from the failing of the prophesied final battle between Christ and the Antichrist and therewith from the delay of Christ's return. Thus Schmitt "knows" that the restrainer exists but he does not know who the restrainer is. Nor does he know who the restrainer was. For that one must be able to name the *katechon* for every epoch does not mean that one can actually name him. From the *Imperium Romanum* down to the Jesuit Order, Schmitt can offer a number of quite different candidates. In historical retrospect his preferred example, the Christian Empire of the Holy Roman Reich of the German Nation, still looks to be a comparatively clear case. Of course, the title of restrainer is no less generously granted to the Byzantine Empire. Are there perhaps two, three, or many *katechons* at the same time? Schmitt seems to incline towards this view. He is also able to imagine "temporary, transitory, dispersedly fragmentary holders of this task." The possibilities are multiplied immensely thereby. Especially as Schmitt cannot decide whether he should suspect the *katechon* in institutions or in natural persons. Was the empire the "holder" of the task? Or were rather the individual office holders? Or were several, while others were not? For example, Emperor Rudolf II of Hapsburg, whom Schmitt names as the restrainer for the period prior to the Thirty Years' War? And how would matters stand concerning the suppressive strength of the *Imperium Romanum* in the "concrete situation" of a Nero? "Perhaps," we learn, "the Jesuit Order was the κατέχων. But since 1814?" But then perhaps it was not. What if against its will the Jesuit Order were to have been a hastener? Anything seems possible. Schmitt does not shy away from also speaking of the old Emperor Franz Joseph at the "end of the superannuated Hapsburg Reich" or the Czech President Masaryk "on a correspondingly smaller scale," or, "for Poland," Józef Pilsudski as "a kind of '*kat-echon*.'" Schmitt's talk and thought, which want to be nothing but "historical," "concrete," "situational," evidently get lost in a generality that can no longer be distinguished from subjective arbitrari-

106. "Vous connaissez ma théorie du κατέχων, elle date de 1932. Je crois qu'il y a en chaque siècle un porteur concret de cette force et qu'il s'agit de le trouver. Je me garderai d'en parler au théologiens, car je connais le sort déplorable du grand et pauvre Donoso Cortés. Il s'agit d'une présence totale cachée sous les voiles de l'histoire." *G*, 80. I am not in a position to determine whether the dating of the conception at 1932 is correct. As far as I can tell, the expression appears for the first time in Schmitt's writings in 1942.

ness. Yet if the notion of the force, *qui tenet*, does not permit a concrete orientation, it nevertheless provides Schmitt, on his own testimony, with a sense of security: "I believe in the *katechon*; for me he is the sole possibility for a Christian to understand history and find it meaningful."[107]

The faith in the *katechon* helps Schmitt to preserve his faith in the truth of revelation and to remain in harmony with himself. How high he estimates the notion of the restraining and suppressive force in this respect is revealed by, among other things, two judgments Schmitt makes of theoreticians to whom he knows himself to be closely related in faith. Of Donoso Cortés he says that the political theologian from Spain "failed *theologically* because this concept remained unknown to him." Because he knew no *katechon*, Tocqueville lacked in turn the "sense of security [provided by] the history of salvation," a security which could have saved his historical idea "from *despair*." Therefore Tocqueville, in distinction to Schmitt, did "not become what he—more than anyone else—seemed predestined to be: a Christian Epimetheus."[108] The notion of the *katechon* achieves three things. First, it "explains" the delay of the *Parousia*, it offers an answer to the question as to why there is still "history." For that purpose, Paul's expression was originally introduced. Second, it protects historical action from despondency and despair in view of a seemingly overpowering historical process that is progressing towards its end. Third, and conversely, it protects historical action from the disdain for politics and history in the certainty of promised victory. Thus for Schmitt the *katechon* is simultaneously the complement and correction of the "genuine, ever-present, and necessary eschatology."[109] For the "living expectation of the immediately impending end seems to rob all history of meaning and gives rise to an eschatological paralysis, of which there are many examples in history."[110] The figure of thought of the "restrainer" forges a link between eschatological faith and the consciousness of "historicity."

Why is it so important to Schmitt that history be prolonged? Why is the supposed *katechon* due such outstanding attention since he "restrains" not only the temporary dominion of the Antichrist, but at the same time the return of the victorious Christ? Does the relative autonomy

107. *LuM*, 11–12, 56 (10, 47); "Beschleuniger wider Willen" [Hastener against His Will], in *Das Reich* (April 19, 1942); *NdE*, 28–36; "Drei Möglichkeiten," 929–930; *G*, 63, 70, 113–114, 253; cf. "Die andere Hegel-Linie" [The Other Hegel-Line], in *Christ und Welt* 10, no. 30 (July 25, 1957): 2; *VA*, 385, 428–429; *PT II*, 81.

108. *G*, 63; cf. 70; *ECS*, 31 (my emphasis).

109. Cf. *DC*, 76.

110. "Drei Möglichkeiten," 929.

of "history" derive from the fact that a state of testing appears indispensable for the confirmation of the moral order? Does only the "idea" of the *katechon*—and especially the thought that *post Christum natum* his position has never gone unoccupied—guarantee the inescapability and unchangeability of the "demanding moral decision" for the entire duration of the Christian eon? Or does the burning interest in the *katechon* spring from the fact that despite everything the end is still to be feared? However that may be, the notion of the *katechon* by no means replaces or represses the eschatological perspective. It fits into the latter and prolongs it, as it were, from the present backwards by making one acutely aware that the battle of decision *could* have taken place in the past. At no point was there the certainty that history would continue, that the end would not suddenly come. "The entire Christian eon" is "a single, prolonged expectation, a prolonged interim between same-times [*Gleich-Zeitigkeiten*], between the appearance of the Lord in the age of the Roman Emperor Augustus and the return of the Lord at the end of time." Yet within the "great interim, new, longer or briefer earthly interims arise which are *mean*-times [Zwischen-*Zeiten*]."[111] In each of these meantimes, which can be seen only in retrospect to be longer or briefer earthly interims that may be followed by others, the question about the *katechon* and about the Antichrist has to be raised anew. And each time the decision for the former and against the latter, or against what supposedly prepares the way for him, has fundamentally the same actuality. The task of knowing the Antichrist is even far more difficult to fulfill by human means than discerning one of apparently countless *katechons* or partial *katechons*, since the Antichrist, on the apostolic and patristic view, can appear only once and, what is more, will make himself into the spitting image of Christ. He is an expert concerning the *mysterion*.[112] The continual error has its roots in the essence of both possibilities of a Christian view of history, the katechontical and eschatological possibilities to which Schmitt

111. *PT II*, 75.

112. 2 Th 2:7. On the tradition of the notion of the Antichrist, the following studies are instructive: Wilhelm Bousset, *Der Antichrist in der Überlieferung des Judentums, des neuen Testaments und der alten Kirche. Ein Beitrag zur Auslegung der Apokalypse* (Göttingen 1895); *Die Religion des Judentums im späthellenistischen Zeitalter* (Tübingen 1926), 254–256; Ernst von Dobschütz, *Die Thessalonicher-Briefe*, 291–296; Norman Cohn, *The Pursuit of the Millenium: Revolutionary Millenarians and Mystical Anarchists of the Middle Ages* (Oxford 1970, revised and expanded), esp. 33–34, 78–79, 80–81, 86. For treatments of the Antichrist-tradition contemporary to Schmitt, cf. Hans Urs von Balthasar, *Apokalypse der deutschen Seele. Studien zu einer Lehre von letzten Haltungen* (Salzburg/Leipzig 1939), III, 30 ff. and Paul Schütz, *Der Anti-Christus. Eine Studie über die widergöttliche Macht und die deutsche Sendung* (Berlin 1933), 7, 18, 22–24, 38–39, 49–53.

refers. For that reason it should be no surprise that devout Christians saw and see forces at work in one and the same historical power that were and are utterly opposed to one another. In the present context it suffices to recall the head of the Roman Catholic Church, in whom Martin Luther believed to have discerned the Antichrist, whereas John Henry Newman, who probably took the threat of the Antichrist no less seriously than any other Christian before or after him, perceived in the Pope and everything truly "Roman" the *katechon* who "preserves" the Christian age.[113] The same Cardinal Newman concluded from the fact that the Christians who thought they knew the Antichrist and expected Christ's return in the near future were heretofore all in error, only that heightened vigilance is necessary. The greater the delay, the more suddenly the event will occur. "True it is, that many times, many ages, have Christians been mistaken in thinking they discerned Christ's coming; but better a thousand times think Him coming when He is not, than once think Him not coming when He is."[114]

For Schmitt's own expectations and for his conceptional action with regard to the "only case that matters," the Antichrist's slogan *pax et securitas*, which originates in 1 Thessalonians, is determinative. It is joined by other prophesies and assumptions from the Antichrist-tradition which were kept alive in the circle of Schmitt's friends, students, and acquaintances.[115] For example, Gregory of Elvira's statement *ipse solus toto orbe monarchiam habiturus est*, which links the dominion of the An-

113. Luther, *Schmalkaldische Artikel*, II, 4 (ed. Clemen, IV, 303), et passim. John Henry Newman, "The Patristical Idea of Antichrist" (1835), in *Discussions and Arguments on various subjects* (London 1872), 51, 87 ff. See in the German edition, *Der Antichrist. Nach der Lehre der Väter*, translated by Theodor Haecker, edited with an epilogue by Werner Becker (Munich 1951), 97, 117, 122–124. On Luther cf. Hans Preuß, *Die Vorstellungen vom Antichrist im späteren Mittelalter, bei Luther und in der konfessionellen Polemik* (Leipzig 1906). Consider "Die Sichtbarkeit der Kirche," 77–78.

114. Newman, "Waiting for Christ," Sermon XVII in *The Works of Cardinal Newman* VI: *Parochial and Plain Sermons* (Westminster, Md. 1967), 237 (cited by Becker in his Epilogue to *Der Antichrist*, 102). The Protestant theologian Wilhelm Stählin argues in a similar way; his view of the Antichrist and the *katechon* agrees with Schmitt's in all essentials: "The very fact that we can identify neither the Antichrist nor the *katechon* with any great empirical, historical, political, or ecclesiastical figures keeps us on wakeful alert not only against the power but also against the cunning of the Old-Evil Enemy and worried that we prove ourselves to be conservative in the sense of the *katechon*." "Die Gestalt des Antichristen und das *katechon*," in *Festgabe Joseph Lortz*, vol. II: *Glaube und Geschichte* (Baden-Baden 1957), 12.

115. From the Catholic side we cite Theodor Haecker, the aforementioned translator of Newman's sermons on the Antichrist, and Werner Becker, who edited those sermons in 1951 and included an instructive epilogue. The latter contains the sentence: "Who is the 'κατέχων' who still restrains the coming of that day? ask our best today" (131). From the Protestant side, Albrecht Erich Günther, who published several essays between 1928 and

tichrist with the establishment of the "world-State."[116] Against this backdrop Schmitt characterizes in 1933 the realization of the unity of the world "within an imperium that spans the entire globe," an imperium in which "the distinction between friend and enemy would wholly cease even as a mere eventuality," as a state in which "men would have achieved the full security of their this-worldly enjoyment of life." The theological significance of such an enterprise, which would "definitively" put an end to politics and make the existence of the bourgeois "obligatory" for everything that bears human features, shines through the more precise determination that Schmitt adds to his characterization: "The old tenet that one is not to expect full security in this life—*plena securitas in hac vita non expectanda*—would be obsolete."[117] After the Second World War Schmitt sees himself only confirmed in his assessment, which he had maintained since his *Politische Theologie* of 1922, that is, that the greatest, the peculiarly satanic danger issues from the "battle against the political." The "faith in the unlimited potential for change and for happiness in the natural this-worldly existence of man" has in the meantime taken on global proportions. The "activistic metaphysics" which unifies the world divided into East and West, has a material power at its disposal for the enforcement of its "giving of meaning" and "making of big plans" as no despotism had it in all of history. The "process-progress," which mankind goes through on its way to the "Babylonian unity," seems to have reached a new stage of hastening.[118]

As the third possibility of a Christian view of history Schmitt names, in addition to the eschatological perspective and the notion of the *katechon*, the Marian view of history, for which Konrad Weiss coined the term 'Christian Epimetheus'. "For Konrad Weiß the merely preserving forces are not enough. He says that the historical conditions are always more to be gained than preserved."[119] With the notion that the Christian is called to historical action in the sense of a humble-daring "anticipation of a commandment that is to be obeyed," the Christian faith in history abandons its defensive stance. It is no longer merely the suppression of the Old-Evil One and the restraint of the end that are of concern. The Chris-

---

1932 on the *Ludus de Antichristo*, and his brother Gerhard Günther, who produced a comprehensive commentary on the *Ludus*: *Der Antichrist. Der staufische Ludus de Antichristo* (Hamburg 1970); (cf. *PT II*, 61; *G*, 218).

116. Cf. *PT II*, 46.

117. *BdP* III, 36; cf. *Carl Schmitt and Leo Strauss: The Hidden Dialogue*, 44–46.

118. *BdP*, 93; *Die Lage der europäischen Rechtswissenschaft*, 32 (*VA*, 426); "Die Einheit der Welt," 1–2, 8–9, 11; *PT II*, 124–126; "Die legale Weltrevolution," 329.

119. "Drei Möglichkeiten," 930–931.

tian Empire was after all, Schmitt reminds us, not only the "holder" of the task of the *katechon*. The "battle against the pagans and the unbelievers" and the mission[120] likewise belonged to its charge, the spread of Christianity no less than its defense.[121] The crusades of the Middle Ages, the mandates issued by the Pope and carried out by the Emperor, mandates for "the land appropriations from non-Christian princes and peoples," can accordingly be regarded as examples of concrete application or, to use Schmitt's terminology, as "creaturings" of this third possibility of a Christian view of history. "The Christian looks back on accomplished events," Schmitt explains the attitude of the Christian Epimetheus, "and finds there the total ground and the total image, in the active contemplation of which the dark meaning of our history continues to grow."[122] Schmitt shows us what we are to understand by such active contemplation in his *Nomos der Erde* with the help of the *conquista*, to which he refers not only as an "enormous historical event" in itself, but which, beyond that, he elevates to a true example of historical action in the Marian spirit. For "the piety of the Spanish explorers and conquerors" bore "the sacred image of their historical deeds within the image of Mary, the immaculate virgin and mother of God."[123] Not quite a decade later Schmitt underscores once more, since he believes that his earlier reference to the "Marian image of the *conquista*" was not appropriately appreciated and that he was not understood,[124] that the "last great heroic deed of the European peoples, the land appropriation of a New World," was "not carried out by the heroes of the *conquista* with reference to the *ius commercii*, but rather in the name of their Christian Savior and his Holy

120. "One does justice to the 'Love thy enemies' from the Sermon on the Mount just as little as to other great realities when one regards it as an ethical demand, thus from the viewpoint of unreality. The Christian love of the enemy is a reality wherever it—cannot be otherwise. Such love enters into this state of 'not being able to be otherwise' where the Church or the individual follow the original commandment of Christianity: to mission. There the love of the enemy becomes the strongest weapon for the conquest of the world, the enemy loved as the future brother." Franz Rosenzweig on Jehuda Halevi's poem "Feindesliebe," in *Fünfundneunzig Hymnen und Gedichte* (1927), *Gesammelte Schriften* (The Hague 1983), IV, 1, 183.

121. *NdE*, 33, 98.

122. "Drei Möglichkeiten," 930.

123. *NdE*, 75; cf. 73 and "Die geschichtliche Struktur," 141.

124. "In a chapter on Francisco Vitoria, the moral-theological critic of the *conquista* (a chapter of my book on the *nomos* of the earth), I recalled the Marian image of the *conquista*. In vain. Right away there was a German professor of international law who dismissed that as 'a lot of Christian decoration' and sought to belittle it." "Nomos-Nahme-Name," 104–105.

Mother Mary. That is the iconographic reality of this unprecedented event."[125] Have we understood Schmitt?

The three possibilities of a Christian view of history which Schmitt falls back on in his battle for the interpretation of history are combined in his thought in one faith in history, which ultimately no longer allows for "concrete" distinctions in reality. Schmitt remains true to the eschatological perspective, and he will not cease watching for potential *katechons*. Might, for example, the guerrilla have some chance of success in counteracting the progress towards the "world-State," from out of his tellurian rootedness, thanks to his heightened political intensity and by virtue of his great mobility? Yet the Christian Epimetheus knows that the supposed restrainer may later prove to be a hastener. Furthermore, he knows that preserving alone is not enough, that there is more to be gained, and that sharpening can be a more successful strategy than defense. But above all he believes he knows that *salvation is, in opposition to all concepts, the decisive meaning of all world history*.[126] In view of such a certainty of salvation, the inponderabilities sink with which the historical agent sees himself confronted. The human uncertainties as to who the restrainer, who the hastener could be, whether the battle of decision is imminent tomorrow or only the day after tomorrow, and against whom one would have to fight, pale in significance. In the certainty of salvation, even that tragedy, which no human arbitrariness is able to conquer, is abolished and overcome in advance. The "silent rock" against which "the breakers of genuine tragedy foam," appears to be the touchstone of faith on the way to final salvation.[127] The secure possession of the truth of faith that promises salvation shifts the weight that bears on the "demanding moral decision," from the right judgment of the concrete historical opposition, only to load it onto the probity of faith. It is therefore not astonishing that self-deception becomes Schmitt's central problem and that the question about the resistance of the Other, the question about the enemy and brother "who cannot be deceived," becomes the most urgent question for Schmitt.

Regarding his own historical role, doubts creep over Schmitt after the Second World War as to whether it might not have been the "pleasure of hastening" that drove, bore, and deceived him.[128] However matters stood

125. "Nomos-Nahme-Name," 104.

126. *LuM*, 58 (48–49). Schmitt takes this sentence, which is central to his faith in history, silently from Konrad Weiss (*Der christliche Epimetheus*, 47).

127. See Chapter I, 11 f. above.

128. *G*, 31.

with Schmitt's inclinations and disinclinations, the faith in history which determined his thought is of such irresistible generality that neither serious errors and individual disappointments nor unexpected events and historical changes could do it any harm. It is resistant to experience and cannot be truly shaken by doubts about concrete persons, actions, or institutions. The most obvious example of this is provided by the "mode of thought concerned with order and formation" [*das "konkrete Ordnungs- und Gestaltungsdenken"*] which Schmitt claimed for himself from 1934 on, or put more precisely: the sole case in which this thought goes beyond the proclamation of its necessity and actually becomes "concrete."[129] On April 1, 1939 at a conference in Kiel, Schmitt presents the conception of an "order of international law based on *Großraum*, with a prohibition of intervention by foreign powers," a conception that proclaims the end of former international law, which took its bearings by the "general concept" of the State, and also bids farewell to the "mere thought of the national State." Instead the conception postulates a new international law that takes the "genuine hierarchy of the subjects of international law" into account insofar as it recognizes a plurality of *Großräume* under international law, each of which has its own political order (domestically) and a prohibition of intervention by "foreign powers" (internationally). According to Schmitt's idea, these *Großräume* would coexist under the political supremacy of leading empires in "a delimitable juxtaposition within a sensibly divided globe."[130] Schmitt's universal plan was bound "historically-concretely" in two ways. On the one hand, it served to justify in terms of international law the political claims of the German Reich as a hegemonic power of order in Central and Eastern Europe, which a few days earlier, in March 1939, had in a manner discernible to all the world turned away from the "mere thought of the national State" by establishing the "Reich Protectorate Bohemia and Moravia."[131] On the other hand, it was expressly tailored to the German Reich, as that historical force from which Schmitt hoped for the most important contribution to the establishment of the new *nomos* of the earth after the end of the "epoch of the State."[132] The complete failure of all historically particular hopes that had driven, borne, and deceived Schmitt's "mode of thought concerned with order and formation," had no repercussions on his historically general expectation that *one* new *nomos* of the earth would finally assert *itself*. In 1943 Schmitt defends the idea of

129. Cf. *DA*, 58, 59, 60, 63, 66, 67; "Nationalsozialistisches Rechtsdenken," 228–229.

130. *VGO*, 64, 69–70, 74–76, 81–82, 85.

131. The last sentence of Schmitt's writing reads: "The Führer's deed gave the thought of our Reich political reality, historical truth, and a great future in international law" (88).

132. Cf. *VGO*, 71, 76, 86–88.

Großraum under international law while no longer naming a specific upholder of it.[133] Far into the Second World War he still named the German Reich,[134] and in doing so the question apparently worried him very little from the start about *whom exactly* he built his hopes *on*. In 1942 Schmitt ends the "world-historical reflection" *Land und Meer* in the certainty that "the new *nomos* of our planet is growing inexorably and irresistibly." Where the "many" see "only meaningless disorder," Schmitt knows that "in reality a new meaning is struggling for its order." Regardless of who will be concretely victorious, there can be no doubt about the meaningful result of the struggle. "Even in the cruel war between old and new powers, just measures arise and meaningful proportions form."[135] Schmitt's faith in history goes so deep that it is above confirmation through historical concretion. He is thus able to live for years and decades in the firm expectation that an order, which will perhaps "preserve" for a time and in any case will be "meaningful," is certain to be reborn soon. He is able to close his essays and books in 1940 or 1941 just as easily as in 1929 or 1932 with a modified quotation of Virgil which expresses this expectation: *Ab integro nascitur ordo*.[136] However much the historical situations may change to which Schmitt directly answers with his "blind anticipation of a commandment

133. "Against the claims of a universal, planetary control and domination of the world, *another* nomos *of the earth defends itself*, the fundamental idea of which is the division of the earth into several *Großräume* which are fulfilled by their historical, economic, and cultural substance . . . The global unity of a planetary imperialism—be it capitalist or Bolshevist—is opposed by a plurality of meaningful, concrete *Großräume*." "The *Großraum* contains the standard and the *nomos* of the new earth. That is its world-historical and international-legal meaning." "Die letzte globale Linie" [The Last Global Line], in *Völker und Meere* [*Peoples and Seas*] (Leipzig 1943), 348, 349 (my emphasis). Cf. "Die Einheit der Welt," 5, 10.

134. Thus in the second, third, and fourth editions of *Völkerrechtliche Großraumordnung*, which appeared—revised in each case—in 1940 and 1941; but also in essays from 1941 and 1942: "New forces and energies bear the new revolution of space, and this time it is the German people that has been given the lead. *Ab integro nascitur ordo*." "Staatliche Souveränität" (1941), 105 (conclusion). "In a powerful change of all historical concepts, new contents and new proportions emerge, new concepts of space arise, and a new law is formed in new orders. This time the order is won by Germany and based on the Reich. But it is not the case, as it seems to those anxiety-stricken and despairing defenders of the former standards, that standard and law would cease altogether today. What ceases is only their old standard and their kind of legality. What is coming is our new Reich. Here, too, are gods that reign. / Great is their measure." "Die Formung des französischen Geistes," (1942), 30 (conclusion).

135. *LuM*, 76 (63). Compare the end of the book with the conclusion of "Die Formung des französischen Geistes" from the same year, which is relayed in n. 134 above.

136. "Die europäische Kultur in Zwischenstadien der Neutralisierung" (1929), 530; *BdP* (1930), 81; *PuB* (1940), 312; "Staatliche Souveränität" (1941), 105. The quotation has been the subject of fantastic interpretations among Schmitt scholars in obvious ignorance of its provenance as well as of the Latin. It is taken from Virgil's *Ecloga* IV, 5.

that is to be obeyed," his faith that divine Providence rules history does not change. Providence does not rule by means of a general law,[137] and direct commands are likely issued only as an exception. It uses historical enmities and friendships so as to bring about order again and again in time and to allow the "*nomos* of the earth" to emerge through the "identifications of the locus" in space. It raises its questions through constellations, situations, or, in the terminology of the *Christian Epimetheus*, through "angulations" which are understood or misunderstood by historical agents as a historical call and to which they "answer in doing" through the creation of new dispositions. The core of Schmitt's faith in history can be indicated by means of an expression Johannes Heckel used for Friedrich Julius Stahl: In the final analysis, at issue is a *theocracy par distance*.[138] God rules "our history," whose "dark meaning continues to grow," through what he allows and through what he does not allow. *Tout ce qui arrive est adorable*.[139]

Schmitt's political theology is unable to provide historical action with any "concrete" orientation. It contributes all the more to the clarification of the fundamental alternatives. For like every thinking that returns to the "most profound connections," it is less attached to its "historical moment" than it apparently believes or would like one to believe, and the insights into these connections that it makes possible, do not remain bound to its own purposes and notions. The concept of political theology itself, which we take up once again at the end of our contemplation, testifies to that. It was not only "introduced" by Schmitt "into the literature," as Erik Peterson wrote in 1935,[140] and thus can be exactly dated historically. As a political concept it has, according to Schmitt's principles of understanding, above and beyond that a "concrete opposition in view." Schmitt appropriates the concept, as we have seen, in his battle with Bakunin. He does not take up Varro and the long tradition of the "*theologia tripertita*,"[141] but answers the challenge of the Russian anarchist,

137. Seth Benardete's *logos* cannot be stressed enough: "law is essentially antitheistic" ("On Plato's *Cratylus*," in *Ancient Philosophy* 1, no. 2 [1981]: 139). Cf. *NdE*, 41–42 on the "disastrous word *law*" and *G*, 274.

138. Johannes Heckel, "Der Einbruch des jüdischen Geistes in das deutsche Staats- und Kirchenrecht durch Friedrich Julius Stahl," in *Historische Zeitschrift* 155, no. 3 (1936): 532–533.

139. See Chapter III, 88 ff. with nn. 59 and 62 above. Cf. *G*, 45, 88, 110, 253. Ernst Jünger reports that the quotation of Léon Bloy was Schmitt's last "non-profane" word (*Siebzig verweht III* [Stuttgart 1993], 575). Compare *G*, 264 and 311 with Jünger's note.

140. Peterson, *Der Monotheismus als politisches Problem. Ein Beitrag zur Geschichte der Politischen Theologie im Imperium Romanum* (Leipzig 1935), 158 n. 168.

141. M. Terentius Varro, *Antiquitates Rerum Divinarum*, ed. Cardauns (Wiesbaden

which in 1922 appears to him to be the most extreme attack on theology and politics. The "concrete opposition" in view of which Schmitt makes the expression 'political theology' into his own concept, is the opposition between authority and anarchy, between faith in revelation and atheism, between obedience to and rebellion against the supreme sovereign. But *authority*, *revelation*, and *obedience* are—regardless of the ways in which Schmitt updates them in detail—the decisive determinations of *the cause* of political theology, which did not come into the world with Schmitt's theorizing. It is as old as faith in revelation, and it will continue to exist, as far as one can tell, just as long as faith in a God who demands obedience continues to exist. Precisely because with his indictment Bakunin negated the "right" thing in the twofold sense of the word,[TN9] Schmitt can transform political theology into a positive concept without it remaining—neither for Schmitt himself nor for any other political theologian—polemically dependent on Bakunin or the opposition to anarchism.[142] Political theology understood as a political theory or a political doctrine that claims to be founded on the faith in divine revelation now becomes a concept of self-identification of the locus and self-characterization. In this sense not only political theologians who take up Schmitt's teaching immediately and with assent use it,[143] but also and ever more numerously those who sharply reject Schmitt's political options and do not share *his* faith: political theologians whose basic attitude is conservative or liberal, who have revolutionary or counterrevolutionary convictions, who profess Christianity, Judaism, or Islam. One is tempted to say that the concept *political theology* found its way via Bakunin and Schmitt to its cause. To be sure, after 1922 it is not only used for the designation of the cause or for purposes of self-identification of the locus. It remains a weapon in the political-theological quarrel. That holds for Schmitt's own use of it, the peculiarity of which lies in his employing the concept of political theology parallel to its "positive recasting" as an instrument in or-

1976), I, fr. 6, 7, 9, 10; pp. 18–20 and 37; cf. commentary, II, 139–142 and see Ernest L. Fortin, "Augustine and Roman Civil Religion: Some Critical Reflections," in *Études Augustiniennes* 26 (Paris 1980): 238–256; further, Godo Lieberg, "Die 'theologia tripertita' in Forschung und Bezeugung," in *Aufstieg und Niedergang der römischen Welt* I, 4 (Berlin/New York 1973), 63–115.

142. See *PT II*, 124–126; cf. *DC*, 9–10.

143. Early examples are the book by the Protestant theologian Alfred de Quervain, *Die theologischen Voraussetzungen der Politik. Grundlinien einer politischen Theologie* (Berlin 1931) or the essay "Politische Theologie" by the Catholic theologian Karl Eschweiler in *Religiöse Besinnung* 1931–32, no. 2: 72–88. In the meantime, the flood of books and essays that include 'political theology' in their titles has become vast.

der to fight the battle with the enemy on his own level, on the level that is determined by Schmitt and on which it is always supposedly only faith that meets faith, political theology that meets "political theology."[144] Whereas Schmitt seeks to make his enemies, as it were, "akin" to himself with the twofold use of the concept, the expression is used by other political theologians frequently with quite the opposite intention: in order to take their distance from political theologians whose political doctrines they disapprove of, and in order to attack political theologians whose bases of faith conflict with their own faith.[145]

Yet more important than the quarrel that divides political theologians is for us the insight that they quarrel among themselves about a cause that unites them and that makes political theology a concept of distinc-

144. See *Carl Schmitt and Leo Strauss: The Hidden Dialogue*, 68–79. In the text of his *Politische Theologie* Schmitt uses the concept 'political theology' exactly three times: on 40, 44, 45 (56, 63, 64). The first and third employment refers to the "writers of the Restoration," the political theologians Maistre, Bonald, Donoso Cortés, Stahl; the second, by contrast, has the concept appear in the context of Kelsen's view of democracy as the "expression of relativistic, impersonal scientificity."

145. The most famous example of this practice in our century is Peterson's treatise on monotheism, which culminates in the oft-cited thesis of the "theological impossibility of a 'political theology.'" In the guise of a learned book in the center of which stands the critique of the political theology of Eusebius, Bishop of Caesarea, Schmitt's long-time friend resolutely rejects political references to theological notions that he considers a misuse of Christian theology. The Christian theologian reaches the conclusion that through the Trinitarian dogma "in principle the break with every 'political theology' was effected that *misuses* the Christian Proclamation for the justification of a political situation" (99; my emphasis). Regardless of however one may assess the persuasiveness of this assertion from theological and historical viewpoints, it is obvious that the treatise attacks a *certain* kind of political theology. Its verdict is aimed at the theological legitimation of political dominion—at least to the extent that the author disapproves of this dominion politically-theologically—for example, based on the formula "One God, one ruler of the world." Peterson's theological writing is an attempt to exert influence in a purposive manner both politically and within the Church (on this point see the informative dissertation by Barbara Nichtweiß, *Erik Peterson*, 764–779). It contains a clear warning directed to his old friend, who in the meantime had made himself an advocate of the National Socialist revolution. And last but not least it represents an attack on Judaism and paganism: "There can be something like a 'political theology' only on the ground of Judaism and paganism" (99–100; cf. Löwith, *Mein Leben in Deutschland vor und nach 1933* [Stuttgart 1986], 94, and see n. 55 above). Thus it is a highly political treatise, by a political theologian of high rank, as any unbiased reader of his works can see. (Cf. *Der Monotheismus*, 70, 95–97, further "Kaiser Augustus im Urteil des antiken Christentums. Ein Beitrag zur Geschichte der politischen Theologie," in *Hochland* 30, no. 2 [April–Sept. 1933]: 289–299, esp. 289 and 298–299, but also *Die Kirche aus Juden und Heiden* [Salzburg 1933], 24–26, 31, 34, 40, 42, 56, 62, 64, 71 n. 28, as well as the book that immediately followed *Der Monotheismus*, namely, *Zeuge der Wahrheit* [Leipzig 1937], 14–15, 20, 22, 39–45, 58, 60, 68. Nichtweiß has presented a wealth of additional material from Peterson's unpublished papers which shows just how much he was a political theologian; cf. 789–790, 797–798, 805, 807, and esp. 820–826; see also Chapter I, nn. 25 and 63 above.)

tion beyond all historical polemics. We have already named the cause: a political theory, political doctrine, or a political standpoint for which, according to the self-understanding of the political theologian, divine revelation is the supreme authority and the ultimate foundation. Political theology becomes a concept of distinction, insofar as the determination of its cause distinguishes political theology from political philosophy, and in fact not after the manner in which two scholarly disciplines or two relatively independent domains of human thought and action may be distinguished from one another. Rather, they are severed by the insuperable opposition in which their answers to the question *How should I live?* stand to one another. The opposition establishes an overall difference, in the way of life, in the positions on morality, politics, revelation, and history. In the confrontation with political theology, political philosophy can therefore gain clarity about its own cause. Its identity is neither determined nor guaranteed by political theology, but the contours of philosophy's identity become sharper for it when philosophy knows what it is not, what it cannot be, and what it does not want to be. The contribution Schmitt's political theology makes to such a clarification is for us his greatest lesson. *Inter auctoritatem et philosophiam nihil est medium.*

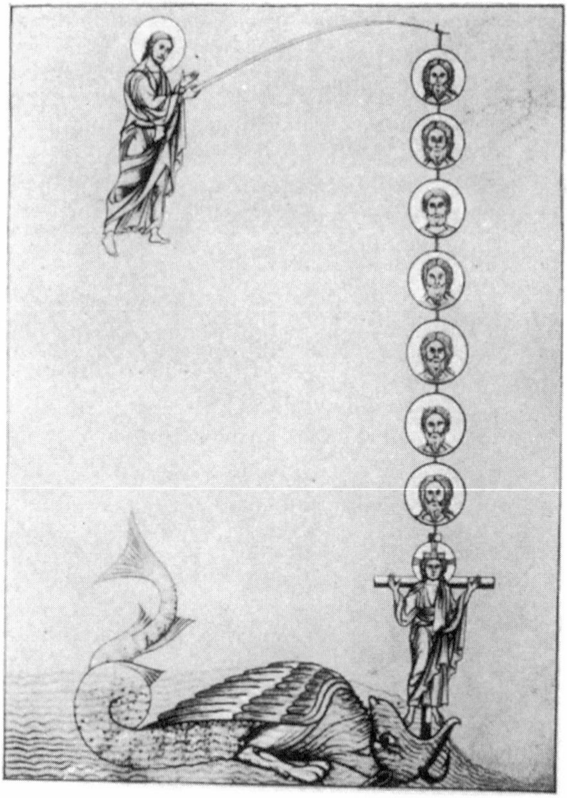

The Leviathan on God the Father's hook, with portraits of Jesus' ancestors and Christ as bait. *Hortus Deliciarum*, by Herrad von Landsberg, late twelfth century. *Below:* Illustration from the dust jacket and the last text page of Carl Schmitt, *Der Leviathan in der Staatslehre des Thomas Hobbes* (Hamburg 1938). See 114 n. 139 above.

TRANSLATOR'S NOTES

TN1. The German prefix *ent-* denotes 'removal from', 'reversal, undoing', 'degradation, reduction', and in English may be expressed by prefixes such as 'de-' and 'un-'. *Ent-Entungen* is a neologism coined by Schmitt and marks the culmination of a series of reversals—'detheologizations' (*Enttheologisierungen*), 'depoliticizations' (*Entpolitisierungen*), 'dejuridifications' (*Entjuridifizierungen*), 'deideologizations' (*Entideologisierungen*), 'dehistoricizations' (*Enthistorisierungen*)—which he lists ad absurdum. The absurdity of these reversals, as Schmitt sees them, is made apparent in their intensification: *Ent-Entungen* could be translated literally as 'de-deings'. However, although it was possible to use the prefix 'de-' in translating the rest of the series, it was thought preferable to underscore the effect of the foregoing terms, rather than the nonsense of *Ent-Entungen*; hence it has been rendered as 'un-doings'.

TN2. Throughout the text, *Staat* has been rendered as 'State' (a sovereign political entity) in order to distinguish it from 'state' (a condition, disposition, or mode of being), which renders *Zustand*. By extension, the adjective *staatlich* has been translated as 'State', so that, e.g., the phrase *der staatliche Souverän* reads 'the State sovereign'. In the few cases in which this solution proved awkward or threatened to obscure the author's meaning, 'civil' was used. The substantive *Staatlichkeit* is used by Schmitt in his designation of the modern age, namely, as *die Epoche der Staatlichkeit* (the epoch of the State).

TN3. The noun *Ordnung* is translated as 'order'. It is to be distinguished from *Befehl* (command), which in turn is to be distinguished from *Gebot* (commandment).

TN4. In the present volume 'instance' renders *Instanz*. It never means 'example' or 'case' but rather is to be taken in analogy with the legal sense of the word, that is, as a judging authority or a court of jurisdiction.

TN5. The adjective *geistig* may be translated, e.g., as 'intellectual' or 'spiritual'. The latter word was chosen to set it off from the intellectualism of the liberal age on Schmitt's understanding. It should be taken in the broadest sense as pertaining to mind, thought, intellect—such as in the translation of Hegel's *Geist* (spirit)—and not as a religious determination. By contrast, the adjective *geistlich* is always translated as 'religious'.

TN6. Since it looks like a normal German word, a simple composite of *vor-* and *Gebot*, and one might therefore assume that it has currency in everyday or scholarly German, one might be tempted to translate *Vorgebot* simply as 'pre-commandment'. However, Schmitt does not avail himself of a common German word here but rather adopts a neologism coined by Konrad Weiss; its meaning is determined by the context of the latter's thought and exceeds the usual understanding of its component parts. In order to retain the resonances of its original use—as Schmitt intends—a direct translation was not possible; instead it was necessary to convey them by means of a paraphrase. Thus, following the solution employed in *Carl Schmitt and Leo Strauss: The Hidden Dialogue*, *Vorgebot* is translated as 'anticipation of a commandment that is to be obeyed'.

TN7. The two senses of *das Maßgebende* (what is authoritative) are, on the one hand, 'that which sets the standard' (*das Maß gebende*) or 'provides orientation' and, on the other hand, 'that which is decisive' or 'compelling'. See, e.g., Chapter II, 36 above.

TN8. In order to distinguish it from 'nation' (*Nation*), *das Volk* has been translated as 'the people', just as the plural form *die Völker* reads 'the peoples'.

TN9. The two senses of *das Richtige* (the right thing) are, on the one hand, that which is in itself right—for Schmitt it is the authority of God and the State which Bakunin negates. On the other hand, it is the thing the negation of which enables Schmitt to transform 'political theology' into a positive concept and thereby to reverse the value of a concept which in Bakunin's parlance is thoroughly negative. It is the "right thing" because its negation is just what Schmitt needs in order to appropriate it for his own purposes.

TN10. *Das Schwarze Korps* (*The Black Corps*) was the official weekly newspaper of the SS.

TN11. The *Amt Rosenberg* was led by Alfred Rosenberg, the chief ideologist of the NSDAP, in his capacity as "the Führer's representative responsible for the surveillance of every aspect of the intellectual and ideological education of the NSDAP." The task of the Party department was to monitor the "ideological purity" of intellectual life and to keep the opponents of the National Socialist weltanschauung under surveillance. The January 8, 1937, edition of the *Mitteilungen zur weltanschaulichen Lage* (*Reports on the Ideological Situation*), published by the *Amt Rosenberg*, contained a "confidential" 14-page dossier on Carl Schmitt. A later critique, which reproached Schmitt for his political theology, appeared in July 1939 in the journal *Bücherkunde*, also published by the *Amt Rosenberg*. Written by a high official of the Party, the attack bore the title "Ein Staatsrechtslehrer als 'Theologe der bestehenden Ordnung'" (A Professor of Constitutional Law as "Theologian of the Status Quo").

INDEX